D1599068

RED EARTH

RED EARTH
Race and Agriculture in Oklahoma Territory

BONNIE LYNN-SHEROW

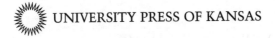 UNIVERSITY PRESS OF KANSAS

Published by the University Press of Kansas (Lawrence, Kansas 66049), which was
organized by the Kansas Board of Regents and is operated and funded by Emporia State
University, Fort Hays State University, Kansas State University, Pittsburg State
University, the University of Kansas, and Wichita State University

Library of Congress Cataloging-in-Publication Data

Lynn-Sherow, Bonnie.
Red earth : race and agriculture in Oklahoma Territory / Bonnie Lynn-Sherow.
p. cm.
Includes bibliographical references and index.
ISBN 0-7006-1324-2 (cloth : alk. paper)
1. Oklahoma—Race relations. 2. Oklahoma—environmental conditions.
3. Oklahoma—Social conditions. 4. Frontier and pioneer life—Oklahoma.
5. Agriculture—Social aspects—Oklahoma—History.
6. Land use—Social aspects—Oklahoma—History.
7. African American farmers—Oklahoma—History.
8. Indians of North America—Agriculture—Oklahoma—History.
9. Human ecology—Oklahoma. I. Title.
F705.A1L96   2004
305.8'009766—dc22   2004003030

British Library Cataloguing-in-Publication Data is available.

Printed in the United States of America

10 9 8 7 6 5 4 3 2 1

The paper used in this publication meets the minimum requirements
of the American National Standard for Permanence of Paper
for Printed Library Materials Z39.48–1984.

CONTENTS

(Photo insert follows p. 40)

PREFACE

I am often asked what moved me to study Oklahoma, of all places. My stock answer is I'm not sure, but I would like to think that I was drawn to that quintessential spirit of American optimism that suffused the territorial period when Oklahoma seemed to embody all the best and worst aspects of American society. One thing I am certain of is that historians, particularly environmental historians, have largely overlooked the amazing story of Oklahoma's hell-for-leather transformation at a critical juncture in American history. I suspected that Oklahoma, because it does not fit neatly into either the history of the American West or the South, simply became a footnote in both fields. My suspicions were confirmed the first time I visited the Oklahoma Historical Society and the only other scholar I encountered was another Canadian who had decided that Oklahoma was the ideal venue for understanding U.S. race relations in the twentieth century.*

The more practical truth about my choice of topics is that the story of Oklahoma Territory allowed me to combine my interests in the West, Indian peoples, and agriculture. While working toward an MA at Purdue, I was fortunate enough to study with two noted scholars of Indian peoples, Donald Parman and Donald Berthrong. It was Don Berthrong's suggestion that Oklahoma might be a good topic for someone interested in agroecological change and Indian peoples. My interest in agriculture and the American West later became more refined through my conversations with my major advisor at Northwestern University, Arthur McEvoy, who challenged me to read as much as I could about the environmental history of the Great Plains. After surfacing from the meditations of Turner, Webb, Malin, White, and Worster, it was clear that both agriculture and cross-cultural interac-

*Wickett, *Contested Territory*.

tion were underrepresented in the historical literature. I took my final step in deciding to study Oklahoma as I drove through the small towns and empty byways of the former territory and was filled with wonder at the red earth.

Donald Worster, James Sherow, John Opie, Donald Pisani, Richard White, Sam Hayes, and Carolyn Merchant provided helpful comments early on in my research and later inspired me with their own work. When Art McEvoy took a position at the University of Wisconsin, the late Robert Wiebe saw me through the final stages of writing my dissertation and helping me format it for publication. My biggest regret is that I will not have the pleasure of seeing him grin as I give him a copy of this book.

At Northwestern I received first-rate advice and help from professors and colleagues: Fred Hoxie, James Campbell, Josef Barton, Howard Perkins, Amanda Seligman, and Jared Orsi. Fred Hoxie expanded my knowledge of Indian peoples exponentially by asking me to work with him on an encyclopedia of North American Indian peoples. To these fellow scholars and teachers, I express my deepest appreciation and respect. Somewhere in the mountains of Montana, Dan Flores inspired me to ignore old categories of meaning, put away my books, and find my own sense of place in the red earth.

In Oklahoma I had the good fortune to meet and talk with the late Frank Beneda of Blaine County early on in my research. A lifelong farmer and resident of the county, Frank's work for the oral history project of the Oklahoma Historical Society, "Living Legends," deserves special mention. In 1973 and 1974 he sought out the memories of nearly every living homesteader in his home county. The tapes that Frank made contain priceless gems of daily life generally absent from conventional historical documents.

Tim Curtin, owner and editor of the *Watonga Republican*, loaned me several reels of microfilm of the *Republican* that were not available for loan from the Oklahoma Historical Society. His assistant editor, Darrell Rice, was a friendly and knowledgeable source of information about people and events in Blaine County. The staff of the Governor Ferguson House in Watonga patiently allowed me to sit in their attic to pore over dusty assessment books.

Among my Kiowa collaborators, I would like to thank Marilyn Bread and Robert Goombi of Haskell Indian Nations University in Lawrence, Kansas, for their candid reminiscences about their families. Ray Doyah of Anadarko agreed to correspond with me, eventually sharing a wonderful collection of his family's experiences in the early reservation and postallotment era. For these contacts, I owe a great debt to Dan Wildcat of Haskell and Benjamin Kracht of Northeastern Oklahoma University, whose superb anthropological study of Kiowa Religion was extremely helpful in my own work.

Several librarians were consistently courteous to me in my research. Dr. Heather Lloyd, head of Oklahoma State University's Special Collections, introduced me to the Bentley Collection on the Oklahoma Extension Service. Grace Almirez of the New Mexico office of the Bureau of Land Management was always quick to respond to my requests for more survey maps. Librarians and archivists at the Newberry Library in Chicago, the National Archives in Washington, the National Anthropological Archives in Maryland, the National Archives regional branch at Fort Worth, the Oklahoma Historical Society, the Territorial Museum in Guthrie, the Western History Collection at Norman, Oklahoma, and Washburn Law School were invariably helpful in my search for materials. Long overdue is a word of thanks to Tom Kavanaugh of Indiana University, whose Kiowa allotment database, together with the surveys, allowed me to reconstruct land-use patterns.

I owe sincere thanks to my colleagues at Kansas State. Al Hamscher was a careful reader of parts of this work; David Graff, Michael Ramsay, and Sue Zschoche provided moral support. Virgil Dean, editor of *Kansas History*, has been an unfailing friend and helpful critic. Nancy Scott Jackson, editor at the University Press of Kansas, was a pleasure to work with. Her mixture of patience and enthusiasm made the final editing almost enjoyable.

Finally, my greatest appreciation and affection goes to my colleague, best friend, and husband, Jim Sherow. His love of the West, deep sense of place, and passion for making the planet more humane has made me a better scholar and a better human being. His support and faith made this journey possible. Our daughters, Brie, Lauren, Lisa, and Evan, have each added to my thinking in countless ways. For all their hopes and aspirations, this book is dedicated to them.

Introduction

Bloodred earth. Caked on my car tires and splashed across the windshield, the red muck is lurid in the bright light of an April morning sun after a drenching rain. Looking south, red lines transect the green horizon in great gashes and cuts. At my feet, the red earth peeks out from under a lush gray-green palette of grama-bluestem. To the east, thin ribbons of red dirt road empty into the pink sides of gentle hills and crimson "canyons," hiding stream banks and gullies. My own red road stretches gently westward, crests the top of a gypsum hill, and then disappears. The endless surrounding space feels motionless even as a stiff breeze from the north ripples the new grass and sends shudders through a distant grove of cottonwoods. The unclouded blue sky overhead promises warmth later in the day.

A landscape of bright colors and gentle expanses, west-central Oklahoma, formerly Oklahoma Territory, seems void of human industry. It is quiet in an eerie way, like the hush that settles around an abandoned house. But on my road, there are no houses, only frozen oil pumps and rusty windmills, mute sentinels of past activity. Yet a century ago, Oklahoma Territory was filled with activity: the ringing of anvils on new railbeds, the clatter of horse carts laden with new lumber for homes, barns, and fences. Powerful ambitions swept across the landscape, turning prairies into wheat fields, crooked paths into straight roads, and bison herds into Herefords. By 1907, when Oklahoma was admitted as a state into the Union, nearly every element that had characterized the territory at its first opening in 1889 was reordered, displaced, or had disappeared. Under an immutable blue western sky, only the red earth remained.

The legal invention known as Oklahoma Territory lasted only a few decades, from the end of the Civil War through statehood in 1907. It comprised the western half of the present state of Oklahoma, approximately 24 million acres, or an area the size of the state of Virginia. As a region, it was—and has remained—largely rural. The clear exception to this pattern has been Oklahoma City, which is situated near the center of the eastern edge of the former territory delineated today by Interstate Highway 35. From this central place, Oklahoma City sprawls southward toward Norman and east-west along Highway 44 between Tulsa, Oklahoma, and Amarillo, Texas. But Oklahoma City's shopping malls, broad meridians, and Bermuda grass lawns rapidly melt into an open landscape of gentle grass-covered hills that dominate the former territory. Here the crops and animals visible from the highway are those introduced to the territory by white settlers in the 1890s. Wheat and cattle, cattle and wheat blanket the landscape, giving the whole an air of permanence.

Although this contemporary landscape reflects the resource choices made by one group of settlers in 1889, it simultaneously obscures the historical presence of others. Certainly the societies who resided in the territory between 1889 and statehood in 1906 were a very different population from those who occupy it today. Like the territorial landscape, its first peoples were a study in color and contrast. Beleaguered Indian peoples, African American refugees, and optimistic white settlers mixed and mingled in near-equal proportion to one another in the new territory. Their visions for the future often clashed, sometimes violently, as they struggled for control over the region and its resources. Their struggle became the blueprint for the ecology of Oklahoma Territory, and it is that contest—and its consequences—that are the heart of this book.

Before the first land runs in 1889, Oklahoma Territory was being advertised by hopeful speculators as the last, best West, preceding Frederick Jackson Turner's famous frontier thesis by more than a decade. In compensation for the millions of acres they had already seized from local Indian peoples in the mid-nineteenth century, the national government set aside the western half of Oklahoma as a homeland for the Plains tribes. The creation of Oklahoma Territory was formally acknowledged by treaty at Medicine Lodge, Kansas, in October 1867 through the work of the United States Indian Peace Commission. Although the Commission's purpose was ostensibly to bring peace and prosperity to the Indian tribes, its truer purpose was to secure a safe route for the railroads through Indian lands. The terms of the Medicine Lodge Treaty specifically outlawed depredations on white migrants by the Cheyennes, Arapahoes, Comanches, Kiowas, and Kiowa-Apaches, who agreed to live on two large reserves in exchange for government help in becoming self-sufficient farmers. In spite of the tribes' reluctance to enter into the treaty with the United States, the reserves soon became refuges where peace chiefs like Black Kettle of the Cheyennes and Kicking Bird of the Kiowas hoped to live with their bands, unmolested by further white encroachment.[1]

For cartographers, census takers, and the average white American, however, the territory was just an empty space in an otherwise populated and potentially prosperous West.[2] Indian control of the territory did not last long under the pressure of organized groups of farmers and speculators camped along the Kansas-Oklahoma border, demanding the territory be "opened" for their possession and use. African Americans, in disappointed acknowledgment of the grim realities of postbellum southern society, listened hopefully to scouts who returned from the territory with descriptions of a vast agricultural paradise with room enough for them to own land, farm, and live in peaceful seclusion from whites. The Medicine Lodge tribes, meanwhile, struggled to retain some control over their fate in the wake of a devastating series of wars with the U.S. Army that had laid waste their possessions, killed warriors, women, and children, and imprisoned their leadership. By 1889, the only thread that these red, white, and black Americans held in common was an ardent desire to work and live in the new territory.[3]

It was never an equal contest. Oklahoma Territory's environmental and cultural transformation from the time of the land runs through statehood was not the proverbial march of progress from field to farm. It was instead a fixed race to see who would determine the fate of the territory. Power regulated the discourse of different peoples and thus shaped the inevitable intersections of culture and ecology. The details that make up the dramatic changes in the territory's ecological and social landscape cannot be found in sweeping generalizations about development or progress. The transformation of Oklahoma Territory was instead a protracted struggle, as one people's relationship to the red earth came to dominate the landscape, banishing all others to the far edges of historical memory.

In this study, three distinct county settlements serve as case studies in the ecological and social transformation of Oklahoma Territory. They are introduced in chronological order on the basis of the year they were made legally available for farming by non-Indians. Situated northeast, northwest, and south of Oklahoma City, Logan, Blaine, and Caddo counties are geographically close to one another (it is possible to drive from one to the other in the space of a few hours), but they encompass much of the region's ecological variation. Each county contained very different human populations during the territorial period—populations that attempted to order their environments according to their own vision of the future. At times they followed larger, identifiable patterns and at other times, they reflected their own circumstances.

Logan County, founded in 1889, lies just a few miles northeast of Oklahoma City. It quickly became home to Oklahoma's most successful black town, Langston, which was surrounded by a large hinterland of black-owned farms. Blaine County, two counties west, was home to a large population of Cheyenne and Arapahoe peoples before it was opened for general settlement in 1894. Within a few years, it emerged as a largely white community of native-born Americans and German-speaking immigrants centered around the county seat of Watonga. Caddo County, directly south of Blaine, is still home for many Kiowa families in places like Anadarko and Mountain View. It was one of the last portions of the state to be opened to homesteaders (1902–6), and the Kiowas were one of the last Indian nations to be allotted individual farmsteads. Together, these three places and peoples tell the story of Oklahoma Territory's dramatic and often violent rebirth as a commercial agricultural region.

The emergence of Oklahomans, Boomers, and Sooners has been celebrated in song—including Broadway—and story. According to anthropologists Howard Stein and Robert Hill, Oklahomans even now strongly identify with images of friendly people, cowboys, Indians, farming, and football, in that order.[4] In the secondary literature on the history of the state, the story of Oklahoma agriculture is inseparable from the story of white settlers who saw an opportunity for land ownership and prosperity and worked hard to make it a reality. The stories of black and Indian farmers, on the other hand, cannot be found in textbook histories of Oklahoma Territory. There are individual tribal histories and a few excellent studies of black Oklahomans, but these works do not focus on agriculture or environmental change. This study seeks to place these forgotten farmers back into the story of Oklahoma Territory's agricultural settlement and to describe how their hopes and dreams for the landscape were temporarily made manifest—or as Annette Kolodny has elegantly defined it in her own study of frontier women and landscape, "rendered and assimilated into meaning."[5]

The ecology of Oklahoma Territory did not determine the agricultural systems that would emerge after 1889, but it did present obstacles and opportunities for the communities of people who wanted to live there. Dialectical by nature, human being–natural world relationships are forever caught in the dynamics of ecology, economy, and culture as they transform one another over time. According to one theorist, "separating the strands of change into identifiable threads"[6] is what makes environmental history distinct from conventional cause-and-effect interpretations of the past. Everyday human decisions, such as whether to hunt bison or plant the ground to cotton, are made according to our most recent experiences with the resources we have and the economies we are engaged in at that moment. Standing at the threshold of a new century, the red earth under their feet, Oklahoma Territory's farmers—Indian, black, and white—were as uncertain about what the future would bring as farmers are today. Then, as now, they looked to the recent past and gamely pushed ahead.

For the Indian peoples of central Oklahoma, notably the Kiowas, Comanches, Apaches, Cheyennes, and Arapahoes, the nonhuman environment was familiar and vital. They had witnessed the destruction of the bison herds, but they tenaciously held onto their horse herds. They knew where the best grass and water could be found. Indian women gathered wild plants and cultivated others. They pronounced some places sacred and others profane. Native-born white farmers, European immigrants, and black sharecroppers, new to the region, were less familiar with the landscape but believed it would respond to agricultural development just as in Texas, Missouri, and Kansas. This was also the opinion of the first scientists employed by Oklahoma's new agricultural experiment station in Stillwater. Years before the territory's first crop had been raised, collective belief in the region's potential for agriculture had made it a valuable commodity in the national marketplace.

It was essentially the marketplace that white Oklahomans in particular looked to when assessing their homesteads. Yet historically, the ways in which any people use and distribute natural resources through their work is an "economy" with its own unique suppliers and consumers. Economies can be internal or external to a society and can encompass several independent but related economies. The unassigned lands were "opened" in 1889 to add the resources of the region to the national economy—or in other words, to bring it into the larger market. But that does not mean the national market was absent from the territory before 1889. The demand for bison hides in the East for carriage robes and in industrial manufactures had already affected the economies of several Indian tribes. When the population of bison declined precipitously after 1850, the social systems dependent on that resource also changed.

For whites wanting to farm or simply speculate in real estate, the most valuable resource in Oklahoma Territory was the land itself. The unassigned lands, the initial parcels opened for settlement in April 1889, were disbursed in 160-acre quarter sections in fee simple title, making each quarter section a fungible commodity on the open market—available for trade, sale, and investment. Individual landowner-ship was the ideal, harking back to Thomas Jefferson's agrarian ethos. Indeed, the mandate of the Land Grant College system to teach "scientific" agriculture to new farmers expressly supported and promoted individual land ownership.

Broadly speaking, "culture" is the expressed and intuited values of a society expressed through its relationships. Or, as Clifford Geertz once borrowed from Max Weber, "man is an animal suspended in webs of significance he himself has spun."[7] Culture determines significance and therefore determines what is and is not a valuable resource. Although external manifestations of any community's values are easy enough to locate in material culture (possessions, works of art, tools), the links between culturally determined ideals, resource use, and environmental change are rather more difficult to trace over time. One way in which to approach this kind of history is to consider Marshall Sahlins's theory that cultural persistence is actually the product of a synthesis of responses as each generation vainly attempts to keep things as they were before. This view of cultural change in this context is what Sahlins calls a "negotiated response" to new situations.[8] New elements are fit into previous categories of meaning, creating a cycle in which the more things change, the more they seem to stay the same.

It seems apparent that ecological, economic, and social systems also maintain and renew themselves in measurable ways. Animals reproduce, grasses reseed, and seasons return. Economies too have a reproductive capacity. Patterns of exchange in any given society tend to maintain themselves insofar as certain resources and values attached to them remain in place. Finally, as Sahlins inferred, culture itself is reproductive. The ties that govern people's lives—kinship relations, gender roles, institutions—are inherited and maintained. Reproduction serves as the engine making the dynamic relationships between ecology, economy, and culture both creative and historical.[9]

Historians have sometimes overlooked this dynamic in the wake of large events, and this is especially true of the history of Oklahoma Territory. The time period covered by this study, 1889 to 1906, is often cast by agricultural and environmental historians as the start of the golden age of agricultural production in which millions of acres of virgin soil were brought into production for the commercial market. This activity in turn is presumed to have caused the environmental catastrophe of the 1930s dust bowl. This major event in environmental history has long overshadowed both Oklahoma history and identity. Oklahoma still suffers from the image of the broken Okie migrant immortalized in John Steinbeck's *Grapes of Wrath.*[10] One purpose of this study is to lay before the reader the environmental and social history of Oklahoma Territory as a period of significance in itself, not simply as a prelude to later events. In doing so, I hope to raise new questions about turn-of-the-century agricultural development and its relationship to environmental and social problems today.

In 1996, while in Anadarko in Caddo County to attend the Kiowas' Black Leggings Dance, I met Ray Doyah, an enrolled member of the tribe and great-grandson of Chief Apeahtone. He asked me how it was that a white farmer and an Indian farmer could start farms near one another, but in a few years, the Indian farmer was broke and the white farmer had a new house, trucks, and tractors. I asked myself a similar question later that year while on the campus of Langston University, an historically black college in Logan County. Where were the black farmers that once surrounded the school? What had happened to their homesteads, their lands, their hopes and dreams?

These were not the questions that I had come to ask. I wanted to learn how the ecology of Oklahoma Territory had changed after the land runs. I was fairly sure that it had to do with technology, land use, laws, and markets. I had not considered how changes in the landscape might be traced to different groups of people. Did the ecological simplification of the territory through commercial agriculture affect only plants and animals, or did it also simplify the human population? Was the ecology of Oklahoma Territory more diverse when farmers of different cultures and backgrounds lived and worked side by side? Was the ordering of the elements of the territory into a rationalized agroecology inevitable? Whom did the mythology of opportunity serve, and whom did it discard? These are some of the questions I have posed in *Red Earth: An Environmental History of Oklahoma Territory* and that I explore through the stories of real people who won and lost in their gamble with the red earth.

1

THE PRAIRIE

The late dreary wilderness [cross timbers] brightened into a fine open country, with stately groves, and clumps of oaks of a gigantic size, some of which stood singly, as if planted for ornament and shade, in the midst of rich meadows; while our horses, scattered about, and grazing under them, gave to the whole the air of a noble park. It was difficult to realize the fact that we were so far in the wilds beyond the residence of man.

Washington Irving, October 20, 1832

In his long trek alongside William Clark across the continent in 1803, Merriweather Lewis described "immence herds of Buffaloe, Elk, Deer and Antelopes" feeding in the central plains between the Mississippi River and the Rocky Mountains as "one common and boundless pasture."[1] A quarter of a century later, Washington Irving, the novelist, left behind a strikingly similar description of the mixed-grass prairie that would become Oklahoma Territory. Amazed by its "wildness," Irving fondly compared the grass-covered hills crisscrossed with rivers and gallery forest to a European estate.[2] It did not occur to him or to Lewis that Indian management practices had in fact created the park-like scenes they found so appealing. Thus began a long series of misunderstandings regarding the peoples and the environments of what would become Oklahoma Territory.

These early written accounts, in spite of their shortcomings, chronicled an ecosystem that was rapidly disappearing. Compared with these early descriptions, the "virgin" prairie so coveted by Euro-American and African American settlers at the Territory's opening in 1889 was practically lifeless. Unknown to these hopeful settlers, recent changes in the ecology of the mixed-grass prairie had altered the region dramatically, leaving only a fraction of its former system of plants, animals, and human beings for them to observe.

More than a century after Irving's visit to Oklahoma, Walter Prescott Webb, an influential historian of the Great Plains in the twentieth century, would explain the development of the plains as one of human progress and civilization in the face of unexpected environmental obstacles.[3] Webb extolled the powers of human adaptation and ingenuity in a vast and inhospitable region that he defined through the measurable parameters of rainfall, vegetation, and climate. Webb's grand view, groundbreaking in his day for even considering the role of environment in human history, made sweeping generalizations about the ecology of a vast geographic area. But in reducing the area to a few common elements, such as lack of water and the tough prairie sod, Webb obscured the historic grasslands' variable nature.[4] This was nearly unavoidable in Webb's day, as twentieth-century agriculture and industry had wrought changes in the northern and southern plains environments so rapid and comprehensive that an intimate knowledge of how the presettlement prairie operated could no longer be gleaned from its fractionalized remnants. More recently, ecologists' experimentation with restored prairie in Kansas and Oklahoma have uncovered the complex nature of presettlement grassland systems. Paired with nineteenth-century travelers' accounts, recent scientific theory about the nature of grasslands is helping to provide a more concise picture of the central and southern plains before agricultural settlement. In short, our understanding of the vast complex known as the Great Plains is more comprehensive than ever before.[5]

The caveat, of course, is that scientists' observations of so-called natural processes have themselves undergone numerous revisions since the historical period began.[6] This was also true of visitors to the Plains, who routinely overemphasized certain features of the environment or compared them to environments elsewhere. Depending on the observer's account, Oklahoma Territory was a desert and an oasis, flat and hilly, wet and dry, hot and cold. Today, environmental historians can reconsider these varying descriptions in light of ecologists' work, which suggests that even relatively small areas—the size of a single county, for example—are composed of numerous and highly variable microenvironments operating within larger systems. In studying the history of human resource use, this new understanding of ecosystems means that localized conditions as much as the workings of the larger environment have influenced human behavior in countless ways. In turn, different peoples have actively worked to reorder their environments to meet their own needs and expectations.

Even that most manifest characteristic of the Plains—grass—is wonderfully disparate in species diversity and distribution. Oklahoma Territory is part of the mixed-grass zone of the southern Plains, considered to be one of the most diverse and important biomes on the planet in relation to humans.[7] Mixed-grass prairies are especially rich in plant species containing both tall grasses, which require a minimum rainfall each year to fully mature, and short grasses, which persist under drought conditions. The mixed-grass prairie zone follows an irregular north-south path between the tallgrass prairies of the old midwestern states and the short-grass high plains (steppe) west of the hundredth meridian. Mixed-grass prairies are the most diverse in terms of plant species; they host tallgrass varieties, such as big bluestem, Indian grass, and switchgrass, which thrive in the moist lower elevations, and the short grasses, blue gramas and buffalo grass, more common to the drier uplands.

Like all grasslands, the mixed-grass prairie of Oklahoma is not a plant community "climax" that evolved from the static conditions of soil and climate. The actions of human beings have also helped to shape the prairie. According to recent ecological theory, all plant communities emerge as a consequence of "spatial and temporal variability in light, water and nutrients, driven by a combination of topography, fire history and climate."[8] Before 1700, for example, prairie flora developed and expanded their ranges in response to the regular presence of fire and large ungulates. Changes in available light and nutrients depended largely on ungulate species, whereas fire events were dependent on anthropogenic management. In the mixed-grass region of Oklahoma, this largely depended on bison and Indian fire practices.

Grazers—bison, elk, mule deer, pronghorn, and even prairie dogs—were central to the historically functioning prairie ecosystem. Because of their mobility, the effect of these herbivores on specific plant communities varied from year to year depending on climate and human disturbance. Not surprisingly, the erasure of millions of bison from the Great Plains is regarded by prairie ecologists as the most significant change in Plains ecology in the last two hundred years.[9] This makes the bison population before the historical period a crucial factor in measuring ecological change.

Confoundingly, estimates of bison populations and their movements before 1800 continue to elude historians' and ecologists' efforts to document presettlement conditions on the Plains. Depending on the sources used, guesses have ranged from 5.5 million to 1 billion bison on the Great Plains before 1750.[10] Some scholars, borrowing a page from early animal management textbooks, have attempted to quantify bison numbers on the basis of the prairie's carrying capacity. The first estimate of this kind came from Ernest Thompson Seton (cofounder with Lord Baden-Powell of the Boy Scouts) in 1929; he based his estimate on the observations of Colonel Richard I. Dodge and the actual number of cattle, horses, and mules that were being grazed on the Plains according to the 1910 census.[11] After making allowance for land taken up in agricultural settlement, Seton arrived at a figure of 60 million bison that formerly lived on the mixed-grass and high plains regions from Canada to central Texas. This figure has fallen into disrepute for several good reasons. In Oklahoma Territory, for example, cattle had badly overgrazed much of the mixed-grass region by 1910, and fires were being actively suppressed. These two factors alone make cattle-carrying capacity an unreliable equivalent for the numbers of bison before 1870.

One problem with estimating bison populations is the large number of variables involved, such as climate, range conditions, competition, migration, hunting, disease, predation, and reproductive capacity. In 1991, environmental historian Dan Flores also used the 1910 census as the basis for his own estimate of the southern herd. According to the sources he consulted, bison are 18 percent more efficient at grazing than cattle, and after taking drought, predation, and disease into account, Flores adjusted Seton's long-standing figure of 60 million downward to 28 to 30 million, with 8 million bison in the southern herd alone.[12] Flores argued that 1910 is a median figure because it predates the effective utilization of the Enlarged Homestead Act of 1909, which would have increased the number of homesteaders and vastly reduced open range cattle ranching. But in Oklahoma Territory, virtually every quarter section of land had been claimed and fenced off by homesteaders by 1901, which makes the 1910 census data immaterial for the purpose of estimating cattle-carrying capacity in the former Territory.

In the 1990s, James Shaw and Martin Lee, zoologists at the University of Oklahoma, further complicated the equation by noting that in the late nineteenth century, the largest concentrations of bison were not on the high plains but on the mixed-grass prairies, particularly in Oklahoma. Their research makes the convincing argument that these animals' habit of discontinuous grazing, taken together with the positive effects of numerous fires, as reported in historical accounts, would have significantly increased the carrying capacity of the southern plains before white settlement. Moreover, data generated by ecologists at Konza Prairie Biological Station indicate that bison eat both warm- and cool-season grasses and therefore require less acreage than cattle. Their research puts the southern herd at approximately 10 million animals, with the greatest concentration in the mixed-grass prairie regions of Kansas, Oklahoma, and Texas.[13] Konza research supports Shaw and Lee's conclusion that Seton's lowest estimate of 40 million animals was closer to the mark, although his initial premise, that cattle and bison are interchangeable, was faulty.

Many other elements and forces beside bison shaped the Oklahoma environment before settlement. Primary among these were climate, water, soils, fire, and human beings. Although Indian peoples interacted with all of these elements, biotic and nonbiotic, their primary influence on the prairies was through their deliberate use of fire. There is little doubt among scholars today that bison numbers were encouraged and sustained through Indian burning.[14] In Oklahoma, Shaw and Lee cataloged every expedition account containing sightings of fire and herbivores into four historical periods: early exploration, 1806–20; the Sante Fe Trail, 1821–32; the Mexican and Indian wars, 1833–49; and the state and territorial surveyors' reports, 1850–57. The routes taken by different explorers indicated the length of their stays in each biome. Animal populations were estimated on the basis of the number of sightings in each biome, the condition of the grasses (based on climate records), and calculated carrying capacity. Fires in each biome were tabulated according to frequency alone, because it was impossible to determine the precise extent of the acreage burned from written observations. Finally, to counter any doubt that most prairie fires were anthropogenic in origin, the study noted only a slight correlation between lightning strikes and the number of reported fires. Shaw and Lee concluded that "without paleo-Indians' use of fire, there would have been no extensive grasslands across central North America."[15]

Historical sightings of ungulates are even more conclusive in measuring the effects of Indian fires on large animal populations. Elk persisted in all three biomes throughout most of the four historical periods, except in the tallgrass biome, where none were reported after 1850. Pronghorn populations did the opposite, remaining low for most of the period and reaching their greatest populations on the short grasses after 1836. These variations were the result of pronghorns' tendency to defensively avoid tall grass, preferring the short grass for greater mobility and visibility over greater distances. Additionally, pronghorn follow prairie fires. As long as Indian fires were suppressed in the tallgrass regions, it suppressed pronghorn populations as well. For both elk and pronghorn, an increase in the human population in eastern Oklahoma after the removal of several Eastern tribes there in the 1830s and a subsequent increase in hunting likely account for the movement of those two species to the mixed-grass and short-grass biomes after 1850.

Like elk and pronghorn, bison movements were highly variable from 1800 to 1850. Both historical accounts and contemporary scientific studies indicate that bison herds migrated over vast distances. Naturalists long assumed that bison herds followed a regular north-south migration pattern: south in winter, north in summer. Newer studies, however, have found a great deal of variation for the first half of the nineteenth century, mainly because bison herds avoided human settlements and lingered in certain areas for long periods of time. Although bison do seem to have traveled great distances before 1800 according to seasonal changes, they were also highly sensitive to other pressures, such as predation, hunting, fires, forage quality, and water sources, making any thorough reconstruction of their migration in the nineteenth century next to impossible.[16] Only one fact is clear: the movements of bison herds and Indians' use of fire were positively linked to one another.

Still other factors influenced presettlement life on the southern plains. Climate was a primary factor in human occupation and resource use on the Great Plains. Anthropologists have theorized that the first permanent residents of the region arrived around AD 500 to farm the fertile river valleys, but settlement on the prairie was sparse because of aridity. Human population on the Plains then took a giant leap at the beginning of what climatologists have labeled the "little ice age" from AD 1450 to 1850.[17] Significantly, the period 1800 to 1850 was a period of very heavy precipitation and lower temperatures, with the wettest years from 1825 to 1849. Although the shift in climate from 1850 to the present has not been extreme, the shift in climate that occurred in the mid-fifteenth century was dramatic and may have triggered both an increase in bison numbers and human occupation on the Plains shortly thereafter.[18]

Scholars have suggested that the Comanches, soon followed by the Kiowas, pushed their way onto the southern plains as early as 1700 in response to climatic changes.[19] By the eighteenth century, the Kiowas were being pushed south and west by European-armed Siouan-speaking peoples who were also moving onto the Plains. In their migrations, these proto–Plains Indians encountered the Utes, from whom they acquired horses. The acceptance of horse-aided bison hunting by the Comanches and Kiowas was rapid.[20] Bison filled the well-watered grasslands, making day-to-day subsistence for Indian people far easier than it had ever been before.[21] The Comanches increased in direct proportion to their growing herds of horses and the availability of bison for food, shelter, clothing, and implements. The people of the Plains had entered a golden era that was to last over a century.

The arrival of the horse-bison complex was not good news for the riverine agricultural tribes that inhabited the future territory. The permanent villages of the Caddoes and Apaches were nearly defenseless against Comanche imperialism in the same way that Pawnee villages became a perennial target of Sioux aggression farther north. The "True Plains"[22] tribes announced a new ecological order completely unlike the spatially limited settlements of an earlier era. Their reliance on bison hunting and the use of fire created the parklike landscapes observed by Merriweather Lewis and Washington Irving only a few decades later.

Like the riverine agriculturalists, the Plains tribes exploited the rich plant communities of the mixed-grass prairies. Horse-mounted Indians throughout the Great Plains, from the Dakotas to Texas, relied heavily on the hundreds of different plants that thrived in Merriweather Lewis's "common pasture" for everything from food and animal care to ritual prayer and ceremony. Wild tubers like the prairie turnip (*Psoralea esculenta*) were a staple food that could be harvested daily as family bands made camp in pursuit of the bison herds.[23] Dozens of other plant species, from the prairie rose (*Rosa arkansana*) to common soapweed (*Yucca glauca*), were prized for their medicinal properties in the treatment of people and horses. Among the Cheyennes, wild rose bark was boiled for tea for stomach trouble, the vapors were inhaled to stop nosebleeds, or it was gargled and swallowed for relief from tonsillitis and sore throat. Among the Kiowas, ragweed (*Ambrosia artemisiifolia*) was applied topically to treat "worm holes" in horses. Soapweed, as the name implies, was used by several tribes for cleaning and to treat lice. As contact with traders led to outbreaks of disease among the Plains tribes, medicine men experimented with dozens of different plants for their healing properties, eventually assembling an enormous pharmacopoeia.[24] Wild plant harvesting directly affected the microecology of seasonal camp sites as Indian peoples dug up, scattered, or propagated certain plant species year after year.

Although Plains peoples had hunted bison on foot for hundreds of years before 1700, the introduction of the horse, an exotic, had numerous unforeseen ecological and social consequences for the mixed-grass prairie. Horses became central to Plains culture and social structure—and at times, a burden. Although scholars have long recognized the release of energy horses provided the Plains Indians, they have rarely considered how horses both limited their mobility and caused them ecological problems at the same time.[25] One important question environmental historians have asked of this system is whether or not Plains peoples had sufficient time and experience to discover how to sustain their newly acquired horse-bison culture before white exploitation of the region began in earnest. New ecological theory would indicate that Indians' historic use of horses and bison for sustenance and trade could not have been sustained indefinitely without some drastic modifications to their populations and lifeways.

Although blame for the destruction of the bison herds has popularly been assigned to white traders, hunters, and sportsmen, Indian peoples, in their individual and tribal pursuit of European goods, were an integral part of the trade from its inception.[26] The Indians' desire to supply bison robes for the trade and to maintain good relations with European traders changed the nature of intertribal relations, altered work routines for men and women, and ended their former dependence on agriculture.[27] All these shifts in Indian political economy changed the ecology of the mixed-grass region of Oklahoma Territory before settlement.

Competition for trade goods also led to an escalation in military clashes between tribal groups.[28] In 1724, Etienne de Veniard, sieur de Bourgmont, a French adventurer and trader, met with a large village of Plains Apache Indians in present-day south-central Kansas for the purpose of persuading them to make peace with neighboring tribes, "that you may trade with one another and be always well treated." The "Head Chief" of the Apaches, or "Padoucas," as Bourgmont called them, responded to his speech by noting that the Spanish "are not like you, who give us a quantity of merchandise such as we have never seen before."[29] By the 1830s, one hundred years later, Plains tribes were clearly seasoned and shrewd traders, highly discriminating in their choice of trade goods, preferring European-made over American-made blankets and guns, not to mention beads made in Italy.[30] One indication of this is that most tribes refused to give up the customary practice of gift giving before business transactions, but still insisted on receiving full value for their horses, dressed robes, and skins.[31]

As resources diminished and Indian peoples found themselves in the economic squeeze between subsistence and trade, raids on Indian and white settlements for horses, captives, and food grew bolder and more frequent. The period 1863 to 1870 saw an intensive series of intertribal skirmishes and raids on white settlements south and west. These highly publicized actions were later used by whites to rationalize the confinement of Indian peoples on reservations and the purposeful destruction of the bison herds.[32] The stereotype of the Indian "savage" would later make it nearly impossible for whites to regard Indians as having any aptitude for civilized pursuits like agriculture.

Intertribal warfare on the southern Plains had some unpredictable consequences for the mixed-grass prairie of western Oklahoma and Kansas. By 1825, as a result of continuous warfare between the numerous Plains Indians and their alliances and the invasion of the high plains bison ranges by the Colorado tribes, the rich mixed-grass prairie biome became a buffer zone or sanctuary for bison that different tribal groups entered with great caution in their quest for winter robes and summer pasturage. Bison became even more concentrated in this area after 1846, when the decline in precipitation and the presence of Indians in the Arkansas River valley caused the bison herds to migrate southward to the mixed-grass region between the Red and Platt rivers. Accounts of intertribal conflict, recorded by white traders and the Indians themselves, and even military alliances between tribes after 1830, reflected an increase in tensions throughout the Plains as different groups tried to stave off the effects of white encroachment, military attacks, a diminishing resources base, and widespread disease.

The introduction of cattle was the next major intrusion into the ecology of future Oklahoma Territory. The era of the cattle trails, that famous two decades from 1867 to 1887 celebrated in American literature and film, was short-lived but had an immense impact on the ecology of west-central Oklahoma. Simultaneous with the decrease in the bison herds from overhunting was a sharp increase in another ungulate: longhorn cattle. From 1867 to 1887, west-central Oklahoma's mixed-grass prairie saw intensive use as hundreds of thousands of longhorns ate their way north from Texas to Kansas. The prairie that would later encompass Blaine County was bisected by two major cattle trails: the west branch of the Chisholm and the Great Western. Three major rivers—the Cimarron, the North Fork of the Canadian, and the Canadian—either bordered or intersected the future county. This made it an attractive stop for drovers looking for campsites and fresh pasturage off the main trails.[33] The unassigned lands, on the western border of the Chisholm Trail within which Logan County was located in 1890, was attractive for drovers because of the absence of Indian claims. This section of the trail contained cross-timbered lowlands and prairie meadows, making the upper Chisholm a good source of fuel and shelter. Captain Randolph Marcy's biographer in 1856 noted that the cross timbers were not a "continuous forest, but interspersed with open glades, plateaus and vistas of prairie scenery."[34] Drovers had to be exceptionally careful in making their way through this area, however, because rounding up a stampeded herd in the tangle of blackjack and post oaks was a difficult and dangerous task.

What would become Caddo County contained the old north-south Indian traders' trail from Fort Sill to Camp Supply. This trail was incorporated into the Chisholm in 1866. Even in this rugged and dangerous area at the foot of the Wichita Mountains, drovers left the main trail in search of forage for their herds. "Little Jim" Ellison recalled that in 1876, "I drove a herd for Ellison and Dewees . . . We went as far, if not farther west than any cattle had ever gone, crossing the Washita about eight miles west of where Chickasha is now located. This was a hard trip. We passed through the Wichita Mountains at the foot of Mt. Scott, and saw lots of buffalo and antelope."[35]

But longhorns grazed more intensely than either bison or antelope did, leaving an indelible mark on the plant communities they passed over.[36] Additionally, cattle trailing suppressed the Indians' use of fire, introduced exotic plants that displaced native grasses on the overgrazed prairie, eroded stream beds at their crossings, and consumed vast quantities of wood for campfires. In 1892, one cowboy noted that along the main trail, "spotting the emerald reaches on either side were the barren circle-like 'bedding grounds.' Each one a record that a great herd had there spent the night."[37] Some drovers thought about life after cattle trailing and took note of other resources in the region, like rich soil for farming or promising mineral deposits. One former trail hand recalled that Jesse Chisholm worked a salt mine in future Blaine County because there was a great demand for salt and no ready supply in the territory.[38]

The herds ate their way through Oklahoma Territory, consuming vast quantities of forage along the trails and creating mile-wide paths in their wake. Although the main trails did not initially transect Logan and Caddo counties, after 1871, spurs leading several miles away from the main trail and occasional links from one trail to another sprang up, increasing the area directly affected by the drives. One spur linking the Chisholm to the Great Western passed directly through present-day Blaine from Pond Creek to Cantonment. Just south of the spur near Cantonment was a well-known campsite for drovers called Cedar Springs. It contained a Cheyenne burial ground and was a great curiosity to the drovers. One branch of this trail continued west to Doan's Spring, and another followed an Indian trail south to Darlington Agency near Concho and then on to Anadarko in present-day Caddo County.[39] This trail later became the foundation of the military road between Fort Supply and Fort Sill.

The movement of more than 10 million longhorn cattle north from Texas to Kansas between 1867 and 1887 required a more intensive use of the Oklahoma grasslands than bison and produced a series of dramatic ecological changes. In 1884, to cite an extreme example, Ike Pryor contracted to move 45,000 animals in one monumental drive. He hired 165 drovers, 15 cooks, and 15 bosses. Each man was given six saddle ponies for a total of more than one thousand horses. Chuck and equipment wagons were purchased for every fifteen hands and stocked with supplies.[40] Incredibly, Pryor's drive was only one of dozens to hit the trail that season.

The quantities of grass, water, and wood the cattle drives required were staggering. Contemporary descriptions of the trail attest to its overuse. The first drive would set the path, which became wider with each season. Erosion by wind and water made deep cuts in the exposed soil, turning it into a mire. Deep cuts also marked river and stream crossings from cattle following each other in single file. As one driver noted, "Once upon this wide bare trail, there was no difficulty in following it: there was no longer any need for wagon tongue or Northern Star."[41] The clearly defined trails created by Indian peoples were largely erased, buried under compacted highways pounded flat by millions of hooves on their way to market.

The next overlay of human activity on Oklahoma Territory was the establishment of military roads and posts in central Oklahoma, a direct consequence of the Treaty of Guadalupe that Hidalgo concluded in 1848. Under the provisions of that treaty, the U.S. Army was given responsibility for maintaining peaceful relations between Indian tribes and an ever-increasing flow of traders and settlers making their way to California, New Mexico, and Texas. Although no major trails, like the Sante Fe or El Paso, cut directly through central Oklahoma, the army did set up a series of posts designed to pacify the Indians and help them along the path to civilization.[42] The posts established in west-central Oklahoma after 1867 were linked by roads that formerly linked Native Americans village sites or had been mapped by early European travelers. The locations of Fort Supply and Fort Sill, for example, were chosen on the basis of their proximity to well-known Indian camping sites and to nearby supplies of good water, fuel, and forage for their animals.

Fort Supply was established in November of 1868 at the confluence of the North Canadian River and Wolf Creek and was the main base of operations for Sheridan's forces in their campaigns against the Cheyennes and Arapahoes for more than a decade. Fort Sill's location was chosen for similar reasons. Fort Arbuckle and Fort Cobb were considered too far away from the camps of the Kiowas and Comanches to be effective, so Sheridan authorized the establishment of a new post on the trail near the main Indian encampment.

In an area known as Medicine Bluff by the Indian guides who first took him there, Colonel Grierson of the Tenth Cavalry (an all-black regiment) suggested it as a possible location for the future post: "The clear, trickling water of Medicine Bluff and Cache creeks assured a pure and ample supply, the whole area was covered by a rich carpet of grass, wild game was seen everywhere, and the rugged beauty of the Wichita Mountains promised an abundance of building material."[43] The establishment of Fort Sill was one of the last links in a military road system used by troops, the U.S. mail service, Indian agents, missionaries, and native peoples for the next quarter century.

In many ways, the transportation routes that crisscrossed Oklahoma Territory before 1889 are an apt metaphor for the layers of human relationships that existed in the region before non-Indian agricultural settlement. Indians, federal agents, missionaries, and the army, although in frequent conflict, worked within a well-defined system of treaty rights and boundaries to help sustain the tribes against the intrusion of white society. In passing through the areas claimed by Indian peoples, the cattle industry was a divisive element in this system, consuming resources, disregarding tribal title to the land, and bringing legal and political pressure to bear on the territory's Indian inhabitants to give up their resource rights.

By the 1870s, cattlemen were defiantly grazing their cattle on Indian lands without compensation to the tribes. The near-starvation condition of many Indians and the constant presence of such a large supply of meat predictably led to violence and theft. On one occasion, Indian agents for the Cheyennes and Arapahoes and the agents for the Kiowas, Comanches, and Apaches called on the army for help. The agents charged the cattlemen with trespass and confiscated two hundred head of cattle, which they then turned over to the Indians for rations. The cattlemen were outraged, but, recognizing their extralegal status on the reservations, eventually agreed to be compensated at 3.5¢ per pound.[44] As western historian Edward Everett Dale noted long ago, cattlemen were dependent not just on Indian grasslands but also on the Indians, the agents, and the military for lucrative beef contracts. The same was true of the white traders who relied on the annuities of the tribe from year to year to provide them a steady market. Last but not least, outlaws and bands of petty thieves who preyed on Indian horses and relieved cattlemen of their animals and traders of their goods parasitized the entire system. Their persistence into the settlement era would constitute a major obstacle to Indian stock raising and farming after allotment.

In the 1860s and 1870s, yet another small but highly influential group of visitors arrived in west-central Oklahoma: the federal land surveyors. The surveyors' purpose in Oklahoma Territory was very different from the groups that had preceded them. Sent to document the region's potential for agricultural development and mineral deposits, the surveyors' assessment—their vision—was shaped by what they believed the region might become, in addition to what it already contained. Their work in Oklahoma, as elsewhere, was predicated on the belief that the landscape lacked order and rationality. Their presence was a prelude to white settlers' efforts to turn the Oklahoma "wilderness" into a garden two decades later.

As Paul Wallace Gates and John Opie have amply demonstrated, the dissection of the public domain into townships, sections, and quarter sections sprang from long-held Anglo notions of land ownership and its best or highest use. It was popularly held that the survey would aid in the even distribution of agricultural lands to ordinary citizens in fulfillment of Jefferson's democratic ideals based on individual land ownership. But as Opie has persuasively argued, the survey's only virtues were "its reliability in locating individual tracts and the trust-worthiness of accurate title to land."[45] In short, verification of legal title became the primary purpose of the survey in Oklahoma. In this regard, the survey was the tool of a larger and older principle in American land and economic policy: the transfer of all federal lands into private property. The "incongruous land system" that Gates so painstakingly documented evolved from numerous schemes and rulings enacted by the U.S. government in its recognition that above all else, land was capital. This was true regardless of the physical limitations of the land itself or how potentially productive for farming it was or was not.

Legally, land ownership was simply a business transaction. It was this mentality, coupled with the government's often confusing and contradictory disposal schemes, that allowed the American Land Company, for example, to preside over and dominate the distribution of much of the midwest in the 1830s and 1840s. The Preemption Act of 1841 and the Homestead Act of 1862, passed to show Congress's support of the ordinary citizen farmer, with its forest and desert variations, did little to stem the tide of land speculation (versus actual occupancy) at any time in western settlement.

By the 1880s, when debate over the Oklahoma Territory was reaching its apex in regard to the average American's so-called right to claim a quarter section of the last, best West, the right of those same claimants to speculate in land (as opposed to simply farming it) was taken for granted. William A. J. Sparks, commissioner of the Land Office from 1884 to 1887, described what he regarded as a completely indifferent attitude toward the legal dispersal of the public domain under his jurisdiction: "Men who would scorn to commit a dishonest act toward an individual, though he were a total stranger, eagerly listen to every scheme for evading the letter and spirit of the settlement laws, and in a majority of instances I believe avail themselves of them."[46] Commissioner Sparks, whom Paul Gates judged the ablest civil servant of the Land Office in American history, was ousted from his position as a result of his uncompromising stance against land fraud.

On the other side of the law, as early as 1850, Plains tribes were acting to preserve the bison range from potential outsiders.[47] Their stance became more strident in 1867, when Texas cattle began eating their way north through Oklahoma Territory. Although some tribal leaders could see the economic and ecological connections between the robe trade, the cattle drives, and the diminishing herds, most tribal leaders did not. Even so, white cattle drovers' accounts of their interactions with Indian peoples clearly indicate that the tribes intuitively understood that the cattle drovers were encroaching on their livelihoods in chasing and killing bison for sport, consuming grass, polluting water sources, and disturbing their pastoral and hunting refuges.

Drovers' encounters with Indians were frequently hostile and hard-bargained. Although some drovers considered the Indians' resistance to the drives unreasonable, others gladly paid their toll in cattle, coffee, and tobacco in recognition of the Indians' prior claim. Disrespectful stockmen, on the other hand, often paid a high price for their lack of consideration. In 1872, George Hindes ran into a group of Osage warriors who demanded a steer for passing through their lands. Hindes quickly reassured them that he had already picked one out—a large animal weighing nearly 1,500 pounds. Another drover, John Redus, was not so well disposed and reluctantly offered the group a crippled steer from his herd of over a thousand animals. After a short council among themselves, the Osages mounted their horses and rode yelling and shooting into Redus's herd. As Hindes recalled, "when the smoke and dust cleared, all he had left was his men and two hundred and fifty head of beeves that ran into my herd where the Indians did not follow them."[48] Another common tactic among the tribes was to stampede the cattle herds during the night and then ask to be paid in either cattle or horses for helping to round them up the next morning. These antics indicate that Indian peoples perfectly understood the economic value of their lands and all that they contained.

As bison became harder to find, the Kiowas, Comanches, Cheyennes, Arapahoes, and Plains Apaches increased their raids on Mexican and Texas settlements. These well-publicized predations in addition to the mixed-grass prairie's commercial value—to cattlemen, the railroads, and would-be farmers—led to a series of military encounters and stricter confinement of the Indians on reservations. Although allotment is often regarded by historians as the primary agent by which native peoples were deprived of their lands from 1880 to 1895, the redrawing of reservation boundaries by treaty account for 60 percent of the acreage that would be subsequently lost in the twentieth century.[49] The nomadic life of the southern plains tribes was nearing an end, setting in motion a new set of ecological relationships dominated by the values of Euro-American settlers and businessmen.

One of the earliest indicators to Indian peoples that Euro-Americans had arrived was the almost overnight construction of railroads through Indian and Oklahoma Territory. A vaguely articulated notion that the territory had been cruelly deprived of its rightful place in the economic development of the West gave Oklahoma's promoters and builders a sense of urgency unmatched by other western states.[50] Once opened for settlement, the "development of railways and urban centers was especially swift."[51] Railroads followed an unpredictable path as investors attempted to take advantage of the territory's unconventional land laws, meet the needs of an expanding national economy, and avoid expensive environmental obstacles.

One frequently made argument in favor of railroad development that would later have a dramatic impact on the fate of Indian attempts at agriculture was that the roads were a civilizing force in western development and would play a dominant role in building the economy of the new state of Oklahoma. The rhetoric was simple: Oklahoma Territory was a savage country waiting for the civilizing hand of roads and markets to bring it into the national economy. Left out of this view, of course, was the fact that the territory was already host to numerous "industries" that employed Indian peoples, explorers, traders, cattle drovers, and employees of the federal government at army posts, Indian agencies, agency schools, and land offices. Even would-be Oklahoma settlers, or Sooners, illegally camped along the region's borders for more than two decades before 1889, created their own unique shantytown economies. Together, all these elements formed a presettlement economy in Oklahoma Territory that may have seemed separate and elementary but was in fact already highly profitable and deeply dependent on the broader national economy in every way.

In spite of all this very human activity, Oklahoma Territory's white and black settlers regarded their new homes as virtually untouched and untapped by human activity. Yet long before the first settler had turned over a single row of sod, large portions of the parklike landscape observed by Irving in 1832 had become a semidesert of overgrazed grasslands intersected by eroding waterways largely stripped of their tree banks. The introduction of the horse and the substitution of cattle for bison by both whites and Indians, as well as the suppression of fire, further altered the grassland's former plant and animal populations as the resulting fractionalization of habitat zones negatively affected wildlife populations. As the ecotones between grassland and gallery forest disappeared, so too did the animals that inhabited them.[52] Last, a climatic shift to generally drier conditions resulted in numerous adaptations by plants, animals, and human beings. The "virgin" prairie soon to be claimed by farmer-settlers was a vastly different place from the bonanza environment the Comanches and Kiowas had entered two centuries earlier. A new set of cultural constructs, economic attractions, and social relations was unfolding in the mixed-grass prairie of Oklahoma Territory.

2

THE PROMISE

Far away, on the western frontier of the United States, explorers were given a brief opportunity to select the landscape to which their hearts led them. . . . Not the dark forest, waiting to be cut back and replaced with a pastoral landscape of crops and hedges. Not the empty desert flats, good only if irrigated and planted in grass and trees. But the intermediate habitat already in place, a terrain that we ourselves can instantly appreciate: a savanna, rolling gold and green, dissected by a sharp tracery of streams and lake, with clean dry air and clouds dappling a clear blue sky.

E. O. Wilson, Biophilia

Two years before Frederick Jackson Turner gave his famous frontier address, Oklahoma settlers were reveling in their roles as pioneers and discussing the historically pivotal place they occupied. Although they fashioned themselves as latter-day Daniel Boones, Oklahoma Sooners worked hard to shed their homespun image and join the nation's mainstream agricultural economy. Historian David Danbom's description of the average American farmer in 1900 as "part entrepreneur and part Jeffersonian yeoman, . . . at least half anachronism" fits the Sooner identity particularly well.[1]

Neither identity had much use or respect for the territorial landscape as it was in 1889. As Samuel Hays has observed, "Resource exploitation . . . reflected the attitude not merely of corporations, but of Americans in all walks of life. Small farmers, as well as corporate leaders, helped to establish a wasteful pattern of land use. Everyone in the nineteenth century hoped to make a killing from rising land values and from quickly extracting the cheap, virgin resources of the nation."[2] By the time of the first "opening" in Oklahoma to non-Indian settlement in 1889, private speculation in land was a national obsession.

The notion that land was capital and that legal title to it was more important than its potential for agricultural production helps explain why the traditional grid system, indifferent to geographical or environmental factors, was adopted in spite of the unsuitability of the Oklahoma landscape for a system developed in the more humid states. This incongruity did not go completely unnoticed before Oklahoma settlement. John Wesley Powell's vision of the Oklahoma landscape lay in his training as a physical scientist. While others observed the rich grasslands and animal populations, Powell saw inanimate building blocks—soils, geology, and watercourses—and envisioned what the West could become in terms of sustainable communities. "What seized [Powell's] imagination was the inorganic. He sensed a compelling story in that realm, one that would reveal how the West had come to be what it was and would suggest to Americans what they needed to do if they were to make a successful civilization in the region."[3] Powell's newtonian focus on the region's basic elements later would influence both the Reclamation Service and the U.S. Department of Agriculture, but not until well after Oklahoma's pioneering stage had passed.

Powell's other vision—that the General Land Office abandon the township and range system that divided the landscape into quarter sections regardless of the physical properties obtained—went nowhere. Had Powell's revised system of metes and bounds based on the classification of the land according to its unique properties been adopted, the landscape of the West, including Oklahoma, would look far different today. Powell recommended that the landscape be classified and studied and only those portions that were suitable for agriculture be settled. Powell recognized that land needed to be classified in order to determine its value, if not its actual use. On the other hand, his idea that large portions of the West, including Oklahoma, were unsuitable for traditional extractive use was simply too limiting and pessimistic for late nineteenth century politicians and promoters. The result was a national survey that ignored the landscape's irregularities and shortcomings but took note of every potential commodity within its artificially imposed boundaries.

The survey grid created a new landscape; points and right angles that adhered to the rigid columns and corners of the range and township lines. As settlers took up their quarter sections, the location of centrally located services such as grain elevators, mills, gins, and railroad stations followed the logic of the survey rather than the topography of the land. Small towns emerged, not as a consequence of environmentally favorable location, but simply because of their placement on the survey. Older trails and roads did not disappear immediately as a result of the survey, but were eventually subsumed as private property beneath a new system of straight roads and ninety-degree angles. Those few trails not abandoned became the foundation of railroad lines and the modern highway system. Overall, however, Oklahoma's system of rural roads followed the township and range lines of the federal surveys. As farmers took up their claims and fenced them off, travelers were obliged to follow the fence lines to their destinations, lending an uneven landscape the guise of predictability and orderliness.

The introduction of railroads in the 1870s and 1880s symbolized yet another vision of the prairies and woodlands of west-central Oklahoma. Like the surveyors, railroad developers saw potential for the region as a source of revenue for would-be customers, especially farmers. They considered their role essential to the development of the region; railroads were integral to the industrial model of progress. In a 1908 speech to the Trans-Mississippi Commercial Congress, J. C. Stubbs, a railroad executive, ascribed to the railroads almost all the credit for the increase in Oklahoma Territory's value from $73 million to $32.5 billion since 1889. He graciously acknowledged the work of the farmer, the miner, the manufacturer, and the merchant, but claimed that even their success would have been "impossible with the aid of artificial means of transportation. Railroads entered the territory, overcame these obstacles and it may fairly be said were and will be the chief instrumentality in uncovering the wealth of this Trans-Mississippi country."[4]

The railroads, wanting to make the most profit from the sale of land ceded them by federal and state governments, were open to incentives offered them by town developers, sometimes veering off an otherwise direct route in order to pass through particular towns. As a result, the routes taken by the "roads" that entered the territory between 1875 and 1907 were unpredictable because they primarily followed commerce. Where the railroad had been given a right of way along natural watercourses, the roads' land holdings were often the most valuable for agricultural purposes and therefore brought high prices. Where no watercourses existed, the route followed the survey lines, connecting and creating commercially important centers at appropriate junctures.

Pressure to build rail lines through Oklahoma and Indian territories began to mount during the cattle trailing era. In 1870, the Missouri-

Kansas-Texas won a bid to continue its line south from the Kansas-Oklahoma border through Indian Territory, terminating in Denison, Texas, near Dallas. Although the right of way was not granted by the Indian tribes, a general resentment among northern whites against those tribes that had supported the Confederacy during the Civil War gave the railroad the political clout it needed. An east-west route was also authorized in 1870 but not completed. As a result of Indian raids, slow treaty negotiations, and a lack of white settlers, no other railroads were built in Oklahoma Territory before 1889.

The official role of the government in the development of railroads was philosophically consistent with its role in land survey and classification. As historian Carl Degler observed, "all seemed to feel, if one can judge from their actions, that to aid in the construction of railroads was to participate in the destiny of America."[5] Just as the federal government was instrumental in alienating Indian lands through the reservation system and in conducting the land runs, so too did local, state, and national governments subsidize the expansion of the railroads through Oklahoma.

By 1885, in anticipation of the opening of the territory for white settlement, ten separate bills authorizing railroads through Indian lands and Oklahoma were presented to Congress. The most famous line to be built as a result was the Atchison-Topeka and Sante Fe, which ran from Chicago, Illinois, to Galveston, Texas, through the so-called unassigned lands in central Oklahoma. This was the line that many of the original 89ers rode to the first land run. Like the Missouri-Kansas-Texas line, the Atchison-Topeka and Sante Fe became the foundation of a major highway artery through the state: Highways 69 and 77, respectively. Although initially behind other states in terms of railroad development, Oklahoma caught up fast. By statehood in 1907, more than seven thousand miles of track had been laid in the new state—far more track than was economically feasible to maintain. More than any other feature of the changing landscape, the railroads represented Oklahoma's connection to the national economy.

That connection relied squarely on the future work of farmers. Oklahoma Territory was opened for agricultural settlement at the height of a transition in farmers' identity: from yeoman to businessman. Among Oklahoma Territory's first white settlers, pioneering was valued far more for its promise of economic reward than a process in itself. The most respected pioneers in the community became those who had accumulated the greatest wealth—presumably through hard work and self-help. Ironically, the most successful farmers in Oklahoma did not toil alone but relied on extensive kinship and social networks to see them through their initial hard times.

At the time of Oklahoma's opening to non-Indian settlement between 1889 and 1904, the era of self-sufficient farming was functionally over. Territory farmers were temporarily obliged to live in the same rude manner that pioneers had endured a century earlier, but they were not content to remain there. Territory farmers were pragmatic above all else, embracing a world market culture and a new, "progressive" model of farming based on profit, efficiency, and technological innovation in order to compete successfully with other sectors of American society.[6] Adam Ward Rome, an agricultural economic historian, has succinctly summarized that "in the West, even in the earliest settlements, prairie farmers grew crops for profit."[7] Only later did they see their migration as a romantic American adventure—and only then if everything had gone well.

The first run, April 22, 1889, was on the unassigned lands because they had not been promised to any Indian nation during the period of the Indians' removal to Oklahoma from east of the Mississippi River in the 1830s. The second run took place on September 22, 1891, and opened the Iowa, Sac, Fox, and Pottawatomie-Shawnee reservations. Guthrie, the territorial capital and future Logan County seat, was founded near the center of the new county. Agriculturally, Logan County is considered to be within the far eastern edge of the "fortunate" part of Oklahoma, where the red bed plains are fairly level and wheat is the primary crop. The county is approximately 747 square miles or 478,000 acres, most of which is a gentle upland plain that slopes west to east toward a wooded area known as the cross timbers. Numerous creeks, such as Fitzgerald Creek, Soldier Creek, and Bear Creek, flow southwest to northeast through the center of the county, while Skeleton Creek makes its way in the opposite direction, northwest to southeast. The largest watercourse, the Cimarron River, named for its red earth banks and brown water, neatly bisects the county north and south through Guthrie. In addition, thousands of spring-fed streams that flowed only intermittently initially covered the county, creating innumerable microenvironments that supported what native flora and fauna remained in the wake of the now-forgotten bison and cattle herds.

For black pioneers, the new county of Logan was a promised land, a fresh start far from the troubles of the past. Long before the first land opening in 1889, African Americans were a highly visible sector of society in Indian Territory, east of the unassigned lands. As slaves of the so-called five civilized tribes, the Cherokees, Chickasaws, Chocktaws, Creeks, and Seminoles, African Americans had been removed to Indian Territory along with the tribes after the Treaty of New Echota in 1835. John Ridge, one of the Cherokee signers, estimated that in 1826, his nation contained, "13,583 native citizens . . . and 1,277 African slaves." Of the relationship between the Indians and their slaves, Ridge noted, "There is a scanty instance of African mixture with the Cherokee blood" and that "African slaves are mostly held by Half breeds and full Indians of distinguished talents."[8] Although there was a great deal of variability in the way each of the Indian nations dealt with its slaves, the lives of Indian slaves was comparable to that of plantation laborers in Georgia and Tennessee. This system was maintained after the tribes' removal west of the Mississippi to Indian Territory.

After the Civil War, the Cherokees and other tribes who had sided with the Confederacy were forced to give up some of their lands and emancipate their slaves. These "Indian freedmen" founded the first all-black communities in Oklahoma. It was not until after 1877, however, that the majority of these former slaves were officially given any land to cultivate on their own. Frequently educated and skilled, the freedmen of Indian Territory wished to remain on their own lands rather than take up new homesteads to the west after 1889. They resented the migration of what they called the "state negros" wishing to settle in Oklahoma Territory, with their "bowing and scraping and scratching the head."[9] The Indian freedmen, however, soon found themselves suffering equally from discrimination and hostility at the hands of both Indians and whites after 1890.[10]

Other African Americans entered Oklahoma Territory in the ranks of the U.S. Army or working in the cattle drives. After the Civil War, two African American regiments, dubbed the Buffalo Soldiers by Indian peoples, were often engaged in helping to suppress Indian attacks on white settlements in Kansas and Texas.[11] Within the cattle-trailing industry, African Americans held various positions, although they were most conspicuous in their role as trail cooks. As a result, a small but seasoned group of African Americans arrived in Oklahoma Territory for the run in 1889 with a first-hand knowledge of its unique landscape, people, and climate.

It was rare, however, for a black farmer to take up a homestead all alone. African Americans' sense of community was especially strong in the years after the Civil War. In W. E. B. DuBois's 1911 novel *The Quest of the Silver Fleece,* the communal efforts of former slaves to reclaim a swamp and remake it into a productive cotton field becomes "the symbol of community self-reliance and virtue, [whereas] the 'swamp' becomes a source of strength and autonomy."[12] It was this same sense of community, and its intimate connection to agricultural production, that African American migrant farmers from the South carried to Oklahoma in the last decade of the nineteenth century.

African Americans' desire to become farmer-landowners in the decades after the Civil War has been thoroughly and convincingly documented by historians.[13] Even in urban areas where landownership was not an option, blacks worked tirelessly to preserve their local institutions, such as churches, schools, hospitals, and social clubs. In the face of widespread efforts by whites to maintain the inferior economic status of blacks, the African American community forged new patterns of mutual assistance. As David Thelen has submitted, "The welfare of the individual was the welfare of the race in a world circumscribed by whites."[14] In the period 1890 to 1920, both rural and urban blacks considered themselves engaged in a mutual struggle for self-determination against huge odds.

The stories of African Americans' various attempts to obtain land in Oklahoma illustrate the hopes and dreams they had before pulling up stakes and becoming Oklahoma bound.[15] On the basis of court records, interviews, and the reminiscences of Oklahoma's first black settlers, it is clear that most black migrants wanted to become farmers but did not expect to acquire their land in the same way as whites—that is, through the runs or in the lotteries. African Americans acquired their land most often through land speculators, boosters, and individuals who sold them abandoned or unworked parcels, known as relinquishments.

Black migrants' determination to own farms was sometimes exploited by profiteers, both white and African American. Shortly after the 1889 run on the unassigned lands, Marion Blair, a white speculator, advertised lots at Lincoln Town, the "first African town ever started in a civilized country." With the help of two clergymen who hoped to found an academy with freedmen's funds, Blair persuaded a number of black home seekers in Topeka to settle along the Cimarron River just west of Logan County. The land was second rate with plenty of blackjack timber. The assumption was that settlers would sell the timber for cash, hunt wild game, and take up subsistence farming on 40-acre lots. The first group of two hundred settlers was reported to have grown to nearly a thousand inside of a year.[16] Blair's interest in founding the town, however, was short-lived and profit-driven. He expected black farmers to make do with smaller, less productive parcels than any of their white neighbors, and Lincoln Town was soon abandoned.

Some speculators and land "finders" were even more unscrupulous in their dealings with black farmers wanting to come to Oklahoma. W. L. McNulty, a witness to the run on the Cheyenne and Arapahoe reservation in 1892, interviewed a "young white promoter who had accompanied two hundred negroes from Topeka Kansas . . . he boasted of collecting $5 apiece from the home seekers, for which he promised to secure each one a claim."[17] After paying their own train fare to Hennessey, the group walked 16 miles west to the Cimarron River, where they were instructed to make the run along with everyone else.

One Guthrie resident recalled how another group of African American settlers was similarly swindled by two black promoters in Memphis. After paying for lands near Kingfisher and traveling the entire route from Tennessee in a "walking train," they arrived to discover that "there was no land to be had. Those two Negroes had taken the poor peoples' money and had given them nothing in return . . . There are only a few left who took part in those times, and they do not wish to mention it, they were so disappointed."[18]

Most African American migrants, however, were fully aware of promoters' schemes and avoided outside organizations. These settlers came in fairly large groups made up of whole communities or in extended kinship networks in much the same fashion as earlier migrations to Kansas in 1879. One of the best-known organizers of such a party to Logan County was Sandy Dickens. The son of a black slave mother and a Seminole father, Sandy was raised in slavery in Alabama. After the war, Dickens traveled with Booker T. Washington in his campaign to raise funds for the founding of Tuskegee Institute in Alabama. While on the road with Washington, Dickens learned about the opportunities for blacks in Oklahoma Territory.

Dickens immediately returned to his home in Alabama and organized the entire community into an "immigration" party. The ensemble arrived in Guthrie in January 1892 and settled on farms to the west and south of the city in Logan County.[19] "With Sandy Dickens as leader, they were active in building churches and schools . . . and took an active part in the civic, political and religious affairs of Guthrie and Logan County."[20] Dickens died in 1910, a revered patriarch of the Oklahoma African American community.

Mary Brown Williamson's family also traveled as a group. As she put it, "We did not have to leave Memphis, Tennessee, but it was our desire. There was so much mobbing going on we wanted to get where it was a free country, so we would not be so afraid for our lives, and where we could live a straight life." A group of nearly four hundred formed an "Immigration Organization," with Thomas Holland as its treasurer. Mary's family came by team and wagon, but "some walked every step of the way." They were fed and cared for by the people of the towns they passed through on the two-month journey. Upon their arrival in Kingfisher, just west of Logan County, "there was nothing for us to do, only scatter out and settle where we could." In spite of the hardships of the journey and the work of making a farm from scratch, Williamson claimed with pride that she was glad they had come, even though "we were offered less assistance in Oklahoma than anywhere on the road."[21]

Eventually Mary's family moved to Oklahoma City, where her father became a teacher in an all-black neighborhood. In recalling her family's trials, Mary drew parallels between her uncle's and father's Old Testament teachings about Israel and the promised land and her own family's exodus to Oklahoma. "I began to look on this as the promised land," she explained. "We tried to help the people coming in. Very often we'd have tents in the back yard, people camping there until they could get a place . . . We tried to help others get a start."[22] Once in Oklahoma, migrant groups tended to settle near one another so as to continue to offer one another assistance and support.

Extended kinship groups often formed the foundation of long-lasting communities of blacks in Oklahoma Territory. Edna Randolph Slaughter and her family all migrated from Tennessee. Her maternal uncle migrated to Oklahoma first and then sent for the rest of the family. "My father talked it up in the family and finally about seven families decided to make the move." The family first went to Purcell, where her uncle lived, because "There was a big dugout on my uncle's property . . . Several families of us moved in there."[23]

Although the early 1890s saw the largest influx of black settlers, the stream continued steadily up through the turn of the century and beyond. By the mid-1890s, the pattern of group migration and solidarity in helping new arrivals get a start was well established. J. H. Crowell of Orlando in Logan County was following a well-worn path to relocation in Oklahoma when he arrived in 1894 at his sister's farm in the southeast corner of the Cherokee Strip. Here he helped his brother-in-law with the farm and attended school for the first time in his life. "My parents were slaves and I had never had much of an opportunity so when the first school was organized near my sister's home I went to it for one term. There were white and colored children attending there; later another school was built and colored children were separated from the whites."[24] Although his experiences in Oklahoma were largely the result of his own hard work and initiative, Crowell's individual economic success started with his connection to his sister and the community they settled in.

The vast majority of African American hopefuls present for the 1889 run were not native to eastern Oklahoma and were attracted to the territory by the promise of free homes. There is some uncertainty about the numbers of blacks who entered homestead claims in the original 1889 runs, primarily as a result of the way in which claims were entered and litigated and also because the federal census of 1890 is no longer extant, which would have counted farmers living on homesteads according to race.[25] John Womack's comparison of the federal land tract records with the 1890 territorial census found only forty-two blacks who made successful claims under the Homestead Act. These were concentrated in an area just north of Kingfisher and a few miles west of Guthrie.[26] The number of African Americans who successfully participated in subsequent land runs and lotteries was also small. Although the *Langston City Herald* claimed that "nearly a thousand colored families secured homes"[27] after the opening of the Sac, Fox, and Pottawatomie-Shawnee reserves, the number of black families that staked claims under homestead laws was much lower. The major obstacles for blacks who attempted the runs were white obstructionist tactics up and down the "lines," or entry points, and the subsequent difficulty of obtaining legal right to claims at the land office, or, if contested, in the territorial courts.

In September 1891, in a prelude to the second run on the territory, the *New York Times* reported that about fifteen hundred "mostly Negroes" had gathered at Langston to make the run into the Cimarron Valley, but "many white settlers, among them being numbers of cowboys, object to the Negroes' plans, and will take desperate chances to preempt choice claims in the very face of the negro host." On the day of the run, September 23, the *Times* reported that a group of Negroes who attempted to make a start at the north end of the line near the best agricultural lands "were warned away by the whites, and, fearing for their lives, went back south among those of their own color."[28] Violence was commonplace during the runs, and African American settlers were wise to avoid confrontation.[29] Federal marshals stationed along the starting line could barely control the crowds of white would-be claimants. The marshals' primary task was bringing back Sooners—claimants who snuck into the territory before it was officially opened and then claimed that they were there "sooner" than the others.

For those blacks who did stake claims, there was always the risk that it would be contested by a white settler and all their investment lost. A. M. Capers, who staked a claim near Orlando in the northeast portion of Logan County, recalled that immediately after he and his brother staked their claims, he was charged with being a Sooner. Fortunately for Capers, he had bought a pony at public auction in Waco, Texas, on the day he was accused of having illegally entered the territory. By furnishing the local land office with affidavits from Texas auction officials, he was able to retain title to his claim.[30]

One ex-slave born in Macon, Mississippi, in 1855 who migrated to Oklahoma in 1891 made the run but ingeniously avoided all the paperwork of the land office. William Stewart, carrying only a blanket and a gun, simply walked west into the territory until he encountered two men on a claim they had staked but did not want. They offered to sell the claim to Stewart for $10. Stewart agreed but said he would give the money to Messrs. Coil and Smith, who owned a general store in Guthrie. The men were to give the transfer papers to the merchants. "The next day, Mr Smith went with me to the Land Office to see that the claim was approved and properly transferred to me." Stewart remained on his 160-acre claim, 23 miles east of Guthrie, for the rest of his life. His claim was twice contested by whites after he bought it, but he held onto it with the help of Coil and Smith, who Stewart praised as "wholesale grocerymen and cotton dealers and fine men and they certainly were nice to me."[31]

Stewart's and Capers's experiences illustrate several realities for black settlers: they were not as well equipped to make the land runs as many whites were; they purchased, rather than staked, their claims; they often required the help of whites in maintaining their claims legally, and their lands were often located in less desirable agricultural areas. Taken together, these factors worked to locate black settlers in the most environmentally sensitive portions of Logan County—a fact that would lead to changes both for the ecology of the area and black farmers' social and economic networks.

By statehood in 1907, there were at least twenty-five all-black towns in Oklahoma.[32] Some lasted only a short while, some remained predominantly black, and others became home to both black and white residents. Twelve miles east and north of the territorial capital of Guthrie in Antelope Township, Langston was the best known of the black towns populated by migrants to Oklahoma between 1890 and 1920. Named for John Mercer Langston, a black congressman from Virginia, the town was founded in 1890 by politician and entrepreneur Edwin P. McCabe, who purchased the land from a white speculator, Charles Robbins of Guthrie.[33]

As in other portions of Oklahoma where black farmers settled, Langston contained only second-rate soil and plenty of cross timber. This made the section less than ideal for farming, but it was well situated as a town site, flanked by the Cimarron River to the north and two major creeks to the east and west. More important, the new town was conveniently located on the main road between the territorial capital at Guthrie 12 miles to the west and the newly established Agricultural and Mechanical College at Stillwater in Payne County just 30 miles to the east.

McCabe, already a well-known figure in Kansas where he had served two terms as state auditor from 1882 to 1886, and William L. Eagleson, a newspaperman from Kansas, began publication of the *Langston City Herald* in 1890. It was not long before copies of the paper were being circulated throughout the South. As a result of the papers' advertisements for homes in Oklahoma in the weeks before the 1891 opening, Langston's population swelled to nearly two thousand people—most of whom were migrants who hoped to stake claims. A similar pattern of population growth preceded the land runs of 1892 in the Cheyenne-Arapahoe lands and in 1893 when the Cherokee outlet was opened for settlement.[34] Thereafter, the town's population steadily declined until 1897, when the Oklahoma Territorial Legislature authorized the creation of a Colored Agricultural and Normal University under the provisions of the Morrill Act and located it just west of the town.[35]

Even after 1900, local black newspapers continued to carry glowing reports of the salubrious social and ecological climate of the territory in order to attract newcomers. In April 1901, the *Oklahoma Guide*, a black paper edited by G. N. Perkins of Guthrie, was advertising the formation of a "Colored Immigration Bureau." The purpose of the bureau, according to Perkins, was to furnish members with information on the opening of the Kiowa reservation, to instruct colored people in getting homes, and to provide all necessary information about Oklahoma Territory. Upon the opening of the Kiowa reservation, Editor Perkins, who was also president of the bureau, advised that "if the negro would wake up and get a move on themselves, at least 2000 of them could get 160 acres of this fine land almost free, which is worth from $250 to $5000."

Perkins also noted that in the area surrounding Langston, "the colored farmers are doing excellently . . . They raise from ten to sixty bushels of corn per acre, from one-fourth to one and one-half bales of cotton per acre, from ten to thirty bushels of wheat per acre and all other kind of produce in abundance." The reason for farmers' success, according to Perkins, was the favorable climate. He reported in tongue-in-cheek fashion, "Oklahoma is not disturbed much by hot winds or drought, it is a subtle fact now that Oklahoma is assured of a crop each year, as any state in the union."[36]

City boosters like Perkins knew that black Oklahomans brought a taste and knowledge for certain agricultural products with them from their former homes and tried to appeal to them on that basis. As a culture, the South had long been associated with certain agricultural products and food preparation techniques, especially for corn and pork, the staples of the southern diet. Variations and additions beyond the numerous pork and corn dishes, common to most southerners, depended on the socioeconomic status of the individual. Wealthy white southerners tended to eat more beef, lamb, and dairy products. Poor whites and blacks ate fewer eggs and poultry, more game, sweet potatoes, turnips, peas, and beans in addition to their regular rations of corn and pork. Accordingly, these were the crops initially planted by black settlers to Oklahoma. According to Sam Bowers Hilliard, the southern environment was so conducive to agriculture generally that "whatever deficiencies the soil might have had it was much more apt to affect the growers choice of money crops than his attempts at subsistence."[37] Space and the price of feed were the limiting factors for blacks in the South—a fact that made Oklahoma all the more attractive.

A presumed escape from social tyranny was another reason for black farmers to migrate to Oklahoma, and for a while, this looked possible. Mack McClelland, a black migrant from Tennessee, took up a claim of

80 acres, most of it in cross timber, near Kingfisher and moved his family there in 1893. "Several colored families agreed to get claims near each other," he recalled, and "we named it the 'New Dora' Settlement." McClelland's nearest neighbors were the Erlenmaiers, a Dutch family that settled in New Dora at about the same time. "He managed to get hold of one old horse and I got one. We would put these together and have a team. We would get a load of wood, cut and take it to El Reno. There we would trade it for two sacks of corn meal and come home."[38] Stories like these kept black settlers hopeful about life in the promised land of Oklahoma Territory.

A. M. Capers, whose fortuitous purchase of a pony allowed him to remain on his claim, recalled his neighbor, W. A. Clinkinbeard, had some young steers that he broke to work with Capers's team to break sod for themselves and their other neighbors for a fee. They also used their combined team to haul crops to Perry and Guthrie, a two-day trip.[39] Other accounts by black settlers near Langston mention friendly exchanges between whites and blacks in the early days of settlement. Roscoe Dunjee, editor of the *Black Dispatch*, noted that "at most of the church socials and social events there was in those days always a sprinkling of white people . . . Those were the great old days that are gone forever."[40]

As earlier noted by black settler J. H. Crowell, rural elementary schools were generally integrated in the territory, as were stores, banks, saloons, and most public conveyances.[41] In more populated townships, however, as in the agricultural areas surrounding Langston, the density of the black population lent itself to notions of racial isolationism and self-help. Langston residents in particular exhibited a genuine spirit of cooperation and community spirit. In April 1891, the *New York Times* sent a reporter to Guthrie and Langston to investigate the numerous claims being made by white newspapers in Arkansas, Kansas, and Missouri that thousands of African Americans were making the pilgrimage to Oklahoma from their homes in the South for the express purpose of forming an all-black state.[42]

Southern newspapers had responded to these rumors by depicting black migrants as outcasts of the worst sort, possessing little more than the rags on their backs. In contrast, the *Times* reporter found that the busy town of Langston had approximately two hundred permanent residents and that the most destitute among them "have been cared for by persons of their own race until they could help themselves and help others." On black-owned farms nearby, the *Times* discovered,

"two, four and sometimes eight families, all working together await-
ing the time when more lands will be opened for settlement." Within
the city limits, it was reported "83 acres of land have been broken up
and will this year be used as a cooperative garden by the entire
colony." The *Times* reluctantly admitted that it was the poor white
farmers of the township who were the biggest drain on their neighbors
and the most insistent on government help—not the black agricultural community.[43]

To counter white stereotypes of black shiftlessness and poverty, and
to prepare potential residents for the reality that awaited them in
Oklahoma, the *Langston City Herald* regularly advised black southerners considering a move to "be prepared to support yourself and your
family for up to year, *We make this point strong.*"[44] When the *Times*
asked the new settlers how they were going to get by in their first year,
"the general reply was that they 'did not come here as paupers' and
that they brought enough money with them to live on for some time."
One settler from Missouri said he came with "some little money" and
did not expect to raise any crops for two years.[45] What Langston residents could not have known was the ways in which the physical environment, even more than the social climate, would ultimately shake
their faith in Oklahoma Territory.

Figure 1. Mixed grass prairie near Medicine Lodge Kansas 1892. Smithsonian Institute, National Anthropological Archives, Suitland Maryland.

Figure 2. Homestead, one half mile east of Watonga Oklahoma, circa 1892. Photo courtesy of Frank Beneda collection, Watonga Oklahoma.

Figure 3. Immigrant homesteader in front of dogtrot log cobin with sof roof. Blaine County, circa 1895. Photo courtesy of Frank Beneda collection, Watonga Oklahoma.

Figure 4. Abandoned commercial building, Langston Oklahoma, May 2002. Photo by author.

Figure 5. Abandoned territorial school, Langston Oklahoma, May 2002. Photo by author.

Figure 6. Boarding school house. Kiowa, Comanche and Apache Agency, Record Group 75, Records of the Bureau of Indian Affairs, "Photos of Indian Agency Schools, 1876–1896." National Archives and Record Administration, Washington, D.C.

Figure 7. Encroachment of red cedar on pasture land in northern Caddo County Oklahoma. Photo by author.

Figure 8. The effect of different land uses are dramatically illustrated on this hillside, where each quarter section is under a different regime, i.e., cedar infested pasture, managed pasture, agricultural fallow, and freshly plowed red earth, May 2002. Photo by author.

Figure 9. Bison calf and adults on tall grass prairie preserve, eastern Oklahoma. Photo by author.

3

THE BLACK FRONTIER

The war of races in Oklahoma is sure to come, but it will not be fought with guns and knives. The weapons will be the plow and hoe, which will be wielded by each race upon its own lands. It remains to be seen whether the hot sun of Oklahoma will favor the black cuticle of the cotton and tobacco grower or the white skin of the corn and wheat raiser.
New York Times, April 9, 1891

In 1905, the *Boley Progress* was proudly boosting a new black town 70 miles east of Guthrie as "very productive and well watered, making an excellent farming and stock county. Streams are well stocked with fish while the surrounding forest abounds in deer, turkey and many of the species of the smaller game."[1] In comparison with earlier pamphlets and circulars, these later advertisements were tempered in their descriptions of the territory. Nevertheless, advertisements that described the fecund territorial environment written by men like Perkins, Eagleson, and Roscoe Dunjee of the *Black Dispatch* in Oklahoma City continued to attract new black settlers to the Langston area past Oklahoma statehood in 1907. Anywhere that black families could envision a self-sufficient lifestyle and escape the unremitting cycle of poverty and indebtedness that characterized the southern sharecropping system was bound to look attractive. Although some black speculators saw Oklahoma as an opportunity for quick wealth, the majority of African American settlers came to stay and were encouraged by what they were told about the landscape of the territory. Yet on the eve of statehood, the ecological and economic niches within which black farmers operated had already begun to constrict.

For black farm families, Oklahoma Territory was more than just a place to get ahead. It was an escape from a new and intense wave of racism and violence rocking the nation, a place to put down roots and make a home in relative safety and security.[2] Oklahoma Territory's African American settlers hoped to secure complete independence from their former owners by becoming farm owners and operators. As the *Langston City Herald* put it, "There is no use talking; nothing makes a colored man feel prouder than to stand on his own property and call it home."[3] Ownership, not leasing or sharecropping, was the goal. For nearly two decades, that ideal looked tantalizingly close. For a few black families, it became a reality.

The political and economic limits of black land ownership in the territory had a direct effect on the size of their farms and the ecology of the areas in which they settled. Unlike white-owned county news-papers in the 1890s that only advertised lots in excess of 160 acres for sale, the *Herald* regularly published the land office filing fees on 80 acres ($7) and even 40 acres ($6). The price of land in and around Langston rose steadily after 1900 depending on location, soil quality, access to water, and improvements. Advertisements for farms ranged anywhere from $200 to more than $1,000 in Logan County when J. H. Crowell, a black farmer, purchased a second farm in 1901 for $1,000. The average assessed value for all farms in Antelope Township in 1904, however, was about half of that, or between $500 and $600. According to a U.S. Department of Agriculture (USDA) 1909 soil survey report, the price of poorer sandy land was $20 an acre or less, while prairie farms went for between $10 and $80 an acre, an increase in value from 1890 to 1900 of more than 100 percent. Black-owned farms in Logan County, however, were assessed far lower values and reflected the county's variable soil quality as black farmers purposely sought out the least expensive and, for white farmers, least desirable parcels.

Even so, white farmers were often resentful of their black neighbors. William Eagleson, the future editor of the *Herald,* in March 1890 responded to white threats against black settlers in Oklahoma by declaring, "We propose to exercise our prerogatives as American citizens, be it on a forty, eighty or 160 acre tract . . . We are in this race to finish."[4] Eagleson was not alone in taking a strong stand for black land ownership—it was the rallying cry of freedmen and freedwomen throughout the South. Elizabeth Rauh Bethel, an historian, discovered that in Promised Land, South Carolina, an all-black community of farmers in the 1880s, that "it was not the fertility of soil or the possibility of economic profit that attracted the freedmen to those farms. The single opportunity for landownership . . . was the prime attraction."[5] For former bondsmen everywhere, land ownership was a privilege to be sought after in itself.

Anticipating white resistance to their presence as landowners in the territory, African Americans rarely homesteaded alone. Yet some exceptional individuals staked claims on their own. Their success at remaining undetected was generally the result of the undesirability of their land for crops. Wilson Randle of Tennessee recalled that he "found his place" because "no one else wanted it because there was so much better land without so much timber on it . . . I made a dugout on the place and grubbed out the trees whenever I could find time. I had no horses and had to dig up the land with a grubbing hoe and plant peas, corn and melons."[6] By taking up marginal lands in order to avoid conflict with Anglo-Americans and diversifying their crops beyond the familiar cotton and corn, some African American farmers were relatively successful at maintaining themselves and their families in the years before statehood.

Black farmers were successful largely because of their experiences with living on the social and environmental fringe. The family of William Black of Texas is a good example. After successfully claiming a 160-acre tract in 1892, William Black returned to Texas, where he already owned two "black land" farms. His oldest son Thomas was then sent to live out the residency requirement for the Oklahoma property. Barely twenty years old, Thomas "broke out farm land, dug a well and made a fence of saplings cut from black jack trees." He raised cash money for the land patent by walking 8 miles to Langston to work on roads and building crews for 50 cents a day. On May 3, 1897, Thomas Black paid $204 to the land office in Guthrie and was issued a patent on his property, located in the blackjack country south of present-day Coyle.

Thomas then sent for his fiancée, Mary Horst, from Texas, who had been waiting for Thomas to return from Oklahoma. She refused to live in Thomas's one-room log cabin, so they lived for a time with his uncle and aunt nearby. She did not want her new family to know she was disappointed with her circumstances, so each day she slipped out alone "to the orchard behind their log cabin and cried my eyes out." For Mary Horst, Oklahoma did not represent new opportunity but the loss of a cherished home in Texas. Over the next several years, however, most of the black family migrated to Oklahoma and settled near one another in Logan and Lincoln counties.[7]

By 1900, Langston's black agricultural hinterland in Logan County encompassed three townships of 6 square miles each: Antelope Township, Bear Creek Township directly south of Antelope, and an unnamed township to the east of the city containing the present-day town of Coyle. Of these three townships, Antelope contained the most African American residents at the turn of the century.

When the constitution of the new state was finally approved in 1906, its two outstanding features were the protection of private property interests and the legalized separation of the races. Before statehood, however, cooperation between black and white settlers varied enormously, depending on the locale. In urban centers like Guthrie and Oklahoma City, blacks were segregated from whites almost from the town's founding. But in rural areas claimed by recent European immigrants with little or no experience with either slavery or historic race relations, black farmers enjoyed a high level of tolerance, cooperation, and mutual dependence with their white neighbors.

Yet even those farmers who did not arrive with negative opinions regarding black farm practice inadvertently created restrictions for black farmers by excluding them from their cooperative networks. In the years just before statehood and after the land runs, hundreds of newly arrived blacks arrived to take up farming in Logan County, not as owner-operators, but as sharecroppers. In many cases, these new arrivals were offered contracts similar to contracts in other southern agricultural communities. A lifelong resident of Logan County of German ancestry, Otto Flasch, whose family still owns and operates hundreds of acres of land in Logan County just east of Langston University, expressed disdain for the way some white landlords after 1900 had duped black tenants into working cotton farms that paid them little or nothing but brought a tremendous annual profit for the landowner. The German community in Logan preferred to see African American farmers in better circumstances, but according to Flasch, concern did not mean that blacks were invited to join their support network of shared labor, machinery, marketing, and insurance against natural disaster. The German families of Logan helped one another out in times of crisis (illness, fire, or other hazard), but this help was not extended to their black neighbors. Flasch ventured that the German community would have aided a black family only if they were tenants of a German landowner.[8]

Given the exclusionary behavior of even the most benevolent white farmers in Logan, then, it is no wonder that black farmers chose to settle near one another, with predictable ecological and social results. Black farms were smaller and more intensely farmed than larger white-owned farms, and they were located in clusters on marginal lands that were subject to a number of environmental problems, the worst of which was erosion. More important, many black-owned farms were unoccupied—that is, the owner did not live on the land he or she farmed. In keeping with their community-oriented pratices, many black families chose to live in an all-black town and travel to their farms to work them. This too would prove to have an adverse effect on whites' perception of black farm practice.

Anecdotal evidence of these trends is confirmed in the records for the county. According to the twelfth federal census, there were thirty-three black farm families living in Antelope Township in 1900. Of these, twenty-six families owned their farms, while the remainder rented their land. One group of six families lived 2 miles south of the town, and another eight families were spread out on individual farmsteads east of Langston toward Coyle. The balance of the township's black farmers lived within Langston's city limits in homes clustered around the business district and the newly founded all-black college. In 1904, the total population of Antelope Township was 958 persons, 623 listed as "white" and 335 designated as "colored." But only 108 "colored" residents lived outside of Langston City, compared with half the families in 1900 who lived on individual rural tracts. This means that more than two-thirds of the black population lived in Langston, although the vast majority of Antelope's black residents were listed as farmers in both the 1900 manuscript census records and in the 1904 township assessments.[9] The pattern of settlement in Logan County is clear: black farm owners commuted to their farms from their homes in Langston, which offered them greater security and access to a social life through the local church and the new agricultural school.

Regardless of where they lived, whether in town or on their farms, African American farmers used similar strategies to support themselves. Most important for black families in this period was subsistence farming, which provided a base of support from year to year regardless of economic or climactic conditions. Next in importance was supplying nearby markets with localized commodities like firewood, vegetables, fruit, poultry, eggs, and dairy products. More established black farmers in Antelope entered into staple crop production, if only on a small scale, raising a combination of cotton, corn, and wheat. Finally, throughout the territorial period and beyond, African

American farmers worked for cash wages as casual laborers in towns, on white-owned farms, for the railroads, or with harvesting and road construction crews.

Subsistence agriculture had its roots both in necessity and in cultural experience. The rudimentary character of Oklahoma's economy and services in the 1890s required most farmers, regardless of race, to provide their family's basic needs in the form of gardens, livestock, poultry, and dairy products. Most farmers supplemented their home production by hunting, fishing, and harvesting wild plant foods. As in other sections of Oklahoma Territory, wild turkey, quail, prairie chicken, rabbit, squirrel, prairie dog, and deer all found their way to the black settler's table. After raising 8 acres of cotton on a corner of his sister and brother-in-law's Logan County farm, J. H. Crowell bought a disputed claim for $150. He did not own any implements or draft animals, so he traded two pigs for a mare and cooperatively used his brother-in-law's harness and plow to get his start. He raised a mixed crop of corn, cotton, melons, and vegetables and hauled them two days to Guthrie for sale. In the winter, he hunted and trapped rabbits, opossums, and raccoons, which he "used for meats and I sold the furs, the income from which I used to get things I needed."[10]

Mack McClellen of Udora recalled that in the mid-1890s, "we had a time trying to get enough to eat. There were plenty of wild turkeys and quail, prairie chickens and deer. We had meat when we had loads for the gun, but how to get corn meal and flour was the question." The McClellens often ate prairie dog too, because "they are clean meat as they'd not eat anything but roots and berries. They are good as squirrels." African Americans had little trouble substituting game animals in Oklahoma for the animals they had hunted in the Old South.[11]

The farm products blacks near Langston chose to raise for cash were nearly identical to those they had raised in different locations throughout the southern states. Antelope's black settlers found that their new environment was similar to the South in terms of a long growing season, dense woods (in the cross timbers region), small game, and sandy soils. Oklahoma differed from most of the South, however, in aridity, wind constancy, insects, and soil quality. Nevertheless, black migrants sowed and planted the crops they knew best. Turnips were a staple for most black farmers, especially on freshly broken ground.[12] They came up immediately, providing greens for the table in a few weeks, and the bulbs could be easily stored for the long winter months. J. H. Crowell recalled, "Turnips was a very productive crop and they grew so large—

often measuring twenty-two inches around them but were only worth ten cents a bushel."[13]

Another common crop for Oklahoma's black farmers was melon. These were of several varieties and were eaten fresh or made into sugar syrup. Sweet potatoes, peas, and beans were all common truck crops for black farmers. Sweet potatoes did not do well in Oklahoma, and some black farmers experimented with substitutes. In 1894, the *Herald* reported on a new variety of tubers called chufas[14]: "A recent analysis of a poor sample of chufas at the Experiment Station shows an astonishing amount of nutritive material in the tubers of this almost unknown plant. According to this, 100 pounds of chufas are the equal of 2,365 pounds of corn and the station notes show that over 200 bushels can be grown to an acre, making this the most economical of all foods for hogs and poultry."[15]

Kitchen gardens and flower gardens were also common around Langston. In the South, blacks often planted trees, shrubs, and flowers as part of the "built" environment. Exterior walls were lined with hooks for keeping everyday tools and the spaces just outside the settlers' cabins, or partial dugouts served as extra "rooms" in good weather. Gardens, either vegetable or flower beds, served as boundaries for this domestic space. The grass growing around the front door was commonly grubbed out and the hard ground swept clean to serve as a floor. In addition to their gardens, Antelope's black farm families were particularly fond of orchards, and most reminiscences by settlers include a reference to large orchards of peach, plum, apricot, and apple trees.

But Logan County African American farmers also quickly adopted new crops and methods when they promised to improve the family's self-sufficient lifestyle. "Kafir corn," as it was commonly known, is a drought-resistant grain sorghum that was very popular in Oklahoma at the turn of the century. It has an exceptionally hard casing, which means that it keeps well, but it is inedible for human consumption unless boiled for several hours. Not surprisingly, black farm families in Antelope grew both yellow and kafir corn, which they used to feed hogs and poultry. Hogs were raised primarily for home consumption, and there was no shortage in Logan County. De'Leslaine Davis of Canadian County recalled that corn sold for $0.15 a bushel in the 1890s, while shoats (baby pigs) went for "three dollars per hundred."[16] Left to forage in the blackjack woods, hogs did extremely well on acorns, sand plums, and wild plants in summer and were fed corn, potatoes, grain, and dairy by-products through the winter.

By 1900, Antelope's black farmers were self-sufficient enough to engage in selling at least a portion of their crops to local buyers. In some ways, this strategy was followed from the outset: many black farmers sold firewood cut from their own property as they cleared their land for crops. Firewood sold for between 50 and 75 cents a load, a little more than a day's wage. One enterprising black homesteader dug a deep well in a region where there were few creeks and sold water for more than two years to raise money for fences, horses, machinery, and other improvements. The most common market products, however, were fruits, vegetables, eggs, and butter. These items were sold to grocers in Langston and Guthrie.

Around Langston, the fruit of choice was the peach. In comparison to other counties, Logan produced more peaches than all of the surrounding counties combined. Peaches, of course, were a familiar crop to most blacks, having long been an important component of the southern diet.[17] Overripe or surplus fruit was fermented into wine or distilled into brandy and even fed to hogs. In Oklahoma, the cultivation of fruit was undertaken somewhat more systematically than it was in the lower South. Trees were planted in rows on the leeward side of the house. This afforded them protection from the wind and made cultivation, watering, and harvesting more efficient.

Advertisements and newspaper photographs of local black vendors at the turn of the century indicate African American farmers successfully competed for a share of the peach market in Langston, Guthrie, and Oklahoma City.[18] Commercial peach production reached its zenith around 1904 in Logan County when J. A. Taylor, a white investor, exported a hundred crates of peaches from Guthrie to Liverpool, England. These were reported to have been distributed primarily from the farm of Colonel J. C. Jamison, whose farm was located between Guthrie and Langston. The fruit arrived in England in good condition and netted Taylor approximately $1.50 per half-bushel. Although the Guthrie papers did not specify where the balance of Taylor's peaches were grown, Antelope's black farmers almost certainly participated in the venture.[19]

Subsistence and truck farming, however, were not sufficient to meet most black families' needs, and they planted several different kinds of commercially important crops. These differed from farm to farm and depended on the physical features of the land and the quality of the soil. Corn was grown on almost every farm, as a staple for human subsistence, for animals, and for commercial sale. Other more drought-resistant varieties of corn, such as broomcorn and kafir corn, were not for home consumption but were destined for market as they were harvested or were converted into hogs, cattle, and other animal products.

Cotton was the most common cash crop planted by black and white farmers in Logan County, but unlike sharecroppers, they did not dedicate more than half of their cultivated land to it as farm owners and operators. Cotton was hard on the soil, but the initial fertility of the easily worked land of the cross timber and savanna landscape was hard to resist. Both black and white farmers grew cotton in Logan County with success for more than three decades.

Wheat was raised in modest amounts on most Antelope County farms. It is difficult to know whether or not black farm families expected to make much money from wheat, given the heavily wooded properties they settled on, or whether their neighbors from states such as Iowa, Kansas, and Illinois encouraged them to try wheat growing. It is likely that the small plots of wheat planted by Antelope's black farmers were simply a bonus they did not depend on for their livelihood. Other commercial crops grown by Antelope's black farm families were oats, hay, and the occasional experimental plot of legumes such as cow peas (similar to soybeans), which were beginning to find their way to the farmers of Oklahoma through the efforts of the nearby experiment station staff in Stillwater.

And yet regardless of their efforts to make the farm pay, a quarter of all black farm families in Antelope Township also worked as agricultural laborers. Clearly, the earnings to be gained from mixed farming practices were not enough to provide black farm families with much-needed cash. Farm labor was scarce in rural areas, and black families easily hired themselves out to local farmers and businesses at different times of the year. Nellie Cutler and her husband arrived in Oklahoma Territory in 1892, and in 1893, "we bought a relinquishment from a man who had made the run in '89 but had been unable to make his farm succeed, chiefly because he had no horses nor mules and had no money to buy any. My husband gave him a team of horses in exchange for his right to the land." Cutler and her husband then hired a "colored man for 50 cents a day to do the actual grubbing"—that is, to take out the blackjack cross timbers so that they could plant their first crops of cotton, corn, and kafir corn for their stock. Finding someone to do the labor was not difficult, as Cutler recalled, because "there were quite a number of colored people living in our community."[20] Custom threshers did not generally hire African Americans, but local farmers did hire black workers seasonally to stook or shock wheat and pick cotton.

For several years after the establishment of the Colored Agricultural and Mechanical College at Langston in 1897, black farmers found work in campus construction. Later, as railway companies vied for feeder lines to Oklahoma's newest towns, blacks were hired to help lay track. In 1900, Langston lost its bid for a St. Louis and San Francisco Railroad depot, but the company did lay track through Antelope Township, linking Guthrie to Coyle, a white settlement.[21] In all these different ways, African American farmers in Antelope contributed to the agricultural development of the township rurally and in the expansion of Langston, Coyle, and Guthrie as educational and commercial centers.

The diversity of African American resource use in Antelope is most clearly reflected in the township assessor's descriptions of individual farm families for the year 1904. On the basis of these rolls—the only individualized agricultural records for Antelope extant before statehood—black farm units in Antelope Township were amazingly diverse. Sixty-year-old Rachel Williamson, a recent widow living with her two adult daughters, operated a small family farm that specialized in household perishables and truck produce. Although the entire farm, including "improvements" (buildings, wells, and fences), was valued at only $200, the Williamsons had 60 acres in crops: 25 acres in wheat, 25 acres in corn, and the rest in kafir corn and hay. In addition to these row crops, they owned milch cows and chickens; they produced 380 pounds of butter and $73 worth of eggs and poultry in 1904.[22] Their 1-acre orchard produced apples, pears, peaches, apricots, plums, and cherries, and from the fruit, the family fermented 80 gallons of wine.

Similarly, Robert Slaughter, aged fifty-nine, his wife Mariah, and their five children, ranging in age from fifteen to twenty-one, moved to Oklahoma from Arkansas. The westward move to Oklahoma was their second hop, as Robert was originally from Virginia and Mariah from Tennessee. In the fall of 1904, their farm had 90 acres in crops, including 27 acres of wheat with the balance in corn and cotton. The Slaughters owned $30 worth of agricultural machinery, likely a plow and a horse-drawn reaper and wagon for transporting farm produce to Langston or Guthrie for sale. Like the Williamsons, the Slaughter family had invested in fruit trees: over 200 peach trees as well as cherry and plum trees. Their farm was assessed at $500, the second highest valuation for black-owned farms in Antelope Township.

But the Slaughters were enterprising in other ways as well. In 1892, Robert Slaughter was listed in the Guthrie resident directory as owner and proprietor of the Langston City Hotel. It is likely that the proceeds from the hotel provided the family with the means to purchase their very productive farm later on.

Other black family farms in the township had more modest assessments, although they also employed a mixed economy of subsistence and market farming through diversified agriculture. The Langdon, Tomlinson, and Jones families, each with five to ten members, all raised small acreages of wheat, corn, and fodder; they owned cows, swine, and chickens; and they planted orchards of several varieties. The Dirks family, one of the township's earliest farm families, lived for half a century in their two-room dugout built into the side of a hill. Robert and Amanda Dirks grew most of their own provisions and made their cash living from cutting and selling the lumber on their farm. In an advertisement in the *Western Age* in 1908, Robert Dirks called himself the "Wood Man" because he was "prepared to furnish nice seasoned wood ready to burn." In 1904, the Dirks's belongings, not including their land, were valued at $4, the second lowest of all of Antelope's black residents.[23]

The most market-oriented of all black farm owners in the township was King Neal. He and his son Louis planted the usual farm garden and cash crops—corn and cotton—but rather than planting wheat as a fallback cash crop, Neal invested in fifteen hundred peach trees, together with a few rows of apple and cherry trees. Unlike his neighbors, Neal's quarter section was upland, representing a small break between two densely forested sections of the township on the east and west. Neal's decision to invest in peaches may have been a conscious strategy to avoid competing with his white neighbors. It certainly set him apart from the new population of black sharecroppers growing cotton in the area after 1900, while taking advantage of what looked to be a new crop for Oklahoma that could be marketed locally and nationally. It is also possible that Neal concluded that trees were ecologically suited to his property, making his decision a rational adaptation to the environment as well as a socially and economically sound investment. In any case, Neal's flexibility in his use of the land paid off. By 1932, he had made enough money from the farm to move into town a mile away and build one of the town's first bungalows—a recognized step up from the town's original cellar and log cabin homes, both of which were still common.[24]

Antelope had its share of very poor farm families as well. Isaac and Laura Jefferson and their thirteen children, ranging in age from a year old to twenty years old, eked out a living on a mere 80 acres. The family planted 30 acres each of wheat and cotton and smaller acreage of corn and oats, but they owned less than $10 worth of agricultural machinery. They had a small farmyard of pigs and chickens for home consumption and a few fruit trees. Like many other poor farmers, the Jeffersons were cross-listed in the census under the occupational heading of "agricultural workers." The Jeffersons leased rather than owned their farm and would eventually join the general exodus out of the county after statehood in 1907.

Similarly, the Hand family typified the least stable element of the black agricultural community in Antelope Township. Farm labor was undoubtedly the primary occupation of Willis and Susie Hand and their seven children ranging in age from their eldest daughter, Belle, at twenty, down to Walter, aged eight years. They were sharecroppers and worked off-farm for some years until 1910, when they rented a farm of their own near Meridian. By 1920, however, the Hands too had left Logan County for opportunities elsewhere.

The white settlers living next to Antelope's black farm families also worked hard to become independent farmers. Their use of the land, however, reflected their different experiences, expectations, and resources. For example, Logan County's white farmers were wholeheartedly investing in wheat as a cash crop by 1904. Two families perfectly illustrate the differences between white and black farm operations after 1900. J. B. and Salley Paris and their five children moved from Missouri to Oklahoma in 1896. By 1904, the Parises had 90 acres in mixed crops with 160 acres under fence. They owned virtually no machinery but had planted 140 acres to wheat. They owned livestock valued at $180, which they kept on 70 acres of native pasture. Like many of their African American neighbors, they planted a small orchard of peach, apple, pear, apricot, plum, and cherry trees. Their farm was assessed at $900, three times the average for black families in Antelope. The Parises' neighbors, the Whitleys, from Iowa, had six children. They raised 90 acres of wheat in 1904, along with corn, broomcorn, oats, and prairie hay. Their small herd of milch cows produced 150 pounds of butter, and like many Antelope County residents, they had 3 acres in orchard. Their farm in 1904 was assessed at $800. The difference between Antelope's white and black residents was not so much in the variety of crops they raised as in the quantity devoted to each. In devoting more of their land to wheat, Antelope's white farmers exhibited a willingness to invest in mechanized agriculture and enter into full-scale market production. Although the average value of agricultural machinery owned by white farmers was not much more than for blacks ($20 to $30), the average acreage Antelope's white farmers planted to mechanically harvested crops like wheat was 119 acres, compared with only 40 acres on black-owned and -operated farms. This difference between African American and white farmers in regard to mechanization would have far greater consequences for both groups than either of them could have imagined.

By statehood, the ecological consequences of trying to grub out a living through intensive farming in Logan County were beginning to take root. Problems soon arose in the vicinity of Langston as the fertility of the land decreased and new waves of black farm workers took up sharecropping for white farmers nearby. Economically, a countywide increase in crops like wheat that required the sharing of expensive harvesting equipment suddenly put black farm families outside of the mainstream agricultural economy in Logan County. The growing distinction between Anglo-American and African American farming practices between 1889 and 1907 and the number of black owner-operators who supplemented their incomes by working for white farmers made it easy for white farmers to regard all black farmers as tenants instead of neighboring owner-operators. Black farmers added to this misperception by congregating in and around the all-black towns. By statehood, only a handful of black families had gained clear title to their land. Nevertheless, they had weathered the storms of economic and environmental change and maintained a clear sense of community in the midst of increasing tensions with whites.

One of the forces at work in Logan County that further separated white and black farm practices was the establishment of the Agricultural College at Stillwater. Although it was only a few miles to the west of Langston, the relationship of the college to Logan's black farm population was destined to be far more distant. For white farmers, the college became a positive force in their quest for dominance over the territory. Indeed, Stillwater's ascendancy in shaping farm policy and practice in the state continues even today.[25] Oklahoma's unusual federation of farmers' clubs and organizations—a coalition that emerged in the early twentieth century as one of the most successful socialist movements in the United States—has also been attributed in part to the early organizational efforts of the USDA.[26]

Moreover, the USDA's debt to progressivism's "experiment with bureaucratic order" or, as Alan Trachtenberg has described it, "the emergence of a changed, more tightly structured society" dependent on professionals supported Oklahoma's rapid economic and political transformation from territory to state in the years immediately following non-Indian settlement.[27]

In the mid- to late nineteenth century, a significant proportion of white farmers in Oklahoma were turning to agricultural journals for advice. These journals were forthrightly supportive of new agricultural methods based on so-called scientific farming. In order to maintain a broad appeal and to avoid the taint of "book farming," the new agricultural journals expanded their coverage to include all aspects of rural life, including women, children, education, and domestic economy. Some historians have eschewed the journals as the province of well-to-do farmers and professionals, whereas others contend that the readership of agricultural journals increased throughout the nineteenth century to encompass all farmers. In Oklahoma at least, farm families needed all the help they could get.[28]

Although the new territory's climate made farming a more tenuous proposition than in the East, farmer-settlers hoped it could be made to sustain a traditional self-sufficient family farm economy. In spite of surveyor John W. Powell's 1878 report on semiarid lands that bluntly stated that beyond the ninety-eighth meridian "agriculture is not successful," the Department of the Interior's 1880 report on agriculture asserted that "the lands of the sub-humid region have already been taken up, and are under cultivation with varying success." The report noted that large portions of the region were still open for settlement and it was hoped that they would "be found to have a somewhat wider adaptation to agricultural purposes than is assigned them by Major Powell."[29] Ironically, Powell's recommendations were severely undermined by the onset of an unusually wet climatic cycle that coincided with the arrival of Oklahoma's first settlers in 1889. The newly plowed plains produced abundant crops, and the land boom was on.

From this auspicious beginning arose an official confidence in the future of agriculture in Oklahoma Territory. Policy makers, agricultural experts, and settlers alike trusted in the genius of humanity to overcome all natural obstacles to commercial agriculture. On the other hand, very little of what either promoters or experience told the territory's settlers was adequate preparation for the backbreaking, confusing, and unpredictable job of sodbusting. Hence, there existed a clear gap between farmers' aspirations and the practical knowledge they required to attain their goals. It was precisely this gap that the Oklahoma Experiment Station scientists hoped to fill.

The Oklahoma Experiment Station in Stillwater, Payne County, published its first bulletin, on the history and purpose of the college and station, in December 1891. By the spring of 1892, staff entomologist Earnest Bogue had collected enough specimens to publish a second bulletin identifying Oklahoma's most common insect pests.[30] Other bulletins that year reported on the results of field trials in several varieties of oats, corn, and spring wheat as well as a tentative soil analysis. Thereafter, territorial newspapers hungry for local copy carried the station's regular press releases and summaries of bulletin reports, and a few printed the station's bulletins and annual reports in their entirety.[31] Public demand for station publications doubled after 1894, with the director, George Morrow, reporting an average circulation of 13,500 copies per bulletin in 1899. By statehood in 1907, the mailing list had increased to 25,000. By this measure alone, the Oklahoma station had realized Congress's intention that it "diffuse among the people of the United States useful and practical information on subjects connected with agriculture."[32]

Public interest in the work of the station grew in direct proportion to the increase in precipitation after 1896. A drought that plagued Oklahoma's new settlers from 1889 to 1894 finally ended in 1896. A new wave of settlement followed the rains, extending Oklahoma's pioneer era well past the turn of the century. In 1899, 3 million acres of land remained unclaimed in western Oklahoma Territory, but by 1907, nearly every available acre had been filed on.[33] Continued good weather, high yields, and rising market values for staples like corn, wheat, oats, and cotton seemed to justify the hardship and uncertainty of the past and led Oklahoma's farmers to regard the future with renewed optimism.

The Oklahoma Experiment Station's primary architect during this period of rapid growth was John Fields. Born in Iowa and educated in Pennsylvania, Fields joined the station staff as an assistant professor of chemistry in 1896. Also hired that year were Earnest Bogue (entomology, Ohio State University) and L. L. Lewis (veterinary medicine, Iowa State University). Frank C. Burtis (horticulture, Kansas State University) and Oscar Morris of Oklahoma A&M's first graduating class were hired in 1899. Burtis replaced a young Frank A. Waugh, who would go on to write numerous books about horticulture and the role of the agricultural college in American society.[34] Walter Shaw (Stanford University) replaced Bogue in 1900. Burtis hired Llewellyn Moorhouse (agronomy, Ontario Agricultural College) in 1902. Together, this young and energetic group became the core of the Oklahoma Experiment Station's work for the next decade and beyond.

In spite of its short history, the Oklahoma Experiment Station was already in desperate need of revitalization by 1899. Like so many other territorial government considerations, Oklahoma A&M College appointments had become the political plums of a provincial and self-serving legislature. College president George Morrow became station director in 1896, taking over for the lackluster James C. Neal, a well-intentioned but inexperienced administrator who owed his appointment to his friendship with territorial governor George Steele. It was Morrow's successor, college president Angelo Scott, who noticed Fields's talent for organization and recommended his appointment as head of the station in 1899.

The new director ran into trouble with his superiors at the state and federal level almost immediately. The gregarious and articulate Fields, who was only in his twenties, did not fit the conservative mold of Neal's directorship. A. C. True, national director of the Office of Experiment Stations, was alarmed at the change in personnel and immediately contacted F. J. Wikoff of the Oklahoma A&M Board of Regents to confirm Fields's appointment. To Fields, True wrote, "I was naturally surprised and called his attention to some considerations which I feared the Board might not have taken into account." But Fields was not intimidated by this lack of faith, having already witnessed how overmanagement by the board and the national Office of Experiment Stations had retarded the station's progress.[35] Fields's first priority as director of the Oklahoma Experiment Station was in protecting and maintaining the Station's reputation among local farmers. He believed it was his job to provide settlers with everyday practical advice and help in the most effective and timely manner he and his staff were capable of. In gaining the farmers' trust, Fields believed the scientific work of the station could be implemented on a broad scale, making Oklahoma a model of scientific agricultural practice. He was quick to recognize that conditions in Oklahoma made the agricultural population uniquely open to suggestion and direction from agricultural "experts," a situation he consistently exploited during his tenure with the USDA and much later as the editor of the *Oklahoma Farm Journal*.

Nearly all of this new change in direction for the station was lost on the black farmers of Logan County. The 1896 *Plessy v. Ferguson* (separate but equal) decision had a direct impact on black farmers in Oklahoma when the territorial legislature immediately voted to open a Colored Agricultural and Mechanical school that same year. Langston was chosen as the site for the new college, and local fundraising for the new college began with the first classes meeting in 1897. But Langston's mission was hardly identical to that of Stillwater. Illiteracy among many poor Oklahoma farmers was high in 1897, and Langston's first graduates were teachers equipped to deal with that problem. Inman Page, the first president of Langston University (renamed in 1941) further removed the curriculum away from scientific agriculture. Page eschewed the Washington-Tuskegee model of black education based on industrial training and instead emphasized a broad educational curriculum.

In spite of unwavering support from the black farm community, Langston University's growth was excruciatingly slow.[36] Twenty-five years after its founding, only eleven of four hundred students were taking college-level classes. The rest were enrolled at the elementary and secondary school levels and in practical courses such as bookkeeping and typing. Students complained of heavy schedules, poor equipment and facilities, and a lack of trained teachers in some areas. Federal funding for the school followed formulas common throughout the South, with all-black schools receiving far below their proportion of funding based on population.[37] The tragedy for Oklahoma's black farmers was that after 1897, most whites at the station and elsewhere were satisfied that black agricultural education was being taken care of at Langston, regardless of the inequities.[38] Outreach from the experiment station at Stillwater would thereafter bypass the black farmers of Logan County.

Agricultural extension and the now-familiar county extension agent system began more than a decade after the founding of colleges at Stillwater and Langston. The migration of the boll weevil from Mexico to Texas was the real impetus for the appearance of the county "demonstration" agent after 1900. Although virtually ignored by historians of extension, Oklahoma played a central role in the development of the county agent program. Seaman Knapp, universally regarded as the father of extension, had long advocated that the USDA needed a special program to reach southern farmers. A longtime farmer and agricultural educator, Knapp's first experiment in demonstration work was in Louisiana, but his most famous experiment was the Porter Demonstration Farm in Terrell, Texas, started in 1903.

Knapp astutely observed that the experimental plots of the agricultural colleges were disregarded by farmers as too artificial to be of any practical use. In Terrell, Knapp persuaded a group of local businessmen to underwrite a demonstration of cotton raising on the Walter Porter farm. Knapp provided advice and guidance, and Porter supplied the rest. At the end of the season, Porter reported that he had made $700 more following Knapp's advice than he would have on his own, and this was after boll weevils had eaten half his crop. Knapp had found a highly effective way to reach farmers: let them convince one other.[39]

Oklahoma was quickly drawn into the demonstration work on cotton culture, as it was also threatened by the boll weevil. One of Knapp's first agents, William Bentley, would become a fixture in Oklahoma extension for more than two decades. Bentley, a successful farmer in Illinois, moved to west Texas in 1890 in order to have a larger farm. Through diversification and careful management, he had become one of the most successful farmers in his county. In February 1904, a railroad representative of Knapp's called and asked if Bentley would like to join the demonstration work on a sixty-day contract. Impressed by the potential significance of Knapp's ideas, Bentley threw some things into a suitcase and boarded the train. He retired twenty-five years later, director of the Oklahoma Extension Service.

Bentley was one of six other agents—the first extension agents in the nation—charged with recreating the educational results of the Porter demonstration farm. Agents spent long days riding in horse-drawn buggies or taking the train from farm to farm, signing up demonstrators (farmers that the agent would be giving direct advice to) and cooperators (farmers who worked on their own according to written instructions and then reported the results). Although his original justification for the agents was preventing the spread of the boll weevil, Knapp saw in this new system a means for rejuvenating southern agriculture in general.

As the program increased in scope, Knapp proposed a list of ten "commandments" for agents to teach farmers, including deep plowing, seed selection, harrowing, simple rotations, fertilizers, optimal livestock-to-pasture ratios, home production of staples, and, last but not least, the "need for reducing operating costs through the efficient use of labor . . . horse power and better machinery."[40] In 1907, Bentley was the supervising agent for northwest Texas and all of western

Oklahoma. The following year, the demonstration work was reorganized, and he was given the entire state of Oklahoma as his territory.

By 1909, Bentley was supervising a team of eleven agents. By the end of 1912, Bentley had a force of forty county agents, two district agents, and eleven women agents with a budget of more than $40,000. In addition to adult demonstrators and cooperators, agents were instrumental in forming boys' and girls' corn and cotton clubs. Their efforts directly contributed to the formation of 4-H clubs in Oklahoma. Knapp's advice for agents—to avoid talking politics or religion, "never put on airs, be a plain man,"[41] and always demonstrate practical common sense, proved key to agents' success with farmers. Knapp also understood that farmers were suspicious of book farming and insisted that his agents not be recent graduates of the agricultural colleges, but older men with an abundance of practical experience on their own farms. As an added safety measure, agents were directed not to serve in their home counties.

Demonstration work was boosted by Knapp and his supporters as a universal program for the farmers of Oklahoma. This, however, was not entirely accurate. Knapp's ideal "well-rounded, progressive" farmer meant Americans of Anglo-Saxon ancestry almost exclusively. In an early address to the Mississippi Agricultural and Mechanical College on practical education, Knapp stated that as a result of unbalanced education, New England had fallen victim to the Irish and German immigrant. "It is not decreased fertility nor the competition of the West which has caused the New Englander to transfer his ancestral home to the foreigner." Similarly, Knapp warned, "An invasion of the barbaric millions from orient and occident has commenced, which will be more baneful to our republic than the hordes of Attila and Alaric to the Roman Empire."[42]

Knapp's nativist tendencies extended to other racial groups as well. As a southerner, Knapp was deeply suspicious of the ability of African American farmers to join the movement toward progressive, scientific farming. His deep-seated racial bias stemmed from the seeming connection between blacks and tenancy throughout most of the South. Among agrarian reformers, tenancy was considered the biggest obstacle to progressive farming. Knapp was initially opposed to appointing black agents because he feared prejudice against African Americans among whites would give the general program a poor reputation. A successful partnership with Tuskegee through Booker T. Washington eventually convinced him of the need for black agents to help educate other black farmers. But to his own agents in Texas and elsewhere, Knapp directed that in appointing blacks, they should "go slow."[43]

Much to the credit of Walter Bentley, Oklahoma did not go slow, and it appointed its first black agent, J. A. Council, in 1909, six years before the appointment of the first black agent in Texas. Council was a recent graduate of Tuskegee Institute and a tireless worker for black farmers. In his annual report for 1910, Bentley recorded that in only six months, Council had already traveled 326 miles by rail and over 2,000 miles by team to sign up black farmers for the work. Bentley's assessment of Agent Council that year was, "For colored people, all right."

But Oklahoma's admission to statehood in 1907 had already set in motion a series of obstacles that would make black demonstration work less effective than it might have been. In 1910, Bentley invited Council and another new black agent to attend the annual agents' meeting in Oklahoma City. Bentley later reported that the hotel had refused to give the black agents entrance. After that, Bentley avoided the situation altogether and met with his black agents once a year independently in their home counties. The founding of the Colored Agricultural and Normal College in Langston in 1897 further separated the black agents from the regular training that took place on the State A&M Stillwater Campus. It made no difference that the new school at Langston was inadequate to train agents, to perform experimental work, or to distribute farming information.

In many ways, the discrepancy between Euro-American and African American agents' training and access to information was not considered a problem by people like Knapp. In agricultural education circles, it was generally understood that most black farmers were tenants, not commercial operators, and that the best that black agents could (or should) do with them was to improve their daily lives in "live at home" campaigns.[44] Black farmers were instructed in how to dig wells for clean water, build sanitary drainage systems, save money through the planting of gardens and thrifty use of manure for fertilizer, screen their doors and windows, and whitewash their homes and fences. Needless to say, these simplistic measures did nothing to prepare black landowners to compete against white farmers on the open staple crop market, cooperatively purchase seed and supplies, or mechanize their farms. The black farm extension program in Oklahoma ultimately owed its outline to Knapp and the economic conditions found in the lower South. The same program he advised for southern sharecroppers was applied to Oklahoma's black farmers, regardless of their status as sharecroppers, tenants, or landowners and operators.

Another reason for blacks' alienation from the growing wheat economy of Oklahoma, not related to the demonstration program or to the environment, was white Oklahomans' expectations of black farm practices, or lack thereof, in regard to mechanization. An overview of graduate theses submitted to Oklahoma's land grant schools at Stillwater and Norman in the 1920s and 1930s revealed that the history of "Negro" agricultural practice was a popular topic of study among agriculture majors in those two decades. These early attempts at explaining the African American experience in Oklahoma are valuable both for useful statistics no longer available and for the way their conclusions reveal something of the white community's attitude toward black farmers. Typical of these studies was Asa Dagley's 1926 University of Oklahoma study of "Negro" farming practices in central Oklahoma. Dagley concluded that the black farmer "is much more fitted to plow in a little bend in the creek with one mule and a broken plow than he is to turn the sod of the broad prairies of the state where it is necessary for him to handle four horses and operate a piece of good machinery."[45]

Dagley's assessment of black farmers' capacity for modern agricultural practices was based on a widespread belief that the black farmer "would, if left alone, let his crop become hopelessly lost in weeds and grass." Black farmers' lack of competitiveness in the marketplace was, according to Dagley, a result of their inability to relate to "such abstract, burdensome things as duty, or attention to business." This, Dagley explained, was a result of blacks' misconstrued idea of freedom after the Civil War as "freedom from all restraint, and especially from all kinds of work." For Dagley, the inability of the black farmer to retain control of his land was inevitable, and that "one reason the negro of today quits the farm is because he cannot cope with the scientific farming of the white man." If Dagley's explanation of blacks' failure to thrive as farmers is at all representative of thinking in Oklahoma in the first two decades of the twentieth century, then the social environment in which blacks were endeavoring to make a living from farming was as unyielding as the land on which they had settled.

The reality was that the direction taken by black extension in Oklahoma after statehood and the high cost of mechanized farming prohibited black farm families from engaging more heavily in the wheat market. As a group, the black farmers of Antelope Township acquired some horse-drawn implements for harvesting wheat and other cereal crops but did not form cooperatives to purchase self-powered separators and combines. Antelope's white farmers clearly relied on mechanical harvesting of their wheat crops and realized a profit in these years, so why not black farmers?

The reasons for blacks' continued use of animal-powered machinery, tendency toward smaller and more varied crops, and concentration on local marketing of truck produce are numerous. First and foremost was the location and quality of the land they occupied. Almost universally, black-owned and -operated farms were located in blackjack country. According to the first (1906) official soil survey conducted in Oklahoma in Oklahoma County just below Logan, the county contained a number of well-to-do farmers in the better farming areas. These farmers had built good homes and had purchased plenty of machinery. According to the surveyors, all the desirable land had been "well settled by white people, while sandy sections are more sparsely populated with a mixed population of whites and negros."[46]

For the surveyors, soil types determined the kind of settlement and even the settler that could be found in different areas. They reported that on the prairie sections, farmers from the northern states were raising wheat, corn, oats, and kafir corn, and were pasturing stock animals, but in the sandy sections formerly covered in timber and settled with southerners, "a different order of things prevails. The areas under cultivation are devoted very largely to cotton, which is the chief money crop. Considerable corn is grown but is consumed mostly by farm stock. On some of the sandy types, peach growing has become an important industry."[47]

Although the soil survey noted that sandier soil areas were less productive, they had the advantage of being less costly to purchase and contained a ready supply of fuel and building materials. For black farmers, trees had other uses as well. Shady areas served as outdoor rooms for black pioneers busily engaged in outdoor production activities like butchering, fruit packing, wine making—even doing laundry taken in for wages. By laying claim to the cross-timbers region, black farmers were maintaining time-honored cultural practices.

But as several of Logan's settlers recalled, grubbing out the trees from their farms could take years to complete, putting the black farmer on a much longer timetable for producing a profitable acreage of commercial crops such as wheat or even cotton. It also allowed the sandy soils greater exposure to the elements. Arthur L. Tolson, writing in the early 1970s, observed that by 1950, the Langston area was suffering from severe sheet and gully erosion. Mistaking the contemporary rural environment for the historical one, Tolson wrongly surmised that "agriculture in this area resulted in the disappearance of big and little bluestem, grama, buffalo grass and other verdure that originally covered the land."[48] Tolson did not realize that more than half the township had originally been densely wooded, especially around Langston.[49]

By the early 1930s, University of Nebraska ecologist W. E. Bruner had completed a full-scale study of Oklahoma vegetation and faunal zones akin to J. E. Weaver's studies of Nebraska. Bruner's study described the oak-hickory savanna that characterized the blackjack strips near Langston as a transition environment that was highly variable depending on the quality of the subsoil.[50] Today, the Ancient Cross Timbers Project at the University of Arkansas considers the cross timber and savanna environment of central Oklahoma one of the most endangered ecosystems on the Great Plains.[51]

Antelope's black farmers needed their trees for cash and for the opportunity they afforded for landownership as less desirable acreage. Although their use of the land after it was cleared differed markedly from white farmers in terms of diversified, nonmechanized agriculture, removal of the timber caused them the same problems—erosion, soil exhaustion, and insect infestation—that plagued white farmers in the same region. A recent study of farmers in the cross-timber district concluded that farmers unfamiliar with the light, sandy soils of the region had removed the natural vegetation, and by plowing up and down the hillsides, "triggered some of the most serious soil erosion to date in the United States."[52] The increasing infertility of the soil around Langston only compounded the problem. Without intending to, the survival strategies black farmers depended on would make them economically and environmentally vulnerable well into the future.

4

BLAINE COUNTY BEGINNINGS

Folks, there's never been anything like it since Creation. Creation!
Hell! That took six days. This was done in one. Thousands and
thousands of people from all over . . . traveled hundreds of miles
to get a bare piece of land for nothing. But what land! Virgin,
except when the Indians had roamed it. "Lands of lost gods, and
god-like men!"

Edna Ferber, Cimarron, 1930

In 1820, Major Steven H. Long and his small party of ten men were
traveling southeast on their way back from Pike's Peak and into
Comanche country. They were exploring an uncharted trail between
two major rivers, the Cimarron and the Canadian, in present-day
Oklahoma. The level bluffs above the Canadian River were a relatively easy route to follow, although they noted that water levels in the
river were low and the few ponds they encountered were so full of
bison manure that it sickened them to drink any.[1] By contrast, at one
point along the river, the party encountered wild grape vines so lush
they looked like small hills. Continuing southeast, this fertile valley
soon became lost in the tangle of the cross timbers. As they waded
down the riverbed to avoid the thick undergrowth, Long and his men
were nearly driven mad by ticks and flies. Finally, as they approached
the confluence of the Canadian River with Gaines Creek, they surprised several large flocks of herons, cranes, and ducks. In spite of this
varied landscape, Long and the party's botanist, Edwin James, pronounced the area that is now western Oklahoma a wasteland that God
had provided to prevent further American expansion.[2]

Long and his men believed they were charting the Red River, but in
fact, they were following the Canadian. Although Long regretted this
humiliating mistake for the rest of his life, his descriptions of west-

central Oklahoma are among the first glimpses we have of several future counties, including Blaine County in Oklahoma Territory. Without benefit of an Indian guide, the Long expedition frequently became lost in the wide expanse of low, rolling hills, grasslands, and trees. When compasses and landmarks failed them, they made use of bison paths to find their way back to the Canadian River. On August 20, 1821, near the border of present-day Roger Mills and Custer County, Long recorded that they followed a bison track because it would be the most direct path back to the river. He was right, and the party continued along the Canadian for several more miles.

Thirty years later, when Captain R. B. Marcy made his survey of Oklahoma Territory, he noted that the trails he encountered closely followed the topography of the land. He observed that the trails marked the easiest way to traverse the land, going around obstacles such as dense thicket, cuts, ravines, and deep water. Marcy's 1849 survey of a single township in Blaine County near the future county seat of Watonga clearly shows the military road from the Cheyenne Agency at El Reno north to Camp Supply. This northwest-southeast road followed a high ridge of land parallel with the North Fork of the Canadian River, similar in description to the trails that thirty years earlier Long and James had followed on their way back from Pike's Peak. It was still the easiest and shortest route through the area, avoiding river and creek fords, the riparian woodlands on either side of the ridge, and steep ravine slopes. Not much had changed in the variegated landscape of broken red earth, save for the trampled buffalo grass growing in the road bed, shyly hinting at the changing relationships between animals and grasslands, people and place in Oklahoma Territory.[3]

According to the Treaty of Medicine Lodge signed in 1867 between the United States and the tribes of the southern Great Plains, the Cheyennes' and Arapahoes' reservation lands, encompassing just over 4 million acres, lay principally along the North Fork of the Canadian River running northeast to southwest, a portion of which was destined to become Blaine County. Unable to find enough bison on the reservation for either trade or subsistence, and having lost the battle of Adobe Walls with the U.S. Army, the Cheyennes' and Arapahoes' situation by the middle 1870s was grim.[4] From 1867 until the 1880s, the agent at Darlington had tried to encourage the Cheyennes to take up farming, but severe drought for most of the 1870s dictated that their attempts at farming were minimal.[5] Accordingly, in 1880, the tribal agent at

Darlington Agency leased over half a million acres of reservation land to a handful of cattlemen at 2 cents per acre in an effort to raise some cash for the tribes' use. Robert Hunter of St. Louis and G. E. Reynolds held leases for much of future Blaine County between Cantonment and the Indian agency at Darlington, near the present-day city of El Reno. When fully stocked in 1885, the Cheyenne-Arapahoe reservation held an estimated 220,000 animals. According to the terms of the lease, the stockmen were entitled to fence these lands, which they did, using timber from the leased areas for fence posts.[6]

In addition to the white ranchers' herds, the Cheyenne and Arapahoe people also raised cattle on the land reserved for their own use. The tribal cattle herd was small compared with the tribes' horse herds, although they too were reduced in size as a consequence of their confinement to the reservation. The substitution of so many domesticated animals for native ones had a dramatic effect on the ecology of the reservation. Large cattle and horse herds now roamed Cheyenne and Arapahoe land, effectively turning the entire reservation into an enormous cattle ranch in the years leading up to the run on Blaine County.

The 1880s cattle leases to Hunter and Reynolds essentially completed a longer and more gradual transformation of Blaine's mixed-grass prairie system from one based on keystone species like bison and prairie dogs into a domesticated agroecological system of cattle and horse grazing. If, during the period 1867 to 1880, Indian peoples had kept horse herds for self-sufficiency alone—that is, for hunting bison—they might not have significantly altered the ecology of the region. As far back as 1800, however, hunting was not the only reason for horse ownership among the Comanches, Apaches, and Kiowas, nor would it be for the Cheyennes and Arapahoes who made their appearance on the Plains a few years later. Among all these Plains peoples, horses were more than a means of transportation: they quickly became valuable capital and symbols of individual wealth and status.

Throughout the nineteenth century, horses could be traded for guns, metal tools, corn, cloth, and whiskey. Horses were universally accepted as currency between Indians and whites, and southern Plains peoples quickly took advantage of the wild descendants of Spanish runaways and the amenable environment to accumulate large tribal herds. In 1855, a drought year, the Indian agent for the Kiowas, Comanches, Apaches, Cheyennes, and Arapahoes reported that the tribes averaged more than six horses per person, for a total of nearly seventy thousand animals. Donald Berthrong, an ethnohistorian of the southern Cheyennes and Arapahoes, has determined that in 1855 the southern Cheyennes alone had seventeen thousand horses.[7] Beyond their obvious commercial value, horses were a sign of prosperity and status, indicating the relative success of their owner in the trade.

The availability of horses also made Indian peoples more effective hunters of other animals for commercial trade. The 350 lodges of the southern Cheyennes camped at Walnut Creek in 1855 collectively cleared more than $15,000 from their sale to a trader of more than 40,000 buffalo robes, 3,000 elk, 25,000 deer, and 2,000 bears.[8] The number of bison robes alone amounted to thirteen robes per person, twice the estimated number of animals required annually for subsistence.[9] Numbers like these indicate that the commercial sale of bison robes and other hides was putting pressure on the ecology of Blaine County long before the arrival of white settlers.

Even before the demise of the bison herds in Oklahoma Territory in the 1880s, the physical requirements of horse keeping by the Cheyennes and Arapahoes were changing the ecology of the mixed-grass prairie. Large domestic horse herds increased competition for available forage with other Plains ungulates, notably bison, elk, and pronghorn. Continuous cropping of the grasses by horses pushed these ungulates out of the mixed-grass areas and into the high plains, causing further displacement of the fauna and flora in those locations.

Although Indian peoples valued their horses and gave them the best care they could, horses held in captivity often endured severe hardships, especially in winter. As James Sherow has noted, and Indian peoples well understood, the short grasses of the mixed-grass and high plains maintain a higher protein content than warm-season grasses over the winter months, but on the high plains, foraging too far away from shelter was dangerous for both beasts and humans.[10] To keep their horses and themselves sheltered, warm, and fed, Indian peoples resorted to feeding their herds the less nutritious branches of riparian-system willows and cottonwoods found in the riverine valleys. Over time, these small groves of trees were stripped bare of saplings, and places like Big Timbers in western Kansas and Cottonwood Grove on the Washita River ceased to resemble their names. A similar pattern of deforestation obtained throughout Oklahoma Territory.

As Indian populations increased, so did their involvement in bison hunting for subsistence and trade. Increased trade meant a requisite increase in horses, placing greater pressure on the grasslands in an ever-increasing cycle of degradation.[11] The international bison robe trade, made possible through the domestication of the horse, increased preexisting intertribal competition for resources and created stricter boundaries within which human populations existed. A full half century before white settlement, the commercial harvest of bison in Oklahoma Territory was already reaching its apex.[12]

By the 1880s, the bison robe trade was essentially finished, leaving the Cheyennes and Arapahoes with few options for maintaining themselves and their families. If most were reluctant to lease their lands to outside cattle interests, they were far unhappier with a new plan on the horizon for the allotment of their reservation. Just before the Jerome Commission arrived to negotiate with the tribe for the allotment of their reservation, all grazing leases were declared null and void by the Indian Office. Then, in July 1890, David H. Jerome arrived to negotiate with the tribes to accept allotment. Under the provisions of the Dawes Act, or the General Allotment Act, every member of the tribe was to receive an allotment of 160 acres. The so-called surplus would then be opened for white settlement. By employing "hard bargaining, threats, deception and bribery,"[13] the commission was able to obtain the needed signatures for the allotment of the reservation. The allotted tribes kept 529,682 acres of land, leaving 3,500,000 acres available to be opened for white settlement.

Allotment of the reservation proceeded slowly, with the different bands taking up lands near one another along central waterways like the Canadian, South Canadian, and Washita rivers. Then, on April 19, 1892, in response to well-organized lobbying on behalf of homesteaders and speculators, the 3.5-million-acre tract of the Cheyenne and Arapahoe reservation not allotted to tribal members was opened by the federal government for agricultural and town site development. The area claimed in the 1892 run was divided into six new counties, including Blaine, just northwest of Oklahoma City.

The 1892 survey of Blaine County's 36-mile square sections (144 quarter sections in each) paid no heed to either the topography or vegetative patterns within its boundaries. As a result, only a dozen sections contained any viable combination of surface water, wood, and open prairie. Some sections were completely covered in blackjack forest; others were within the flood plain of the north Canadian River. The county seat of Watonga, well known to speculators before the run and founded on the first day of the land run in 1892, took advantage of the district's best features, locating on Section 24 next to the military

road with easy access to both the north Canadian River and ample supplies of wood for fuel and building materials.

For many white Americans, Oklahoma seemed the quintessential
manifestation of the nation's destiny. As one historian has noted, the
land openings are particularly instructive because they remind us that
the settlers "believed that free or cheap land gave everyone a chance,
so it was a democratic concept . . . and made settlers causal agents in
history, not victims or pawns."[14] The perennial American promise of
rural life was its alleged contribution to a democratic society in which
all citizens enjoyed equal opportunity. This ideal, of course, referred to
white Euro-Americans exclusively.

In many cases, white settlers' idealism was inflated and exploited by
boosters and land speculators, who claimed that Oklahoma's soil and
climate were amenable to virtually any agricultural venture. One
pamphleteer claimed in 1890 that Oklahoma had better water supplies
than Ohio, Missouri, Kentucky, or Tennessee and that the climate was
perfect for every kind of crop, with long summers and short winters.
"The rainfall is much greater than either Kansas or Texas and but two
dry seasons have been known in thirty years." Southern crops like cotton and fruits grown in California would flourish in the new territory.
On top of all this, the territory was touted as "a stock raiser's paradise."[15]

About the Cheyenne and Arapahoe reservation lands, the pamphlet
writer added, "Those of the Indians who attempted to farm raised
enormous crops with very little labor." This, of course, was patently
untrue, but no matter. The implication was that Euro-Americans
would do even better in raising crops than the unskilled and culturally backward Indian tribes who recently occupied the territory. Boomer
literature frequently labeled Oklahoma as the "new white man's country," a designation that would have repercussions for Blaine County
society long after its initial settlement was over.

Glowing reports of easy farming and free lands were very appealing
to midwestern and eastern farmers, just as they were to migrants to
Kansas a generation earlier. But "free land" was and continues to be a
relative concept. Clarence Danhoff in the 1940s estimated that it took
a minimum investment of $1,000 to start a 40-acre farm in the mid-
west. Since then, agricultural economists and historians have become
increasingly more sophisticated in their reconstruction of farm operating costs in the late nineteenth and early twentieth centuries.
According to one study, the average price in 1860 in the northeast for

a 160-acre farm, implements, animals, house, furnishings, and initial savings for food in the first years before a crop could be made was $4,654. In the midwest, the same farm would cost $2,893, and in sparsely populated areas like Oklahoma Territory, the cost was only $1,248. Although new research has refined Danhoff's preliminary estimate to show that the cost of a western farm was only a quarter of the cost of a farm in Pennsylvania, his basic conclusion still stands. Farming free land required a capital investment far beyond the means of the average wage worker.[16]

Of course, the price of a western farm was only one factor in settlers' determination to pull up stakes and make the run for a homestead in Oklahoma. A few idealists in the 1880s still clung to the notion that farming was best pursued for its ameliorative influence on American society. The editor of *American Agriculturalist* in 1880 complained that farmers were losing sight of their primary purpose and that "farming is yearly becoming more of a mercantile business." But by 1892, on the eve of the run that would create Blaine County, the same publication reprinted an article by C. Wood Davis entitled, "The Present Situation of American Agriculture: Its Relation to the World Food Supply, an Estimate of American Production and Requirements and the Apparently Brilliant Future." Davis's article brightly concluded that "the farmer will *very soon* be by far, the most prosperous member of the community, *wherever,* in the world."[17] By the time of Blaine's opening and initial settlement, farmers everywhere were in accord with the notion that the new territory was a sound economic investment.

Given the general optimism of the time, it is not surprising that the question of whether or not the Oklahoma environment could safely sustain commercial agriculture was not a major concern for most settlers. In keeping with a long tradition of social and moral regeneration through the subjugation of the wilderness, Blaine County settlers considered themselves archetypal noble pioneers, prepared to suffer the consequences of their decision for the improvement of the territory, the nation, and themselves. Unaware of the environmental changes the region had witnessed, they regarded the new territory as untouched and unspoiled, created for their exclusive use by a wise and benevolent God. In reality, the region had undergone several recent significant ecological events and was about to enter into another climatic cycle of diminished rainfall.

On his tour of west-central Oklahoma in 1832, Washington Irving had encountered beaver, bears, and wolves in the riparian woodlands and bison, elk, and deer grazing peacefully in parklike meadows of grass.[18] Similar description of southern Blaine County can be found in the writings of military explorer J. W. Abert. Abert wrote of the valley between Greenfield and Geary in Blaine, "The country was beautiful, gracefully undulating with long swells and the prairie covered with luxuriant growth of grass . . . Bands of buffalo were feeding on every hillside and deer and turkey unusually abundant."

In contrast to the abundant landscapes encountered by early white explorers, Blaine County settlers in 1892 found only high grass, prairie dogs, snakes, jackrabbits, and quail. These, however, did not last very long. Tom Mosely's family arrived in Blaine in 1893 when Tom was eleven. "First thing I noticed was the prairie dogs—whole section down in there. Most enjoyable thing as a boy—watching them prairie dogs standing up and wiggling their little tails."[19] Another early settler, Dick Rice, recalled that there were a lot of quail, a few turkey, and fewer deer, but "it wasn't long before they were gone."[20] A. R. Cook remembered that when he arrived in 1900, there were more large trees, less brush, and "big stacks of prairie hay." Cook also noted that he never saw native hay in such abundance again.[21]

Although Euro-American farmers came to Blaine County for numerous reasons depending on their former occupations and experiences, they did have one thing in common. Lacking any accurate historical memory of the environment, these settler-farmers regarded the land as ecologically primeval and often made erroneous assumptions regarding the region's climate, water, and soil quality. They similarly made mistakes about the nature of the area's indigenous plants, animals, and people. Myrtle Sizelove remembered that her parents moved to Oklahoma after spending "the coldest winter of my life" in Kansas. Oklahoma, her parents thought, did not suffer from such severe temperatures. Dick Rice's father decided to move to Oklahoma after seeing "one of the biggest corn crops ever raised" on a visit to Blaine. The senior Rice "really thought he was coming to Paradise."[22] Having arrived with certain notions of what constituted a conducive climate and a productive agricultural landscape, Blaine's Euro-American settlers noticed only the raw materials they would need to recreate the ordered and established rural landscapes of their former homes and conveniently ignored those elements that were unfamiliar or unpleasant.

Shortly after setting up their farms, however, Blaine residents discovered that the new territory had several unique features not mentioned in the advertisements. They noted that vestiges of earlier economies based on bison hunting, cattle trailing, and cattle rustling were apparent everywhere. These included old carcasses, well-worn paths and trails, wallows, eroded stream banks, caves, and dugouts. Early residents took advantage of some of these, collecting bison bones by the ton for shipment back east, as well as the dried dung left behind by the cattle drives, which they burned for fuel.[23] Some took over the dugouts of the former drovers and bandits that had occupied the region.

The settlers who found dugouts on their claims were lucky, as most original white residents never forgot the hard labor and discomfort associated with soddy life. Fred Turner's parents migrated from Missouri to Loyal, Oklahoma, in Blaine County where Fred was born in a soddy in 1895. Asked about his earliest childhood memory, Turner easily recalled the dirt and discomfort and his mother crying over and over, "Oh why did we ever come to Oklahoma?"[24]

Making the best of a difficult situation, Blaine's first white farmers were quick to turn the region's native resources into cash in order to pull through in the years before their first crops were harvested and sold. But their short-term efforts had long-term consequences for the ecology of the county. Solomon Bill, born in Blaine the youngest of thirteen children in 1898, recalled that enterprising settlers became part-time lumbermen, harvesting the salt and red cedar trees that covered the gyp hills in the western portion of the county. "No one raised much at first, so they cut posts and took them to Old Oklahoma" (the unassigned lands).[25] Quail hunting was another popular way to raise cash. Ross Nigh, who arrived in Watonga in 1900, made a living for two years hunting quail. Nigh received $1.80 per dozen birds, which were a delicacy in eastern cities like New York. Quail hunting paid for his ammunition and still left him a good profit, but business did not last very long because the birds were quickly overhunted.[26] Dick Rice similarly recalled that prairie chickens were "pretty dumb" and "we soon got rid of them too."[27] The same fate awaited the wild turkey and bobcat populations.

According to numerous settlers' accounts, Blaine County also contained plenty of leftover human beings—generally of the undesirable sort. Some of the most famous outlaws of the era—the Doolin, Dalton and Black, and Yeager gangs among them—had hideouts in the gyp hills of Blaine County and regularly relieved local farmers, banks, and trains of their food, horses, and valuables. Years later, Blaine County settlers competed with one another for the best outlaw story as the true measure of a real pioneer, thereby turning their efforts into a morality play that ignored the larger realities of their own negative effect on the region.

In addition to the heartbreaking toil of starting a farm, accidents, illnesses, and violent deaths were fairly common among the first generation of settlers to Blaine. Domestic homicides, flu epidemics, and farming and hunting accidents became seared into the memories of many of Blaine's first settlers. An unpredictable frontier justice system also detracted from the social environment. In 1896, the *Blaine County Herald* reported that a vigilante group had located a local widow's missing calf tied to a thicket. Hiding behind a clump of trees, they "saw Jim Gifford approach; take the calf and several wads of buckshot from the committee." In the same vein, a Watonga lawyer advertised a warning to the thief who took his dun pony to "commit suicide before he is overtaken."[28] Although accounts of accidents and criminal violence may have been exaggerated, a sampling of newspaper reports and reminiscences suggests a fluidity in early settler society that allowed both vice and virtue to coexist and even flourish.

Blaine's early social instability was made even worse by its chaotic local credit system. The Farmers and Merchants Bank, established in Watonga in May 1894, was the first official repository for Blaine and Dewey counties. Three months after opening, the bank mysteriously failed. Bank president J. N. Beacom arrived from El Reno to learn that his son Charles had embezzled the bank's assets and was now vacationing in the Caribbean. Humiliated and bankrupt, the senior Beacom committed suicide, leaving the county without a bank or other source of local credit for another four years.[29] Hardships such as these pushed the cost of homesteading ever higher emotionally, making it nearly impossible for the first generation of pioneers to measure their impact on the environment of the county with any detachment.

Transportation lines, particularly railroads, were of major concern to Blaine farmers, underscoring their rosy expectations of Oklahoma's future role in the national economy. Although some smaller lines were laid before the turn of the century (the Chocktaw and Northern and the Enid and Anadarko Railroad Companies), the county had to wait until 1900 for a railroad with intrastate connections. In spite of almost constant lobbying by local merchants, farmers, politicians, and newspapers, the Rock Island Railroad did not begin surveying for roads from Kingfisher to Watonga and Geary until 1899 and did not begin construction of a road until after 1900. At one point, the *Watonga Republican* editor suggested that Blaine residents take up a subscription themselves to finance a line to Kingfisher rather than wait on the whims of the railroad to dictate their future.[30] As a future county seat, Watonga was able to survive economically without a railroad by virtue of the local land office, trade with the local Indian agency, and a rapidly developing agricultural hinterland.

In contrast, the founding of Hitchcock, 10 miles northeast of Watonga, was entirely the result of the coming of the railroad. In fact, the town did not even exist until the announcement of a line. Emil Schneider recalled, "The first thing that got started was the saloon, then we got a few stores."[31] The town's first residents were farmers who came in to find work on the road, build the depot, and put up the commercial structures for businessmen who quickly bought up town sites in 1900. The same scenario held true for many other Blaine County towns, including Homestead, Longdale, Greenfield, and Eagle City. Conversely, several towns bypassed by the railroad companies, such as Ferguson, Darrow, and Bickford, soon ceased to grow and were eventually abandoned.

Although the landscape was surprising and the lack of transportation distressing, the hardships and risks involved in settlement were not unfamiliar to most white migrants. Many of Blaine's first settlers had migrated from rural communities in neighboring states, where calamities such as prairie fires, grasshopper plagues, and cyclones were expected, if not hoped-for, events.[32] An environmentally based folk culture quickly sprang up among the homesteaders. During the early 1890s, a running joke in Blaine accused Oklahoma farmers of only praying when they were in their cyclone caves; the rejoinder was they only prayed when there was a cyclone, and they were still a half mile from the cave.[33] In another yarn, a farmer reported that while in Texas buying cattle, he saw his own rain barrel blow past. Another settler joked that the gyp water on his claim was so hard, you "couldn't cut it with an axe." One cultural geographer has wryly concluded that "Oklahoma developed a sense of humor which played on the lightness of living and the ironies of hope versus reality."[34] Kidding aside, Blaine farmers' faith in their own ability to reorder the territory remained the foundation of both their humor and their resolution.

The hardships settlers endured the first decade of farming in Blaine may have created a form of regional humor and a neighborly connection between Euro-American farmers, but it took a heavy toll on other relationships in the county. Indians and blacks, although numerous in the county, were quickly discounted as serious agriculturalists by their white neighbors. For Blaine's white population, Indians were a novel curiosity, and black farmers were tolerated for their limited usefulness. Both groups were later displaced as the value of marginal lands increased and crops promised better returns.

In Blaine County, the Cheyenne and Arapahoe Indians had been granted allotments in severalty a number of years before the opening and had been confined to their reservation since 1872. Like the Kiowas, they had experienced numerous disappointments in attempting to farm their allotments. Stock raising seemed a likely occupation before 1892, but later agents working for the Office of Indian Affairs would not let go of what they saw as the needed connections between row crop agriculture, private property, and "civilization."[35] Poor weather, a chronic lack of seed and equipment, and white encroachment made commercial agricultural production by the Indians an unattainable goal. Indians, unable to farm commercially and discouraged from raising their own stock, leased the majority of their lands to white farmers as soon as they became available in order to generate some small income for tribal members. Blaine residents interpreted the Cheyennes' and Arapahoes' unimproved farms, tribal encampments, and refusal to live in government-built housing as proof of their inability to become productive agriculturalists.

Stereotypes of "poor lo" (reservation Indians) went unchallenged as most encounters between Indians and whites became limited to annual festivities and commercial exchanges in town. For their part, Indian peoples lived in large self-contained groups that did not foster one-on-one relations with individual white residents. Indians' insularity actually made Euro-Americans more comfortable in general. As one Blaine resident explained, "They associate with their own kind and never intrude upon the society of the white people unless invited to do so. As a result of this distinguished trait, the white people of Blaine County never think of having a celebration, fair or other festivity of that nature without asking the Indians to help them."[36] The astonishing implication, of course, was that the Indians were recognized for their good manners at staying away from the white community and only coming into town when invited.

Euro-American settlers had a greater degree of contact with the "squaw men," or white husbands of Indian women, who frequently owned trading houses on the military roads between the Indian agencies in Cantonment in Blaine and Darlington near El Reno. Whites living among the Indians were regarded by the white community with a mixture of curiosity and envy for the economic advantages they enjoyed. The presence of the squaw men was, like the leasing of Indian lands, interpreted by whites as further proof of the full bloods' lack of acuity for business.[37] For most white settlers, the annual distribution of cattle to the Indians by the government was proof enough of the Cheyennes' and Arapahoes' savage nature. Settlers recalled with relish their reaction to watching the Indian women drag the beeve carcasses onto the prairie for skinning and carving. Local beef distributions and annual parades, where tribal "chiefs" dressed in full war regalia and performed dances for money, were the most common contact point between whites and Indians in Blaine County. Although historians have documented that the Cheyennes and Arapahoes made a strong effort to take up agriculture within their traditional authority structure, local whites were oblivious to Indian farming and other self-sufficient resource practices.[38]

Agency rules certainly caused whites some confusion. Dick Rice recalled that Indian parents camped near their children's boarding school near Cantonment and at the end of spring term packed up their children and headed south in single file back to the Indian agency in El Reno. Unknown to Rice and other whites, the high incidence of disease and death that plagued most Indian schools caused Cheyenne and Arapahoe parents to camp close by the school to monitor their child's health and safety. White settlers like Rice assumed the Indians' movement between agencies precluded any fixed farming practice when in fact half the Cheyennes and Arapahoes were living full-time on their allotments in 1892. Some whites also made the erroneous connection between the Indians' annuities (paid to them from the sale of their lands) and their children's attendance at school. Susie Temple believed that the Indians put their children in school because the government paid the tribe to have them there. In fact, it was just the opposite: Indian agents often withheld food rations and other treaty benefits from families who refused to send their children to school in Cantonment.

It was also widely believed by local whites that while Indian children were in school, their parents simply loafed. Dr. Earl McBride related that Indian women would visit the towns but never stay overnight. "Indian women—real fat—spread a blanket out on the wooden sidewalk, cross their feet and swing their feet over the edge and sit there for hours."[39] An early historian of the county noted that instead of working his farm, the Indian man "sits quietly smoking, content to let others work and worry."[40] When whites did acknowledge Indians' industry, it was not the ordered and planned work of a civilized people, but an instinctual reaction to physical need. According to Dick Rice, every Indian "rustled [begged] a lot, hunted and the government issued beef every so often."[41]

The most positive and direct contact settlers had with Indian peoples was on a personal basis. Earl McBride took his Indian schoolmates "for granted as little boys . . . [it] suited us later that we did this because we had a lot of connection."[42] Morgan Prickett, a store owner, traded with the Cheyennes and Arapahoes through purchase orders from the Indian agency. Instead of cash, the tribes would present coupons worth a set amount. Prickett then sent these orders to the agency and was reimbursed in cash. For Prickett, dealing with the local Indians was better economically than relying on local farmers, who were frequently behind on their credit for a year or more at a time.

Even so, whites were not predisposed to investigate Indian farm practices in general because popular notions of a vanishing race did not allow for progressive Indian farmers in their midst. In her 1928 history of Blaine County, Marjorie Bennett Everhart expressed several common beliefs about the Indians' past and future. In her description of a Fourth of July parade in Watonga, Everhart watched the brightly colored and mounted parade with a sense of nostalgia and pity: "While we watched him ride by we wondered what was in his heart, Did it throb in memory of bygone days? Did he ponder the question of race amalgamation and assimilation and does he wonder what the future has in store for him or has our civilization crushed his courage and individuality until he felt that he was but one of a vanishing race?"[43]

Not every resident of Blaine County was as romantically inclined as Everhart. There was a great deal of discontent among whites over the lands the Indians had chosen for their allotments before the opening. Any positive effort the Indians were making at farming their allotments was therefore not likely to be advertised or praised by local settlers. As early resident Elmer Epler disparagingly stated, the Indians "picked out allotments along the streams."[44] As times got tough during the extended drought of the 1890s, settlers suddenly realized that the Indians held the best land along the only year-round watercourses. Taking this view in a message to the Washington, DC, Indian Office, territorial governor A. J. Seay wrote that "there was unrest among the settlers because the 'shiftless, indolent and unprogressive' Indians took the 'best land' leaving only the 'second rate' land for settlement."[45] Not surprisingly, Blaine County became the site of some of the most outrageous land swindles against Indian peoples in the nation.[46]

African American settlers in Blaine were in a very different position from the Cheyennes and Arapahoes. The vast area opened for settlement in the 1892 run was not immediately taken up by whites, as in previous runs on the unassigned lands. Much of the northwest corner of the county was considered too arid for conventional farming and attracted few homesteaders. Watercourses in the western part of the county were often too saline for use on fields. Poor soil, rocky outcrops, and gypsum and salt deposits just beneath the surface of the soil kept potential settlers away. For many African Americans, however, the lack of competition for land was precisely the kind of opportunity they were looking for.

The majority of black homesteaders, like many poor white homesteaders, were at a physical disadvantage during the runs because they often came on foot. The daughter of an original black claimant explained that during the 1892 run, "the folks from Kansas had horses and buggies, but people coming from the south had nothing but their feet. And that's why they didn't get any close in, good land."[47] African American farmers in Blaine tended to settle near one another in three areas: near the salt mines at Ferguson, south of Hitchcock in the crosstimbers region, and on the south side of the Canadian River. The best wheat lands in the eastern half of the county were overwhelmingly populated by whites.

Most African American farmers grew cotton and corn in order to take full advantage of the soil's initial fertility. They arrived with very little in terms of animals, seed, or implements, which meant that they waited a long time before their claims turned a profit. Lavinia Jones recalled that her father, Charlie Graham, walked to Kingfisher, 20 miles distant, every Sunday night to work for wages and walked back home on Saturday mornings to work his claim. "All the implements he had was a shovel—worked in the evening trying to spade up his garden and his fields—get his farming ground together." Unable to afford seed, Graham would collect the seed corn that passing whites dropped to the ground when they fed their horses at noontime on the road to Kingfisher. These seeds provided him with his first crop. "A few years after that he got a team—several years after that he built a home."[48]

As a result of the county's sparse population and general lack of resources, Blaine's first schools were integrated, and black and white children attended together in most rural areas. It was through the schools and in commercial exchanges with whites that African American farmers were made aware of their white neighbors' intolerance. White Oklahomans considered their treatment of blacks far superior to that in the deep South, and most believed that in Blaine County anyway, it was live and let live. After statehood and the codification of Jim Crow in the new state constitution, however, this sort of statement was more wishful thinking than reality.

Blaine County was indeed better, at least initially, than the places blacks had migrated from. As Lavinia Jones explained, "Our folks tried to live happy, so they wouldn't think about where they came from or wanting to go back. They knew they had a hard time back there and they was trying to build this up so their children would have a better way of goin' when they grew up."[49] Although the common poverty and mixed origins of Blaine's white population meant that blacks were initially tolerated as farmers, the presence of southerners was keenly felt. Violence and racial discrimination had indeed followed African Americans to Oklahoma, even if it was not readily predictable.

The ambivalence felt by Euro-Americans toward blacks in Blaine created some indelible memories. Emil Schneider recounted, "The first thing I remember about is I got a whipping. There was some neighbors went to school with us and I called them niggers. He [the schoolmaster] caught me at it and he give me a whipping. We walked to school with them every morning."[50] Ken Robertson, whose family migrated from Kentucky to Blaine, recalled that his father "would walk away from a job rather than work in the same field with a black person."[51] Lavinia Jones's older sisters complained that at school the teacher would whip the white children when they misbehaved, but when the black children misbehaved, she took them by the hair and knocked their heads against the wall. The girls did not object to being disciplined, but declared, "she should whip us all the same."

Some encounters between African and Euro-American settlers were not so tame. Blaine residents recalled rapes, shootings, and lynchings against blacks in the county in the late 1890s. Asked if there was much crime around Ferguson (a predominantly black community) when he was a boy, Solomon Bill, the son of Russian immigrants, replied, "No crimes I can remember other than people getting drunk. A couple of rapes committed on Negro women—no one got too upset."[52] As a boy, Ross Nigh watched a "colored" woman crowd a white woman off a sidewalk in Watonga. The white woman attempted to retaliate, and an African American man came over to mediate. Immediately, a group of white men chased him away to the depot, where he "jumped on a moving freight train and didn't come back."[53]

In 1895, another African American man was not so fortunate. A prisoner, arrested for allegedly killing a white southerner who had refused him a ride in his wagon, was lynched by a mob who stormed the county jail with an 8-foot log. Tom Mosely recalled that a mob of twenty-five or thirty people "took this here old boy out there and they hung him from a blackjack oak just east of main street. My father had to cut him down—said he was dead before they hung him."[54] Another settler recalled seeing a white drifter shoot an African American man at point-blank range in the back as he was crossing the street in Watonga. The gunman then nonchalantly walked over to the train depot, got on a car, and left town without being questioned.

Although blacks were generally accepted as part of the local agricultural community, the number of incidents recalled by early settlers indicates that blacks' safety and security were tenuous. If blacks came to Oklahoma to escape being treated as second-class citizens, they were disappointed. And because black farmers kept to themselves, it was easy for whites to generalize about their condition and ascribe their behavior to race. Most important for the ecology of Blaine County, black farmers' mixed farming practices were regarded by their white neighbors as proof of their lack of initiative and failure to progress into the cattle and wheat culture.

Some of Dick Rice's family were late arrivals in Blaine, not coming until 1908, when land prices were fairly high. Consequently, the Rices bought land on the south side of the Canadian River, where, as Rice recalled, "half the farms around us were colored." The Rices represented a second wave of agricultural settlement in Blaine by families who could afford to purchase land instead of homesteading it. African American claims were coveted by these new arrivals for their lower prices and basic improvements. As white pressure and discrimination increased, many black farm families sold their farms and took jobs in places in Oklahoma City where there was a large black community.

Still, some black families stayed. Twenty-year-old James A. Rouce Sr. of Arkansas made the 1892 run into the Cheyenne and Arapahoe reserve. He and another black settler, Pashalt Zeigler, staked claims near each other about 5 miles east of Hitchcock. Rouce later married one of Zeigler's four daughters and was appointed a regent of the new Colored Agricultural and Normal University at Langston by the governor, Tom Ferguson. Zeigler was also very successful, becoming the college's first farm manager. When he died, Zeigler had acquired enough land to leave a farm to each of his children. Rouce and Zeigler were both recognized by whites and blacks as outstanding agriculturalists.

One of the keys to their success was their location. Each had farms that contained above-average land in an area with generally poor soil. But their choice of neighbors, Old World Europeans, turned out to be even more important. Frank Beneda recounted that his grandfather Frank Strack migrated to the United States from Austria. Together with his wife Rosina and his mother-in-law, the three family members bought claims together in the east-central portion of the county in 1893. Elsie Strack, Frank and Rosina's daughter, recalled that some of their neighbors were Indians (Mose Coon and Brave Turtle) but that the vast majority of their neighbors to the south were "colored." Charlie Graham, a black settler, was the Strack's closest neighbor. He and Frank worked together to build frame houses on their claims in the late 1890s. They sent their children to the same schools and shared horses, supplies, and equipment. Lavinia Jones, Graham's daughter, recalled that after a while, Frank got a threshing machine and Charlie became one of his main hands. "Frank Strack and Charlie Graham were pals . . . They traveled around—almost clean back toward Guthrie up to Okeene. He was one of the main men on that."[55]

As a result of his early investment in mechanized farming, Frank Strack became one of the most successful farmers in Blaine County— so much so that his activities were a subject of local news interest. In September 1911, the *Watonga Republican* considered it newsworthy to report that Frank Strack was cutting kafir corn. According to his grandson Frank Beneda, Strack bought, sold, and traded land his whole life and at one time owned or leased twelve quarter sections of land, or nearly 2,000 acres. At the time of his death in 1922, Strack owned seven quarters of land debt-free.

Sadly, in spite of their long association, the Graham family did not attend Frank Strack's funeral for fear of rejection by other white families. The Grahams later regretted their decision because the Strack family "let it be known that they were very hurt." Graham's daughter Sallie recalled, "It's a tough feeling when you like people and know they like you . . . and yet think the others wouldn't want you."[56] For the most part, however, cooperation and friendship with the Strack family meant respectability for the Grahams and other black families nearby. Predictably, the African American families with the longest tenure in the county lived around the original Strack claims.

Just as Blaine farmers arrived with certain social expectations, their experiences with other environments deeply affected their relationship to their new homes in the territory. Census records reveal that the majority of Blaine County's first white farmers were from Kansas or spent some years there before moving to Oklahoma. This makes the Kansas experience highly influential in the initial settlement of the county. Fortunately, some generalizations about Kansas farm culture in the years leading up to the 1892 runs can be made from the work of James Malin, one of Kansas' most capable, if irascible, scholars. An early historian of the Plains environment, Malin was fascinated by the process of human adaptation to new environmental conditions. By using primary documents overlooked by other historians, Malin detailed the way in which farmers functioned in his home county of Edwards.

Malin's first discovery was that most Edwards County farmers were native born from New York and Pennsylvania. Most owned modest-sized farms of less than 200 acres, with a small group owning much more. Malin concluded that these elite farmers, with holdings of more than 400 acres, took on the task of instructing recently arrived smaller farmers on what and how much to plant in their first seasons. Edwards County farmers raised cash crops but did not rely on one crop exclusively from year to year. Malin noted, "Even though these farmers were discussing money crops almost exclusively, the fact is inescapable that they were living a relatively self-sufficient existence."[57] The minutes of the Edwards County farm club also revealed that learning how to farm the mixed-grass plains was a process of trial and error. In other words, the farmers of Edwards County were deeply engaged in how to understand and overcome their environment. The two things they felt they lacked most were capital and better agricultural advice.[58]

This pattern held true even after these farmers relocated to Oklahoma Territory. From almost every social, cultural, religious, or economic standpoint, the cost of failure in Kansas, and subsequently in Blaine County in Oklahoma Territory, was high. Failed crops meant foreclosure and loss of their homes. Marginally successful farming strategies meant unceasing toil and a low standard of living. For men and women suffering periodic bouts of drought, insect infestation, hail, flood, and other environmental disasters, the specter of out-migration only galvanized their resolve. Oklahoma Territory farmers, like every other sector of American society, wanted to be economically independent, but unlike the more mobile shopkeeper or wage worker, they often espoused their commitment to farming as a way of life. Torn between their desire to settle permanently in their new homes while extracting the greatest profit, Oklahoma's newest farmers would leave an indelible mark on the territorial landscape.[59]

5

LAND RUSH

Conditions about a growing institution are such that station workers have to put in long hours with practically no vacation. They have done this, recognizing the fact that the farmers of Oklahoma need all of the help which the station can give them in their efforts to build homes and develop farms in a section of the country so recently opened to settlement.

John Fields, Director, Oklahoma Experiment Station, July 1905

The run on the Cheyenne and Arapahoe lands in 1892 did not attract as many settlers as the original run into the unassigned lands. The main reasons for this were ecological: the county contained several thousand acres of unproductive gyp land, the creeks could be salty, and annual rainfall was noticeably less than in the unassigned lands. As hardworking and hopeful as Blaine's white and black families were, the environmental conditions of the first few years of settlement caused them severe hardship. Less than two years after the county's opening in 1892, extreme temperatures and a period of low rainfall converged to create severe drought conditions for three consecutive years, from 1894 to 1896.

Although the Stillwater Experiment Station did not begin recording precipitation in Blaine until after 1900, local newspapers printed their own weather reports, and official temperatures were recorded by the U.S. Department of Agriculture (USDA) in Kingfisher and El Reno, just southeast of Blaine. These sources can be used to reconstruct Blaine's climatic history during the drought years. A conservative overview of rainfall and temperature in Blaine between 1889 and 1905 indicates a severe drought beginning in 1894 and ending in 1896. This was followed by a dramatic increase in annual rainfall beginning in 1897 that continued at above-average levels for the next eight years.

Rainfall averages, however, are deceptive in determining past agricultural conditions because crops can be severely affected by either prolonged drought or deluges that arrive at the wrong time. Regular rainfall is always most beneficial to cereal crops like corn and wheat over the winter and throughout the spring. Crops that fail to come up or thrive in the spring from a lack of moisture do not recover following a July downpour. For these reasons, a year of statistically average rainfall can be disastrously insufficient, depending on the time of year and whether it was accompanied by periods of extreme heat and high winds.

A more accurate predictor of crop success is soil moisture. This tends to be cumulative—that is, it either builds with rainfall or is reduced with each year of prolonged drought. Several years of low rainfall can also affect the water capacity of the soil and the ability of perennial root systems to recover even after a period of years.[1] This was the situation in Blaine County in 1895 and 1896, the two worst years of the drought. After the failure of the wheat and oat crops in the spring, farmers planted corn and even some cotton, but these too failed under the unrelenting heat and desiccating winds. At the end of August 1896, the *Watonga Republican* reported twenty-one consecutive days of 100-plus temperatures, seven of which registered 118 degrees. Forever the guardian of the county's reputation, editor and future territorial governor T. B. Ferguson[2] sanguinely reported, "the county's hay crop this year will be the largest she has ever produced."[3] He did not have to remind his readers that hay was all the county would harvest that season.

Not everyone could afford to be as optimistic as Ferguson. Even the most determined settlers did not arrive expecting to live three years without a crop, and the drought years saw a steady out-migration of population from the county. In May 1895, after the total failure of the wheat crop, Ferguson chided local residents to reconsider their plans and not to "sacrifice your claim now." He reminded them that they came to get a claim and they might not ever have the chance again. "The outlook may be dark, but it is just as bright as it was three years ago when we set our stakes in Blaine County. Look back calmly and look forward hopeful."[4]

Ferguson's admonition was hardly needed because most settlers did not choose to "go home to the wife's folks" until their personal resources were completely exhausted. Like so many other white settlers to Blaine, J. R. Cook's parents arrived in Longdale trusting that

Oklahoma would brighten their economic future. The extended Cook family, including Cook's grandparents and the grown families of several of their thirteen children, were in debt in Kansas after an earlier move from Michigan. According to Cook, they "got out just enough to move" to Oklahoma. Living for years in a partial dugout/log cabin, the Cook clan took up wheat farming but remained so poor that they were not able to purchase a tractor until 1927.[5] Like the Cooks, many of Blaine's settlers had no other place to go if they did not make it in the new territory.

As in Logan County, common obstacles drew local residents together for mutual support. During the settlement years, a general lack of material possessions had a similar effect on Blaine's white settlers because the resources of the county's white residents were fairly homogenous. Very rich and very poor were rare in the county before statehood in 1907. Most settlers had the same basic possessions: a horse, a wagon, some household goods, and a manufactured plow.[6] Initial improvements on their land consisted of a soddy or dugout, a well, a cellar, a small garden, and an orchard. All of these improvements were surrounded by a simple fence of double-stranded barbed wire on posts cut from blackjack oaks or Osage orange trees. The numbers of acres farmers had under plow or improved was modest, with the majority of land still under grass as late as 1900.[7] Real increases in improved acreages arrived with the advent of better weather and scientific directions from the Stillwater Experiment Station.

Understandably, the farm families who stayed on in spite of the drought and inconvenience of pioneering were reluctant to relinquish their land if there was any hope of future success.[8] One poignant example of this hope was the unusual persistence in Oklahoma Territory of the "rain follows the plow" theory of climatic change. On May 15, 1895, the *Watonga Republican* printed a popular version of this theory in poem form.

> I heard an old farmer talk one day
> Telling his listeners how
> In the wide new country far away
> The rainfall follows the plow
> As fast as they break it up, you see
> The heart is turned to the sun
> As the furrows are opened, deep and free
> The tillage is begun

The earth grows mellow and more and more
It holds and sends to the sky
A moisture it never had before
When its face was hard and dry
And so, whenever the plow shears run
The clouds run overhead
And the soil that is stirred and lets in the sun
With water is always fed
I wonder if that old farmer knew
The half of his simple word
Or guess the message that eternally true
Hidden within it was heard
It fell on my ears by chance that day
But the gladness lingers now
To think that it is always God's own way
That the rainfall follows the plow

The message of the poem was something every Blaine County farmer could cling to: good things come to those who wait on the eternal wisdom of God. It mattered little to Blaine residents that the scientific foundation of the plow theory as posited by Samuel Aughey of the University of Nebraska had already come under attack. In Blaine County, the idea took on new life, inspired by notions of manifest destiny and divine intervention, as popularized in 1891 by Colonel W. E. Tweedale of Kansas.[9]

But Blaine farmers apparently also believed that God helps those who help themselves, and after 1896, row crop farmers began dedicating an increasing proportion of their land and capital to raising livestock, particularly cattle. Farmers noted that the native prairie grasses, although damaged, had survived the drought in quantities sufficient to sustain their stock. In combination with raising hard red winter wheat, developed at the experiment station in Kansas,[10] cattle quickly became a popular investment among Blaine farmers. When questioned about his purchase of a small herd of twenty-five heifers in 1899, the county sheriff wryly answered, "There is more money in cows than there is in office."[11] By the turn of the century, most grain farmers had also become part-time stock raisers. Cattle became their hedge against the failure from drought of their small grain crops.

Federal agricultural census records for Oklahoma in 1900 indicate that Blaine's local population was fairly typical of the territory's white farmers. Of the new territory's 62,000 farms, 29,000 reported hay and grain production as their principal source of income, and nearly 15,000 raised livestock. A recent survey of families who have maintained their farms statewide for a century or more also reveals a pattern of combined wheat and cattle production, particularly after the turn of the century.[12] Pasturing animals in the spring on the first growth of winter wheat was an unfamiliar custom in 1892 and only came into vogue around 1900. Farmers' acceptance of this new practice—that was good for cattle without damaging the wheat crop—made stock raising even more appealing.[13]

Dairying, too, gained in economic importance after the invention of the cream separator in 1899, and Blaine countians sold their excess cream to city-based ice cream factories and the new cheese factory in Watonga. One highly successful group of Blaine County farmers took up horse breeding at about this same time, earning Blaine a statewide reputation for high-quality purebred draft horses by 1910. Blaine farmers' rapid adaptation to the drought, the return of better weather in 1897, a steadier market, and their partial shift from crops to stock and dairy farming did not, however, immediately result in greater prosperity. Between 1892 and 1899, Watonga Township's population grew by less than ten people, to only 304 persons, and the average income, even after two good seasons, was only $144, an increase of only $7 in as many years.[14]

The truth was, that for all their hard work and effort since they arrived in 1892, Blaine settlers could hardly be said to be any better off in 1900 than when they arrived. This situation was even bleaker for the county's black and Indian residents. Not surprisingly, the county's observance of the new year in 1900 was marked more by frustration than celebration. *Watonga Republican* editor Tom Ferguson, casting off his usual optimism, grimly observed, "This is not the beginning of a new century but the close of the old. We are still living in the nineteenth century."[15] Blaine County residents were ready for a change.

On September 19, 1902, John Fields, director of the Oklahoma Agricultural Experiment Station, reported to National Director of Experiment Stations Alfred C. True that ever since its establishment, "the station has formulated rather than modified agricultural practice."[16] Vanity aside, Fields had good reason to believe the USDA had become a force in Oklahoma agriculture at the turn of the century. Although the official federal mandate for Stillwater was to oversee the scientific analysis of the new territory—climate, soils, and crops—

Fields's personal objective was to secure the trust and cooperation of the small farmer. Fields made it the station's goal to "help the new settler solve the problems presented by his 160 acres of raw prairie in an unknown and untried land . . . the little fellow with no money and no individual influence to speak of."[17] When he left the Oklahoma USDA station in 1906, Fields little appreciated how much a part of agricultural thinking and practice the experiment station had become.

Unfortunately, the "little fellow" that Fields had in mind was neither Indian or African American. Access to new ideas, and to new technology in particular, became the crucial difference between white farm owner–operators and their less fortunate Indian, black, and tenant neighbors. Contrary to popular notions today, agricultural technology in Blaine County did not mean purchasing tractors, at least not before 1925. Although most farmers purchased some horse-drawn mechanical equipment—implements designed for planting and harrowing—harvesting staple crops like wheat was best done by a self-powered thresher or combine. Instead of purchasing expensive combines, however, most cash-strapped farmers relied on the services of custom cutters.

According to Thomas Isern, an historian of agricultural folk life, custom threshing on the Great Plains progressed in three stages. Beginning in the 1870s in settled states like Kansas, farmers relied on animal-powered implements to harvest their wheat crop. Early mechanical harvesting required several hands to operate the machinery, drive animal teams, and pitch grain onto wagon beds. By the 1890s, some farmers had pooled their resources to purchase a steam-powered thresher for use collectively. More entrepreneurial farmers, often in partnership with equipment distributors, purchased equipment, hired a crew, and harvested for local farmers at a set rate per acre. A third period of mechanization took place in Oklahoma around 1924, when a significant minority of farmers were able to purchase their own combines, tractors, and grain trucks.[18]

The second-stage pattern of localized custom work was common throughout the wheat belt of Oklahoma before statehood, including Blaine County. This is reflected in the local assessments for farm equipment. In 1894, the average Blaine settler owned between $15 and $30 worth of agricultural machinery. By 1910, Blaine County farmers owned nearly $200 dollars of agricultural implements, such as horse-drawn cultivators, headers, binders, and threshers. By 1920, this figure jumped significantly, to over $1,000 worth of agricultural machinery.

The average farm size also increased from just under 160 acres in 1894 to nearly 300 acres per farm unit by 1920. This increase in mechanization and in farm size was accompanied by an increase in the average wheat acreage per farm, from 22 acres in 1910 to nearly 120 acres by 1920.

Statistics in this case, however, obscure the fact that very few farmers actually owned $1,000 worth of agricultural machinery, even in 1920. Although some farmers wholeheartedly invested in self-powered harvesting equipment worth far more than $1,000, including tractor-driven combines, most continued to rely on draft animals for their day-to-day farm power. In fact, in 1910, the number of draft animals (horses and mules) in Blaine County stood at seven animals per farm and actually increased to twelve by 1920.[19]

These seemingly contradictory trends—an increase in both animals and machinery—make sense only in the context of custom harvesting. Although nearly every farmer had draft animals for use all year around and set aside some acreage for fodder crops like oats, corn, and hay to maintain them, a small minority of farmers took out loans to purchase steam-powered harvesting equipment, which they financed by hiring themselves and their equipment out to their neighbors once a year. In this way, nearly every white farmer in Blaine County was able to invest in staple crop agriculture, particularly wheat, on a wide scale.

Blaine County farmers had a number of custom cutters to choose from. On June 8, 1893, the *Watonga Rustler* reported that "there are five threshing machines owned by parties here and two of them will be brought in this year . . . a number of our young men will go to Kansas for work as soon as the harvest is done here."[20] Interviews with custom cutters conducted in the 1940s confirmed the *Rustler*'s report. Longtime custom cutters recalled that before farmers bought combines, "wheat was bound, shocked and left until the threshing machine worked its way into the community and threshed for farmers." Threshing crews, made up of "young men, bachelors, adventurers and others,"[21] moved with the harvest a certain distance and then returned to their homes and farms at the end of the season. This localized pattern of custom harvesting in the emerging wheat belt of Oklahoma Territory spread as improvements in harvesting equipment, particularly sturdier trucks, made it easier to transport both crews and machinery greater distances.

Custom harvesting linked this new technology to land tenure through the medium of community dynamics. In the wheat-producing regions of Oklahoma, custom cutters and farmers contracted with one another on an annual basis. Both farmers and custom cutters relied on other farmers' recommendations and personal experience in their decision to contract with one another. A new farmer, for example, would ask his neighbors to recommend a reliable custom outfit. The new farmer would then write the custom harvester requesting his services in the following year. Most of this correspondence took place during the winter. Similarly, the combine owner would make inquiries about the farmer's reputation, his facilities for housing and feeding the crew, and—above all—how many acres he realistically expected to harvest.

Combiners were paid a portion of the harvest per acre, in addition to board and daily wages for skilled crew members. Because it took approximately the same amount of time to set up operations to harvest 40 acres as it did 200 acres, custom harvesters were predisposed to service farmers with larger acreages. If a farmer had only a small portion of land in wheat, he might attract a combiner by lining up contracts with several farmers in the immediate vicinity to increase the anticipated volume.

In spite of all these carefully laid plans, however, neither the farmer nor the custom cutter were legally obligated to honor their agreements. If a custom combiner contracted to harvest a field in Kingfisher County on a certain date but found himself delayed by rains in Garfield County, the farmer in Kingfisher could not hold the combine operator liable for any loss that might result from overripening, hail, or other damage to the crop. Conversely, should an uncontracted combiner be in that farmer's neighborhood at a time when his grain had reached maximum maturity, he was under no obligation to wait for his contracted unit to arrive. Custom cutters did their best to avoid unplanned idleness by telegraphing ahead to say they were on their way.[22]

The potential economic and social implications of the combine contract system were profound, particularly for those farmers who did not share in the technology-based networks that were beginning to emerge. Small farmers—white, black, and Indian—were especially obliged to maintain good relations with their neighbors and combine owners. Small-scale producers faced a built-in bias against attracting a custom cutter to their fields, thus increasing their risk of ruin in any given season. The informal and extralegal nature of the custom cutting contract system left unlucky farmers with unharvested grain, or crops ruined by early frost or hail and no official redress for their losses.

As the wheat and cattle culture began to dominate the county economy, the soil fertility of black-owned farms, planted largely to cotton,
was beginning to play out. All but one of the county's cotton gins had
shut down by 1914, and many black families found themselves in dire
economic straits. The jobs that early black settlers worked at for wages
were no longer available. The local timber was already cut and sold,
the railroads were consolidating, and the market for fresh produce in
the small towns and at the Cantonment army post and Indian agency
dried up as the posts were decommissioned and Indian peoples became
(officially) more self-sufficient. The town building boom that had
employed hundreds of itinerant workers in places like Kingfisher,
Guthrie, and Oklahoma City suddenly busted in 1907, cutting off yet
another source of needed cash.[23] Even African Americans' economic
isolation from whites began to break down in Blaine as rivers and
creeks were bridged, linking white farmers to black-owned areas south
of the Canadian River, and railroads sent out spur lines linking small
communities to larger ones like Watonga, El Reno, and Geary. Black
families began to look for new homes and opportunities elsewhere.

For Dick Rice, as for many other white settlers, economic, environmental, or technological circumstances were not needed to understand
the African American exodus from Blaine. Racial and cultural expla-
nations were sufficient. According to Rice, blacks simply could not
resist making a cash sale for their property, and "commenced selling
their lands as fast as they could" after statehood. Rice rationalized that
black families in Blaine never expected to live there permanently anyway. "Never could make a success of it by themselves. They were tired
of it, ready to leave when the whites moved in."[24]

In addition to affecting the farm population of the county, the custom system directly affected land use on a wide scale. Given the fixed
costs of board and wages, the custom cutting system encouraged white
farmers to plant a larger percentage of their land in mechanically harvested crops in order to get their money's worth. In turn, larger
acreages increased farmers' chances of regularly attracting custom harvesters until they could afford to purchase their own equipment.
Farmers hoping to get ahead by planting mechanically harvested crops
could not afford to keep many idle acres. Like Frank Strack, those
farmers who took the risk of devoting more acres to a single crop and
profited were able to quickly increase their holdings, thus increasing
their chances for even greater profits in the future. These farmers were
the first to demand help from the experiment station, subscribed to a

higher percentage of farm papers,[25] and kept track of prices through the Chicago Board of Trade. They were also the primary clients of a new kind of scientific farming advocate: the county agent.

The experiment station and land grant college in Stillwater were more successful than those of many other states in gaining farmers' interest in scientific farming practices, albeit by unconventional means. Before 1900, in states like Wisconsin and Iowa, agricultural scientists were largely unable to convert their research results into farm practices because of the so-called country-college gap. Some of this disparity was overcome through farmer's institutes, which brought together farmers and scientists for two to three days in relaxed conditions, similar to a tent meeting or agricultural fair. Although station scientists were often the featured speakers, institutes wisely offered classes for women and girls, followed by dances, hayrides, and other social events.

Farmer's institutes were not immediately organized in the western states. In Oklahoma, the institute system was eventually organized under the leadership of experiment station director John Fields in 1904. This was rather late, however, in the institute movement, and the Oklahoma system never enjoyed attendance levels equal to its midwestern predecessors.[26] In some ways, the institutes were not needed to bring the college to the country in Oklahoma. The unusual circumstances of Oklahoma settlement had already opened many farmers' doors to the work of the college and station.

Oklahoma was also less burdened with the view many progressives held about the social bankruptcy of the rural community. In general, reformers of agriculture fell into two groups: those concerned with the quality of rural life and its effect on urbanites, and those, mostly scientists and businessmen, concerned with the economic future of agriculture. The one reform that all critics of agriculture could agree on, regardless of their viewpoint, was "advancing social and economic efficiency and organization."[27] William R. Taylor of the Wisconsin Agricultural Convention put it nicely in 1873 when he said the "guesswork, random efforts [and] 'cut and try' methods that characterize the practice of most farmers [was] a waste of time and strength and substance."[28] This emphasis on efficiency and "system" placed Oklahoma's agrarian reformers squarely in the progressive tradition.

USDA scientists were only one of several professional sectors at that time who hoped scientific agriculture would quickly form the foundation of a new rural order. Even the reclamation service, as practical and technological as it was, professed to "reclaim 'worthless' lives along with worthless desert soil."[29] As a newly formed rural community, Oklahoma agriculturalists believed they were making a fresh start, free of the stubborn traditionalism of older, more established farm communities. This made Oklahoma a special challenge for men like John Fields, who was trained in one of the most progressive schools in the country before his appointment to Stillwater.[30] Although their social agenda was never very far from the surface, the agricultural college administrators who enjoyed the most success in reaching farmers were those whose agricultural agents focused almost exclusively on technical help, virtually "jettisoning the rest of the country-life program."[31] Oklahoma experiment station staff quickly adopted this mode, putting less effort into changing farmers' thinking and more effort into finding practical solutions to their problems.

Eager to turn the prairie sod into cash, Oklahoma's white settlers looked for advice in all corners, especially local newspapers. Several territory newspapers reprinted selected station bulletins in their entirety. The newspaper at Guthrie printed each bulletin as it appeared. As experiment station director George Morrow reported in 1899, "The county weeklies also make large use of the press bulletins and appreciation of this is shown in the letters received from farmers commenting on this practice."[32]

Fields believed in the recently arrived settlers who "knew nothing of farming when they came here" but "by study and hard work come to be far more successful as a rule than the hardened agricultural sinner who has farmed all his life under other conditions."[33] He also realized that the farmers most eager to take up the advice of the station usually needed it least. "The large farmer and ranchman is able to take care of himself," Fields wrote in 1902, "though frequently he is most insistent in his demands for help."[34] In his survey of three successful station directors in Wisconsin, Illinois, and California, Charles Rosenberg noted that many early directors cultivated ties with existing farm organizations, wealthy farmers, and businessmen. Fields eschewed these kinds of contacts, relying on publications, talks, and short courses to reach farmers while wrangling with politicians through college president Angelo Scott. As Fields declared in 1899, "When an opportunity arises for us to do work which is of service to the many . . . all of the facilities of the station are turned loose on it and we do the best we can."[35]

Fields believed, correctly, that the single-section (160 acre) farm was the most common in Oklahoma Territory in 1899. According to census records, of the territory's 62,500 farms, two-thirds, or 42,600, were classified as more than 100 acres but less than 175 acres in size. The next largest category comprised farms between 50 and 100 acres (6,400 farms). Counting farms under 50 acres in size, the census shows that a total of 52,000 of the territory's farms (80 percent) were 160 acres or less. Oklahoma's small farm majority contrasted markedly with Kansas, where in 1900, less than a third of the state's farmers fell into the single-section category (100 to 175 acres), and out of a total of 173,000 farm units, 125,500, or two-thirds, were 100 acres or larger.[36]

Of Oklahoma Territory's approximately 50,000 small family farms in 1900, a total of 29,000 were committed to grain production. Livestock raising was the next largest category, with more than 14,000 farmers claiming cattle raising as their primary source of income. Station bulletins were tailored to these interests even before Fields took over as director in 1899. Of the forty-two publications generated by the station between 1891 and 1897, thirteen were devoted to the cultivation of cash crops such as wheat, corn, and cotton, and six to stock raising (cattle, sheep, and pigs). The remainder covered other practical topics such as well and road construction, weather statistics, planting times, vegetable gardening, and weed and pest control, all basic to the settlers' survival.

After Fields's appointment in 1899, experiments on the station farm and bulletins continued to address farmers' most pressing concerns, with some important additions, such as fruit trees, poultry raising, dairying, and new forage (pasturage and feed) plants such as cowpeas, alfalfa, and Bermuda grass. In many ways, the extended scope of station experiments and publications point to farmers' new economic status and the territory's rapid transition from pioneer farming to mature agricultural settlement. Unlike their predecessors, however, Fields and his staff were not content to rely on bulletins and press releases to direct Oklahoma's agricultural development in progressive counties like Blaine. They expected to instruct farmers in ways that would make a positive difference in their day-to-day lives and futures.

Physically confined to the college and station by his duties as director, administrator, teacher, and scientist, Fields made a herculean effort to reach every farmer who wrote to the station by personally answering every letter no later than the day after it was received. In 1904 alone, Fields estimated that the station had received 10,000 letters. Not every letter required a response—a large proportion were simple requests to be placed on the station's mailing list—and Fields shared the task with staff members better qualified to answer questions specific to their training. Nevertheless, it was an overwhelming burden.

On January 4, 1905, an average day for station correspondence, Fields responded to two requests for out-of-print bulletins, two for cattle vaccine, and one asking him to attend a local farm club meeting. He also dictated detailed instructions on pasturing hogs, transplanting alfalfa, kafir corn varieties, and spraying fruit trees. In addition, Fields wrote a three-page outline of his philosophy of agricultural education in the public schools to a colleague in Guthrie, Oklahoma, in which he articulated a goal he partially realized in 1905.

Occasionally, Fields's frustration at having to "thrash over and over" simple directions surfaced in his response to farmers. In November 1905, Frank Carpenter of Bridgeport, Oklahoma, wrote to request a bulletin and casually asked if the station knew of any cure for "lumpy-jaw" (actinomyces), a highly contagious and fatal bacterial disease of cattle. Fields replied that the "best remedy I know of . . . is to knock the steer in the head with an axe." It is difficult to determine from the distance of nearly a century whether Fields was being sincere or wildly sarcastic. In general, however, letters sent to farmers from the director's office were helpful and courteous.[37]

Yet Fields was still not satisfied. He wanted to know what was happening to all the information he was so furiously dispensing from Stillwater. Early in his directorship, Fields wrote somewhat naively to True, "It is an easy matter to discover what the farmers want: they want it all; but we're finding it difficult to get hold of what the farmers themselves are really doing."[38] It was this impulse that led him to conduct the station's first survey of local farmers. Targeting what Fields considered potentially the most economically important crop grown in Oklahoma—wheat—station staff canvassed local millers for the names of consistently successful wheat farmers throughout the territory and mailed out one-page questionnaires to each of them. The station received one hundred eighteen responses from eighteen different counties. The questions were brief and to the point, asking for acreage and yields, varieties, and planting times. Acreage varied from 15 to 300 acres and averaged about 18 bushels per acre of mostly hard red Turkey wheat. Hardier than soft wheat varieties, hard winter wheat was sown in the fall and harvested in spring, before the heat of the summer months withered the slender plants. Farmers were also asked if they practiced crop rotation, fertilized, or fallowed their fields. Most responded affirmatively to one or all of these measures.

From the results of the survey, Fields was able to draw up four rules of thumb regarding wheat production in Oklahoma: early, deep plowing; planting seed before October 15; the desirability of hard wheat varieties over soft varieties in the western counties; and the regular rotation of wheat fields with other crops. (He later added that manure was beneficial in many cases.) How quickly farmers actually adopted these rules for wheat cultivation is almost impossible to determine, but the results of a survey conducted by the Oklahoma Historical Society's Centennial Ranches and Farms Project suggests that this formula for successful wheat culture was common knowledge by 1920.

Fields's experiment with polling farmers was significant in yet another way. A station bulletin generated not by agricultural experts but by successful farmers clearly demonstrated to the public the station's respect for farmers' practical knowledge of agriculture in the territory, ingratiating the station even more with the farmers. Moreover, by choosing to highlight an economically important but somewhat unfamiliar crop (winter wheat) in this way, Fields declared the USDA's approval of farmers' participation in the staple crop market as a component of progressive farming.

But questionnaires, like bulletins and press releases, were still a fairly passive form of interaction between the station and farmers, and Fields sought to rectify this deficiency in a number of ways. Speaking engagements were one remedy, although as Fields soon discovered, attending farmer's meetings left little time for station work, and farmers who could afford to attend institutes, short courses, and the like were likely already reading bulletins. What Fields needed was an opportunity to demonstrate, in an unmistakable way, the USDA's commitment to the small farmer.

That chance came in 1899 when the station veterinarian received a thousand doses of blackleg vaccine from the Bureau of Animal Industry in Washington to help combat the disease in Oklahoma. The station's supply was quickly exhausted, and Fields decided the problem was grave enough to warrant the manufacture of vaccine at the station for free distribution to the farmers of the territory. Given the character of the disease and the dramatic consequences of infection, it is easy to understand why large and small farmers alike panicked at the knowledge of the infection's presence and willingly enlisted the station's help.

Blackleg (also known as symptomatic anthrax, black quarter, quarter evil, or cold gangrene) was a well-known cattle disease in Europe that was imported to the United States along with purebred cattle. In 1879, French bacteriologists identified the organism (*Clostridium*) responsible for the disease and worked out an effective vaccine by using nonviable cells from the flesh of fatally infected animals in solution that, when injected into healthy animals, produced immunity to the disease. Unlike other cattle diseases, in which susceptibility was clearly linked to some weakened condition in the animal or a change in the environment, blackleg targeted young, healthy cattle, between six months and three years old, during periods of rapid growth, or fattening, in fall and spring. It was also more prevalent in animals bred from recognized stock—that is, from purebred strains—leaving range cattle largely unaffected.

General symptoms included loss of appetite and fever, quickly followed by the appearance of large tumors or hot swellings on the limbs, neck, or head. These tumors spread rapidly, filling with gas that, when lanced, emitted a foul-smelling dark red liquid. Infected animals generally died between twelve and twenty-four hours after the appearance of the first symptoms. Carcasses were a primary source of infection, and farmers were advised to burn them far away from pastures and barns, and then deeply bury the remains.

L. L. Lewis of the Stillwater Experiment Station reported in 1901 that although blackleg was known in the East, the disease was most prevalent in the most recently settled portions of the western United States: Texas, Kansas, Nebraska, the Dakotas, Colorado, and Oklahoma Territory. On the basis of requests from farmers to the experiment station regarding the disease, Lewis concluded it was to be found in every county in Oklahoma and Indian Territory. For single-section farmers, recently proved up and looking to insure themselves against drought and the grain market by raising a few head of purebred steers, the outbreak was terrifying. Blackleg moved like a terrible, swift sword, reducing a farmer's prize herd of young steers, and the investment they represented, to a smoldering heap of ashes, often in less than twenty-four hours.

The Oklahoma Experiment Station staff used Hatch funds to offset the cost of producing and mailing the vaccine free to all who requested it and were soon working overtime to fill farmers' orders. Moreover, because vaccination required farmers to use a proper syringe and sterile technique for it to be effective, the station also distributed inoculation kits for $4 each (postpaid), consisting of a mortar and pestle, a heavy-duty hypodermic syringe and needles, funnel, measuring cup, glycerine, and absorbent cotton. Dried vaccine was distributed in packages of either twenty or twenty-five doses, and every package included complete instructions for the preparation of the solution and inoculation of healthy animals.

Between 1900 and 1913, the veterinary department of the experiment station distributed 1,243,000 doses of vaccine to the farmers and stockmen of the state. A total of 123,620 doses were distributed to over 1,500 farmers in 1901 alone. As L. L. Lewis, the station veterinarian, concluded in 1912, "Vaccination of all young cattle has come to be one of the routine pieces of work on many farms and ranches, and the experience of these men is that the use of vaccine is the only means at hand to prevent losses from blackleg."[39] Perhaps the best evidence of farmers' adoption of the practice, however, came as early as 1902, when the national Office of Experiment Station informed Fields that he could no longer legally use Hatch funds for the distribution of vaccine because it was not related to any research program being undertaken at the station. Fields quickly published notices in the territorial newspapers warning farmers of the program's imminent end and encouraging them to write their representatives to support an appropriation from the legislature that would allow the station to continue to supply farmers with the vaccine. Fields even enlisted the help of A. C. True, asking him for a letter of support as well as making his own recommendation to the legislature that the program be retained or stockmen would suffer widespread loss over the next few years. The territorial farmers' response was overwhelmingly positive, and the legislature voted to appropriate funds at the close of 1902.[40]

As a consequence of the blackleg scare, white farmers came to expect the station's material assistance in a number of other ways as well. The station chemist painstakingly analyzed dozens of individual creek, reservoir, and well water samples sent him by farmers every week. The station entomologist was kept equally busy identifying unknown insect pests sent to him by puzzled farmers, and the station agronomist routinely tested samples of commercial seed sent him from all over the state, to determine the percentage of impurities or weed seeds in each brand. In each case, station staff did their utmost to answer farmers' questions, with the exception of those who sent mineral samples to the station for analysis. These were generally returned to the farmer without comment.

Satisfied to a degree that the experiment station was gaining the confidence of a significant portion of the territory's white farmers, Fields and his staff next attempted to convince them of the benefits of some of the station's "original researches." The most significant of these were the station's experiments with Bermuda grass. Imported to the United States from Africa in 1751, scientists in the South were having good success with it when John Fields began experimenting with it in Oklahoma in 1896. He was soon convinced of the species' adaptability to the Oklahoma climate and soil. It grew rapidly on virtually any well-drained soil, resisted drought, and once it was established, it furnished a fairly high quality hay for winter forage. The grass gained Fields's unwavering loyalty when it was virtually the only field trial to survive a drought in 1901.

During Fields's tenure, the station published three complete bulletins dedicated exclusively to Bermuda grass. Fields even went so far as to supply a hundred farmers with free sod roots (it could not be easily started from seed) for demonstration and had it planted on the grounds surrounding the station and the college buildings, where it remains to the present day. It was not long before Blaine farmers were planting Bermuda grass in their pastures where for years farmers had tried unsuccessfully to recreate the rolling pastures of the East by planting red clover and Kentucky bluegrass. Bermuda grass eventually became the most common domesticated grass in the state, but not exactly in the way Fields had envisioned its use. As better strains of alfalfa and other grasses were developed for semiarid regions at the Woodward Experiment Station in the Oklahoma panhandle, Bermuda grass was less prized for its value as a forage grass and was regarded as a drought-resistant and attractive sod grass, highly suitable for hillsides, parks, boulevards, and lawns.

Not all of the station's activities, of course, were as influential or accepted by farmers as the blackleg vaccine program and the introduction of Bermuda grass eventually were. It took years for Oklahoma farmers to begin serious trials of cowpeas, a plant similar to soybean that the station had recommended as early as 1902 as a substitute for red clover and timothy, neither of which did well in Oklahoma west of Indian Territory despite repeated attempts and station warnings. College short courses, eight- and ten-week winter programs for farmers held at the college and experiment station, were poorly attended in spite of Fields's strenuous efforts at advertising and procuring reduced railway fares. Similarly, Oklahoma did not have a farmer's institute system until Fields initiated one at the turn of the century. Slow at the start, the idea of local farm clubs in which farmers got together to discuss agricultural problems eventually caught on until nearly every county had an institute by 1905. But as Fields was quick to notice, the farmers who attended short courses and farm-club meetings also tended to send their sons to the agricultural college and subscribed to both the station bulletins and agricultural journals—not the constituency he wanted most to reach.

What Fields, and other progressive agricultural experts contemporary with him, wanted to avoid most were the terrible human and environmental consequences of monoculture as it was practiced in the South.[41] Taking as his inspiration the recommendations of a Vicksburg, Mississippi, convention of southern farmers, Fields hoped to see the day when every Oklahoman practiced what he called "diversified farming." Every farmer would have his small herd of cattle, pigs, sheep, and poultry and "a small acreage of each of the many crops that may be grown and is self-supporting." In Fields's vision, this was not the same as self-sufficiency. Crops and livestock in Oklahoma were destined for market, not for home consumption. Fields's version of diversified farming would help insulate farmers from the extremes of the Oklahoma climate and an uncertain market, thus helping them avoid bankruptcy and tenancy.

Fields made this abundantly clear in his correspondence to farmers. There were crops that Fields routinely discouraged on the basis of poor market values, not because of their utility on the farm or their adaptability to the Oklahoma environment. As he wrote to W. E. Robertson of Avery in 1905, "The conditions for the broom corn market are not as favorable as those of the cotton market. Those who grew broom corn in western Oklahoma last year were much disappointed with the return. . . . I fear you would be disappointed if you grew 25 acres." Potential profit motivated Fields to become an ardent promoter of the new territory as a golden opportunity for farmers looking to make money. As he optimistically wrote to Guy Sproul of Lima, Indiana, that year, "All the stable [*sic*] crops of the United States are grown profitably in Oklahoma. I know of no other place where chances for success are so good for farming."[42] The principles Fields adhered to can be summed up in a single sentence that he repeated to the Oklahoma A&M alumni: "Grow many crops, do not depend upon one crop, but utilize stock to the greatest extent and thus secure greater returns and at the same time, keep up the fertility of the soil."[43] The key to Fields's system was helping farmers understand how to make these different enterprises work together efficiently to maintain themselves and their families, their animals, and their land.

In the South, according to Fields, the "lack of method" by tenant farmers over an extended period of time had resulted in widespread infertility of the soil. To prevent the same thing from happening in Oklahoma, farmers needed first to own their farms and make them consistently profitable without ruining the land. Station feeding experiments, for example, were designed to determine the most economical way for farmers to feed their stock without having to purchase commercial feed or plant valuable land to forage crops. Experimental animals were fed wheat straw, cottonseed meal, and all the other by-products of commercial crops, and careful records kept of their progress. In keeping with this same principle, livestock manure was applied to the fields to help retain the soil's fertility. In the case of kafir corn (sorghum), cowpeas, domestic grasses, and other forage crops new to Oklahoma farmers, the station's recommendations were based on two factors: palatability as an animal feed, and the rate at which these crops composted and returned valuable nutrients to the soil, in readiness for more marketable crops like cotton and wheat.

The difficulty with implementing this well-ordered and "scientific" system in Blaine County lay in the average white farmer's lack of resources to carry it out. Fertilizing with manure, practicing crop rotation, even frequent cultivation to help retain moisture, were beyond the means of many small farmers who did not own enough livestock to manure their acreages and could not safely afford to plant even a portion of their land to noncommercial, soil-building crops. The management of several different crops and kinds of animals additionally required improvements (fences and outbuildings) that many farmers could not afford. Diversified farming, as Fields described it, was also highly labor intensive, a very difficult obstacle for small farmers to overcome because "help" on a 160-acre farm frequently meant the farmer, his wife, and their dependent children. Last, Fields's plan assumed that, given enough knowledge and hard work, every section of land could be made to conform irrespective of the extremes of soils and climate in the territory. This was certainly not the case in Blaine County or in most other Oklahoma Territory counties.

Disregard for, or at least a glossing over of, the region's unique environmental features was built into the station's recommendations. "Scientific" farming led scientists and farmers alike to presuppose native prairie plants were less nutritious and made poorer hay than domestic grasses, and encouraged farmers to plow up acre upon acre of healthy buffalo and grama grass for more drought-susceptible fields of alfalfa and Bermuda grass. With the counterexample of southern agriculture always before them, station scientists focused primarily on retaining soil fertility to the near exclusion of more practical problems like aridity and soil erosion from wind and water. When station bulletins did address the region's lack of rainfall, they did not suggest to farmers that some portions of the territory might be entirely unsuited for crops. Instead, their recommendations invariably included deep plowing in the fall and spring and frequent shallow cultivation throughout the year after each rainfall to help retain moisture. Although laboratory experiments with water retention undoubtedly "proved" the benefits of keeping the soil loosely harrowed (to counteract runoff), they did not count on the long-term effects of wind and excessive rainfall on millions of acres of land managed in this way.

Concurrent with the efforts of the experiment station to reach the white farmers of Blaine County, demonstration and extension agents were capitalizing on their connections with the railroads and to local businessmen. With the support of local capital and transportation systems, agents purchased and distributed seed and provided farmers a ready market and facilities for transporting their crop at the end of the season. This idea was not new. As early as 1889, the Chicago Rock Island Railroad had distributed wheat to farmers along its route. The first Rock Island line followed the Chisholm Trail south from Kansas to Hennessey, 20 miles east of Watonga in Blaine County. Here the company distributed twelve carloads of wheat seed to farmers on a simple promissory note. Farmers from several counties responded to the railroad's offer, and nearly all repaid their notes the following spring.[44]

The distribution of free seed fit in well with the new demonstration program's aims, which promoted wheat growing in most of Blaine County over corn or cotton as a staple cash crop. William Bentley reported to Knapp in 1909 that farmers had not had good luck with wheat in the previous two seasons as a result of drought, poor cultivation, and inexperience with soil moisture conservation through deep plowing. As Bentley put it, "This falling off is caused without doubt by continuous cropping in wheat and failure to select good seed and to properly prepare a good seed bed. Our agents are encouraging the planting of wheat and we believe by proper cultural methods the normal yield of wheat may be maintained."[45] Demonstration agents' efforts seemingly paid off the following year. Wheat jumped 27 percent in terms of total bushels transported by the Rock Island Line the following year.[46]

By statehood in 1906, Blaine County was well on its way to becoming a facsimile of the well-ordered farms of its white residents' memories and aspirations. It was also increasingly Euro-American in form and character. According to the *Oklahoman Annual Almanac and Industrial Record* of 1909, the population of Blaine County in 1907 was "14,019 whites, 1703 negroes, 1503 Indians and 2 Mongolians."[47] The *Record* also noted that 5 percent of the population was foreign born, mostly from Germany and Russia. Cultivated acreage was upwards of 200,000 acres, with only 15,000 acres remaining in trees. The county's principal crop was wheat, followed by corn, cotton, oats, kafir corn, broomcorn, sorghum, hay, and potatoes. The county was more successful than most in attracting railroads, with two different lines (the Rock Island, and the Frisco and Orient) having already laid 180 miles of track. Additionally, the county supported several mills and elevators in Watonga, Geary, Okeene, and Hitchcock as well as a large gypsum mine. In terms of resource use, the surveyor's assessment of the land in 1875 had become a reality in the space of a single generation.

In Blaine County, the so-called golden age of plains agriculture, the years between 1900 and 1920, saw better credit, better transportation, steadily rising agricultural prices, new labor-saving machinery, and firmly established communities. According to white farmers in Blaine, their good fortune was self-generated. The good times of the first decade of the century were their reward for the hard work and sacrifice of the previous decade. The settlers' hoped-for transformation of the landscape in Blaine reached its zenith in 1907 with even the poorest claims and relinquishments under white farmers' control.

Their pride at having transformed the "virgin" prairie into an orderly landscape is beautifully captured in the memoirs of Irene Beatty McNulty. McNulty's family staked a claim in central Blaine County in 1892, persevered through the drought, and invested in more land when the prices were low. By 1905, they were highly successful wheat and cattle farmers. Recalling a drive with her mother in a one-horse spring wagon as a young teen through the agricultural basin at the foot of the Gyp Hills in central Blaine County she wrote,

> The Prairie was beautiful. Our part of Oklahoma is a wheat country, and in April the land for miles around looks like one smooth green lawn. The days of dugouts and sod houses were past; settlers were building frame houses now. Many of the farm houses stood near the road, little new frame buildings of two or three rooms, some painted a glistening white. All had sizable front yards where young lilac and rose bushes like ours had been set out ... Most of the farms were fenced with two strands of barbed wire strung tight on posts. Larks sang on the fence posts or soared up into the clear blue sky. The spring was new, the country was new, even the world seemed young and fresh and clean.[48]

6

RAINY MOUNTAIN:
KIOWAS AND THE LAND
BEFORE ALLOTMENT

We had always moved our horses from one place to another, summer and winter, for good grazing; now we learned to move the grass to the horse and to store it in stacks or in bales. This was new to us, but we saw how it worked. Our ponies no longer grew weak and lean in winter, when snow and ice covered the dried grass. If there were good rains, the prairies and hay fields could be cut not once but several times during the season. It was something we could hardly believe. We saw the men who taught us were smart, and had a new kind of power.

Carl Sweezy, Cheyenne-Arapahoe

Having just reburied the bones of his brother after witnessing the death of their father Satank (Sitting Bear) at Fort Sill in 1871, Eagle Plume took stock of the Kiowas' future:

You have to have new things. You have to have new springs to make the grass grow. But grass grows out of the old earth. You have to have old things for new things to have roots in. That's why some people have to keep old things going and some people have to push new things along. It's right for both of them. It's what they have to do.[1]

The Kiowas are one of the most interesting and enigmatic peoples to occupy the southern Plains. They also pose a tremendous challenge for historians of the postreservation and allotment period. Kiowa Indian scholars generally rely on the work of anthropologists, archeologists, linguists, and folklorists as well as the Kiowas' own oral and pictorial histories for their interpretation of tribal history. Anthropological and archeological work on the Kiowas has focused almost exclusively on those aspects of their culture unique to them: the Sundance, warrior societies, and the colorful bison-horse culture. For early anthropologists intent on describing the "other," the Kiowas' adoption of western agricultural methods was not a new and viable cultural response but rather a watering down of true Kiowa culture and therefore not an aspect of Kiowa life worthy of study except within the context of cultural loss and declension.[2]

This bias in favor of precontact cultural practice by scholars has a long history going back to the mid-nineteenth century, when journalists, explorers, and painters in the American West feverishly worked to preserve for posterity the "true" culture of the American Indian before he was assimilated into American society and vanished forever.[3] Indians' demise as a separate people, however, did not take place as predicted. Ethnohistorians, scholars who combine the methodologies of ethnography and history, have recently shifted interpretation away from cultural loss to continuity. As Fred Hoxie has observed, Indian history today must "encompass both domination and resistance, both decline and renewal."[4] Within this more comprehensive view of native history, the measure of Kiowa agriculture practice need not rely on whether the Kiowas were "successful" (that is, commercially profitable) farmers or not. Kiowa farming practice evolved alongside Kiowa identity in the wake of changing circumstances and remains a continuous process without any clearly definable end point.

Regardless of early anthropologists' lack of interpretation of the Kiowas' transition to farmers in the early twentieth century, their descriptions of so-called traditional culture are invaluable for historians recreating the Kiowa way in relation to resource use before white settlement. Oral histories in particular can reveal the dynamics of ecology, Kiowa social relations, and economics that directly influenced the Kiowas' choice of allotments and their experiences as row crop agriculturalists. A brief outline of their preallotment history, social structure, and economies with particular emphasis on tribal resource use remains indispensable for environmental historians' interpretation of their subsequent role in Oklahoma's agroecological community.

The Kiowas were one of several tribal groups who moved into the southern Plains in the late eighteenth century after acquiring the horse. Language specialists locate the Kiowas' origins in the southwest

among other Tanoan-speaking tribal groups. At some unknown juncture, the tribe migrated north to the area historically occupied by the
Crow Indians, with whom they developed a lasting friendship. After
acquiring horses around 1700, both tribes migrated eastward in search
of bison. In the vicinity of the Black Hills in present-day South
Dakota, they met resistance from several Sioux and Cheyenne bands.
The Crows retreated west, but the Kiowas migrated farther south,
eventually stopping in their present location in the foothills of the
Wichita Mountains of Oklahoma in present-day Caddo County.

Like other Plains groups, the Kiowa people did not live in the shadow of the mountains year round. Hunting, trading, and religious observance dictated that they travel hundreds of miles in all directions:
south to Texas and Mexico, southwest to New Mexico, northwest into
the short-grass plains of Colorado and Utah, and north into present-
day western Kansas and Nebraska. In the same manner as the
Comanches who arrived before them on the southern Plains, the
Kiowas adapted rapidly to the dynamic and geographically wide-rang-
ing lifestyle of horse-mounted bison hunters. Tribal economics shifted
to take advantage of those resources that were most abundant in the
region. In addition to their use of the bison for food, tools, clothing,
and shelter, the Kiowas maintained trading relationships with tribes in
the southwest and numerous Missouri River and Arkansas River
bands, particularly the Caddoes and Wichitas, from whom they
obtained food items such as corn, squash, and melon.

These trade relationships were symbiotic in nature—that is, "the
food traffic was locally integrated, involving direct exchanges between
adjacent sedentary and nomadic producers."[5] Although intertribal
trade could be spontaneous, most exchanges followed a formal pattern
that observed established kinship and territorial limits. Hence,
although bison hunting provided the bulk of their material needs, the
Kiowas were dependent on other tribal groups living around them.

Some exchanges between the Kiowas and other Indian groups took
the form of warfare and raiding. The high tribal value placed on horses and captive women and children made raiding an integral part of the
Kiowas' economy. Hunting and raiding led to a division of tasks within the tribe according to gender and social rank. As hunters and
raiders, Kiowa men were divided into at least five different warrior
societies: from young boys (rabbits) to the most revered and respected
members of the Horse Society (qoitsenko).[6] There were also two
women's societies: the Old Women and the Bears. These existed pri-

marily for the purpose of feasting and offering prayers. Women maintained the extended family's material well-being, made the lodges, cured robes for trade, and collected and stored wild foods. Polygamy was common, although few Kiowa men could afford more than two wives, most often sisters. Women were free to leave their husbands if dissatisfied, and young couples generally went to live with the wife's family in their first years of marriage.

In addition to these military and gendered divisions, the Kiowas have also been described as recognizing a class structure based on kinship, material wealth, "dwdw" (power), and military honors. Anthropologist Jerrold Levy's work on the Kiowas' class structure, although controversial, remains the most comprehensive work in this area. Levy ascribed twentieth-century Kiowa social behavior, long after the reservation period was over, to class divisions going back several generations before allotment. According to his observations, the ideal in Kiowa society was that any individual could achieve high status in the tribe or within their band, but "the actuality appears to have been more one of limited upward mobility and almost no downward mobility."[7]

The vast majority of Kiowas were Kaan. This was a step up from the lowest level of "do nothings" but below the Onde class of priests, band leaders, and recognized warriors. Captives, both Indians and non-Indians, could either be treated as slaves or, if attached to an upper-class (Onde) family, be made a favorite and considered average Kiowa members of the Kaan class. These class distinctions became more complicated during the reservation period, but the most elastic form of Kiowa identity—the band, headed by a respected and dynamic leader—remained intact. The introduction of Christianity and the adoption of peyote rituals further divided the tribe into different religious affiliations without regard to caste.[8] At the time that white traders began to regularly infiltrate the southern Plains in the mid-nineteenth century, Kiowa economics, gender roles, kinship obligations, and class structure were well established and distinct from other tribal practices.

The years 1830 to 1875, leading up to the reservation era, were both tumultuous and triumphant for the Kiowa people. From the opening of the Sante Fe trail to the imprisonment of the tribe at Fort Sill, the Kiowas encountered different challenges from other tribes, white traders, disease, and the national government. Texans in particular were hard on the Kiowas' three basic resources: grass, wood, and

water. These forces, combined with the Kiowas' own resource practices vis-à-vis bison hunting and horse raising, made subsistence more
uncertain with each passing year.

Trade with whites initially increased friction between the Kiowas
and the southern Cheyennes and Arapahoes, but the dwindling herds
of bison and increased white traffic pushed these three tribes to forge
a lasting peace in 1840. Other of the Kiowas' enemies—the Sioux,
Osages, and the Pawnees, for example—continued to attack Kiowa
hunting parties and villages right up until the reservation era. The
Kiowas' first contact with the government was the return to the tribe,
by the army, of a Kiowa captive taken by the Osages who had earlier
in the year (1833) attacked a Kiowa village of mostly women and children. In this infamous raid, the Osages had stolen the Kiowas' most
sacred religious icon (the Tai me) and left the heads of the slain in
buckets for the Kiowa warriors to find on their return. This horren-
dous event coincided with their first infection by smallpox, with
smaller outbreaks occurring regularly over the next thirty years. The
origin of the Kiowas' initial smallpox infection is hard to determine,
but trade seems the most likely vector, as Bent's Fort began operating
in eastern Colorado in the 1830s and the Kiowas were regular visitors
and traders there.[9]

As disease and warfare with other tribes increased, the Kiowas responded aggressively to assaults on their well-being and survival. The
Kiowas' several calendars graphically depict a volatile four decades
punctuated by raids, disease, hunger, displacement, treaty negotiations,
religious fervor, and still more treaty negotiations.[10] Although not considered (by the U.S. Army) as recalcitrant as the Apaches, the Kiowas
were nevertheless considered extremely dangerous, capable of tracking
and robbing wagon trains, non-Indian settlements, and expeditions
with deadly results. This reputation obtained in spite of the tribe's relative lack of firearms. Dynamic leaders, like Dohausan, ably guided the
Kiowas through this difficult period, but these same decades, 1830 to
1875, saw the loss or imprisonment of many of the tribe's oldest and
most respected warriors.

The pictorial calendars of the Kiowas, first described by James
Mooney in 1891, are a graphic and verifiable record of the Kiowas'
annual movements over hundreds of miles in search of food, forage,
and safety during these difficult decades.[11] The calendars are also an
accounting of how the Kiowa people responded to numerous environmental and social challenges before 1875. According to the calendars,

the Kiowas canceled their most important all-tribe ritual, the Sundance, eighteen times in forty-five years. This was attributable at different times to warfare, lack of food (grass) for themselves or their horses, and eventually to government policy.

As depicted in the calendars, the generation of Kiowas who came of age around 1850 were acutely aware of the climatic changes that were beginning to be felt throughout the southern Plains. The Sundance of 1855 was not held because the grass withered and died during a prolonged drought. The dance in 1879 was named the "horse-eating Sundance" in reference to the almost complete disappearance of the bison herds and the starving condition of the tribe. The absence of encounters with whites in the Kiowa calendars, except indirectly through the record of smallpox and cholera epidemics, is a reminder that events can be endowed with different meanings by different groups of people. What the calendars demonstrate is that in spite of the increasing presence of Euro-Americans on the southern Plains, the Kiowas continued to measure events according to their own tribal cosmology, values, and experiences.

Kiowa origin stories are another opportunity for reconstructing the tribe's perception of their environment before 1889. The Saynday (pronounced "Sin-dee") stories, collected by Alice Marriott in the early 1930s and subsequently published in several different volumes, reveal that the Kiowas maintained a high level of consciousness about the landscape they inhabited. Stories about Saynday allowed tribal tellers and listeners to live vicariously, breaking taboos, acting in antisocial ways, and outsmarting their enemies.[12] Saynday's antics, and the consequences he suffers as a result, are a lively transcription of Kiowa cultural ideals.

The stories also demonstrate the Kiowas' use of the environment. Most of Saynday's exploits depict the proper relationship of the Kiowas to the other living things that inhabited the Plains. Saynday steals the sun in order to make green things grow for all people, both animal and Kiowa. He brings bison to the Kiowas by defeating the crafty white crow. He files down the teeth of the (mean) deer so they will have to eat green leaves and grass, and he explains why the ant is nearly cut in two. In one instructive story, Coyote disguises himself with sunflower sap and milkweed to look mangy and tricks Saynday out of some soup, which Saynday had stolen from someone else. Although reflective of many nuances of Kiowa culture, the Saynday stories clearly reveal two important aspects of Kiowa/environmental relations: not all aspects of the environment (plants, animals, people) were held in equal esteem or importance, and much of their lore and identity was based on an intimate knowledge of the ecology of the region they inhabited.

The moral imperatives of the Saynday stories—respect for family, unselfishness, intelligence, loyalty, generosity, and courage—were also reflected in the religious beliefs of the tribe. Kiowa values were translated through the different forms of "power" young men hoped to receive during their vision quests and in the social status of those individuals that emulated Kiowa ideals. For example, Crow, Saynday's enemy, was equated with both winter and selfishness. When the Kiowas heard Thunder (associated with the sun, summer, and war power), they said that the Crow and Thunder were in battle with one another. The Kiowas made supplication to Thunder in their quests for power, but not to Crow because they did not like the cold.[13] Thus, Kiowa environmental and social relations were learned, reinforced, and reinvented in overlapping ways.[14]

Saynday was a pragmatist, and this is also reflected in the Kiowas' relationship to their environment. More than a century of pastoralism on the southern Plains had given the Kiowas a broad body of knowledge in terms of the needs of their ponies and the region's ability to meet those needs. In terms of horse keeping, the Kiowas' collective memory of their environment has yet to be fully explored.[15] We do know, however, that the Kiowas did not discard their knowledge of other environments before coming to Oklahoma.[16] In 1939, two Harvard botanists, Paul Vestal and Richard Shultes, published an extensive ethnobotanical investigation of the Kiowas, one of the first of its kind. They found that the Kiowas had not only become expert at identifying hundreds of different grass and forage plants suitable for the maintenance of their horse herds, but that a great deal of their knowledge of plants predated their adoption of the horse, including dozens of wild edible plants.[17] In terms of environmental history, Vestal and Shultes's work significantly broadens historians' understanding of Kiowas' resource use beyond the traditional horse-bison culture most visible to anthropologists and historians of the preallotment era.

On the other hand, there is little indication that the Kiowas' pre-1875 economy, primarily dependent on bison hunting, the robe trade, horse raising, and raiding, could have been sustained indefinitely, regardless of their knowledge of the native flora. The tribes' fierce protection of the grasslands from wagon trains and cattlemen indicate that some Kiowas, at least, were aware of the limits of their resource base. Plains tribes' rapid adoption of certain practices also provides some sense of the difficulties they were grappling with in the prereservation years.

In the decades leading up to 1875, Indian peoples were the undisputed keepers of the central Oklahoma landscape. The Washita River valley, running through present-day Caddo and Kiowa counties, was initially avoided by white explorers because it was rumored to be populated by dangerous Comanche, Kiowa, and Apache Indians. In 1853, Amiel W. Whipple[18] of the U.S. Corps of Engineers on a surveying expedition for a railway route to the Pacific could not convince either Jesse Chisholm, the well-known trader, or Black Kettle, a Delaware chief and experienced scout, to accompany him any farther west or south of Fort Arbuckle for lack of water and fear of Indian attacks.[19]

Whipple continued on alone and soon discovered, thirty years after Long's initial forays into the region, that native guides were still essential in negotiating the highly variegated landscape. After dodging raging prairie fires for several days, he accepted the help of an unknown Heuco warrior to guide the expedition westward. Unfortunately, the guide took advantage of the Americans' vulnerability and led them southward into a stand of dense cross timbers and ravines and promptly abandoned them. A Kichai warrior who happened upon the group several days later led them out into the expansive Canadian River valley and was generously rewarded by Whipple. In both cases, the ease with which the Heuco and Kichai warriors found their way around without aid indicates they were in territory well known to them.

The first trails pointed out by Indian guides and mapped out by military expeditions followed centuries-old paths, crossing at the same fords and noting the same landmarks. These military roads served as the basis for numerous trade routes between eastern settlements and the far west. Jesse Chisholm's famous north-south trail began as a trade route from his store in southern Kansas to present-day Anadarko in Caddo County. The trail's origins have long been disputed, but it is clear that Chisholm's trail followed an established route to the southwest that was later taken up by Texas cattle drovers after the Civil War.

Joseph P. McCoy, who popularized the Chisholm Trail, was one of the first entrepreneurs to suggest that the surplus of Texas cattle left over from the war might be profitably driven north to the railheads in Kansas. McCoy became a promoter for several Kansas terminals, including Abilene, Ellsworth, and Dodge City. The section of the trail that extended Chisholm's original trail south from Anadarko to Fort Sill was originally called the Trader's Trail because it was used by freighters trading with the Indians before the Civil War.

By the time the Treaty of Medicine Lodge was signed in 1867, the sustained presence of Euro-Americans, African Americans, and Mexicans on Indian lands was already causing problems for the Kiowas. As early as 1870, Lawrie Tatum, federal agent for the Kiowa, Comanche, and Apache tribes under President Grant's Peace Policy, warned U.S. Army Colonel Benjamin Grierson of Fort Sill that he feared trouble if cattlemen were not restrained from moving their animals across reservation land.[20] In choosing first to protect their bison hunting ranges in the west from white hunters, Indian peoples responded to the cattle drives in numerous ways. One strategy was to burn drovers' campsites, forcing them to look elsewhere for game, wood, and water.[21] Cattlemen for their part tried to suppress prairie fires, which they felt allowed valuable fodder for their animals to go to waste. The Kiowas' use of fire as a deterrent against the cattlemen was a clear effort to manipulate the environment for their own gain.

When Indians did encounter passing cattlemen on their lands, they exploited the situation as best they could, with varying results. One drover recalled that on a drive in 1884, his herd cut across the Comanches' reservation, and horses and provisions were demanded. The drovers struck a bargain, and when the cowboys' horses subsequently became bogged down in crossing the Canadian River, the Comanche men "fell right in with our boys and helped in every way to pull the horses out, and when this work was finished they gave us an exhibition of their riding."[22] This same party later encountered a group of Kiowas who were not so easily placated. Unimpressed with the drovers' offer of two horses, flour, sugar, coffee, bacon, prunes, and canned goods, a group of warriors surrounded the trail boss. One trail hand recalled, "He had drawn his pistol, but was unable to use it because of the vise-like grip that held him. At the same time forty or fifty buffalo guns in the hands of the Indians were leveled at his head, and for an instant things looked bad."[23] The trail boss, George Saunders, escaped harm, but the drovers were eventually forced to take up a defensive position against another Kiowa attack. The Kiowas withdrew from a full-blown gunfight but in retaliation the next day shot ten head of cattle in a different herd passing through nearby.

Kiowa raids on cattle drovers, U.S. Army soldiers, and Texas settlers eventually forced the U.S. Army to bring the Kiowas in to stay within a prescribed area. Within four years of Satank's death, all of the Kiowa bands that had fled Fort Sill westward onto the inhospitable staked plains had made their way back to the agency. In September 1874, a combined camp of Kiowas, Comanches, and Cheyennes were routed from their hidden camp in Palo Duro Canyon by the U.S. Army. The soldiers killed only three warriors, but they destroyed everything in the camp, leaving the tribe to face the oncoming winter without food or shelter. By April 1875, all of the so-called renegades had returned to Fort Sill.

Kicking Bird's camp, which had stayed behind at Fort Sill in 1871, was allowed to camp along Cache Creek, but the rest of the Kiowas were shut up in an unheated stone horse corral at Fort Sill for the rest of the winter. Rations were poor, and several children and old people died. The hardships the tribe endured while confined became a touchstone in the tribe's history and a new source of memories and stories for those who lived through it. From that point on, no raids on white settlers by Kiowa warriors are recorded in the daily log of the army stationed at Fort Sill. This was hardly the end of violence around Fort Sill, however, for as Colonel Nye later put it, "The profession of illegal homicide was taken over in an able fashion by Negroes and white men."[24] Subduing the Kiowas was only one of the army's law-and-order duties in the new territory.

Several other major events covering the period 1875 to 1901 help place the Kiowas' ecological decisions into perspective. The warriors that had been imprisoned at Fort Marion, Florida, for raiding were finally released in 1878 and returned to Oklahoma to take up their former roles as medicine men and band leaders. In 1879, Lone Wolf the elder died of malaria, and Mama-day-te, or Lone Wolf II, took over as principal chief. James Mooney similarly recorded 1879 as the last year the Kiowas were able to find any bison, with the last bison bull shot on the reservation in 1890. That same year, Satanta, who told General Sheridan in 1867, "I love to roam the prairies . . . When I settle down I grow pale and die," learned he was not going to be released from his prison in Huntsville, Texas, and committed suicide by jumping out of a fourth-floor window. The 1880s also saw the last attempts by the Kiowas to hold their annual Sundance.[25]

Now militarily subdued, the Kiowas were obligated to interact with non-Indians on a daily basis. Their experiences with non-Indians in these years had a direct effect on Kiowa relations with both white and black settlers after allotment and subsequently on the ecology of Caddo County. The Kiowas' first official agent under Grant's Peace Policy was Lawrie Tatum, who arrived at Fort Sill in 1869. Before long, Quaker Tatum was advocating military solutions to the problems he encountered with the troublesome Kiowas. Exasperated by the Kiowas' utter disregard for his presence, he appealed to the army at Fort Sill to help him, declaring the Kiowas were "wards and paupers of the United States and should be treated as such." The Kiowas' wily strategy of being cooperative before the food distributions and raiding directly afterward prompted Tatum to conclude, "The natural ability of the Indian is little, if any, inferior to the Anglo-Saxon, and he should be held responsible for his actions."[26] Not surprisingly, Tatum, whom the Kiowas called "Bald Head," made little progress in inducing the Kiowas to farm.

Given the climatic conditions at the time, however, it is doubtful that the Kiowas could have been persuaded to farm anyway. Even agricultural tribes like the Wichitas and Caddoes were unable to raise crops in the early 1870s. The Wichitas' crops regularly failed as a result of drought between 1870 and 1875, leaving that tribe in even worse condition than the Kiowas. As they had in the past, the Kiowas responded to the shortage of food by raiding south into Mexico for horses and people. The people were ransomed for cash that was then used to buy food and ammunition from local traders. The horses were also traded for goods needed by the tribe. Raiding took on even greater importance as the drought caused the remaining bison herds to move north and west—out of the legal range of the newly formed Kiowa, Comanche, and Apache (KCA) reservation.

Raiding for horses and captives in Texas had long been a Kiowa practice, but now it took on a desperate quality as the tribe's basic subsistence resource, bison, became harder to find. Captives were taken for many reasons, but it is clear from the memoirs of the first agents and the records of the army that they were a source of quick cash. The Kiowas were used to receiving as much as $1,000 ransom for each white captive that they returned. This money allowed the tribe to purchase food and ammunition from the hoards of traders who frequented the military posts. This was especially important because after each raid, the government agent was directed not to supply the Kiowas with either guns or ammunition. The agent also had the authority to withhold rations for as long as the raids continued, thereby creating a vicious circle of hunger, raiding, ransom, and hunger again.

But raiding also served as a defense against white horse thieves, who had become exceptionally bold in their depredations on Indian stock. Here the Kiowas' notions of reciprocity and Euro-American legal codes came into direct conflict. Kiowa warriors did not always punish the same individual whites that stole their ponies but struck out at the nearest white settlement in response to any white depredation. This was not illogical, given their collective or tribally based sense of justice. The Kiowas simply recognized different "tribes" rather than individuals, whether they were Indian, white, Mexican, or African American. As far as the Kiowas were concerned, the whites had not kept their earlier promises to capture and punish anyone who committed depredations, Indian or white.

In 1869, General Sheridan had declared that "when white people do wrong—commit murders and robberies—we always punish them, and if you commit any crimes I am going to punish you just the same as the white people are punished." This did not turn out to be the case, and Satanta was quick to remind Sheridan that the Utes, Osages, and some enlisted men had killed several of his warriors, to which Sheridan replied, "I have nothing to say to you on that subject now."[27] For the Kiowas, the government's failure to prosecute white thieves on their reservation released them from their earlier promise not to raid in Texas, and so they no longer felt bound by it. To make matters worse, white horse thieves sometimes dressed up as Indians while robbing their white and Mexican neighbors in order to cast blame on the tribes. Fort Sill Commander Grierson soon found himself in the impossible position of trying to restrain the Kiowas from raiding in Texas, while the Texas authorities did nothing to stop their own citizens. He wrote to the Texas legislature that while they were passing laws to control Indian marauders, they "should also devise some means of suppressing the organized band of white thieves who infest their state and steal alike from Indians, citizens and the government."[28]

The numbers of horses, mules, and cattle the KCA, Cheyennes, and Arapahoes lost to white thieves was substantial and continued unabated for the next thirty years. Even Lawrie Tatum, who was appalled at what he described as the Kiowas' "evil intentions," reported that after 1875 a number of the Kiowas were prepared to "do something at farming and raising cattle." The biggest obstacle to their success in these years, according to Tatum, was "the horse thieves from Texas and Kansas." He cited Agent Haworth's report for the year 1875 that among the tribes living near Mount Scott, "I think the estimate of two thousand head of stock—horse, ponies and mules—as stolen from the Indians of this agency is not too high."[29]

Stock thieves notwithstanding, the Kiowas' vocational preference was as stockmen; horse and cattle raisers. Grass became the new medium of trade after the Kiowas were confined to their reservation. As longtime pastoralists, the Kiowas were well aware of the value of their grass for livestock. A regular migration of different bands to new locations within the confines of the reservation was now a response to the needs of their horse herds for forage as access to adequate pasture meant the difference between subsistence and starvation for themselves and their herds. For some members of the KCA who were under the federal watch of the combined Indian Agency at Anadarko, cattle grazing became one way to compensate for the loss of the bison herds. Quanah Parker, a popular Comanche leader, was the most visible member of the KCA agency to embrace cattle raising as an alternative to bison hunting and raiding.

Heavily supported by cattlemen in Texas who wished to lease millions of acres of grasslands from the tribes, Parker and other tribal leaders, such as Kicking Bird of the Kiowas, made the most of the resource base they still controlled. Although many Kiowas refused their "grass money" from leasing reservation lands, the pro-lease faction, led by Parker, were able to supersede this majority and effectively play the cattlemen against each other in their bids for leases. Parker's biographer William Hagan argues that "Quanah was learning what the whites wanted, and where that agreed with his own interests and those of his people, he was happy to cooperate."[30]

Access to grass became a contentious issue that some band leaders used to vie with one another for prestige and control on the reservation. When Thomas Battey replaced Lawrie Tatum as the agent for the Kiowas, Kicking Bird and his band were constantly being harassed by a group of hostile Comanches who thought Kicking Bird too solicitous of whites. Exploiting the environmental weaknesses of Kicking Bird's more sedentary style of leadership, the Comanche band consistently camped adjacent to Kicking Bird's and allowed their immense pony herds to graze nearby, forcing Kicking Bird to find new grass every few days. This caused Kicking Bird a great deal of trouble because he did not want to move too far east of Fort Sill, where whiskey traders and white horse thieves would make his small band even more miserable.[31]

While tribal and band leaders were doing their best to determine how to live in the future, whether as farmers or ranchers or businessmen, the Kiowas' everyday use of their reservation's resources remained largely unchanged as women maintained a subsistence regime consistent with prereservation life. Jim Whitewolf's (Kiowa-Apache) autobiography indicates that although life was not easy on the reservation, his mother and grandmother were adept at providing for the family by gathering the wild foods that the Kiowas had always depended on, making the transition to life on the reservation less traumatic than it might have been.

These customary subsistence regimes were supported by the persistence of traditional kinship roles. As young men, Whitewolf and his cousins were taught in the traditional way by their grandfather to hunt deer and other game and even to run down wild turkeys.[32] Whitewolf recalled that traveling to the agency at Anadarko for beef and clothing distributions were taken as a matter of course and were not central to their daily lives. Similarly, row crop agriculture, as it was introduced through the mission schools and at the Indian agencies, was just one more new element in their daily lives, not an end to their identity as tribal members. As in other periods of their tribal history, when confronted with new circumstances, the Kiowas saw agriculture as both a challenge and an opportunity for survival. It was a challenge they approached on their own terms and in keeping with what they already understood about the environment they occupied.

Even though the Kiowas worked hard during the reservation period to make a place for themselves within Euro-American culture, their farming practices were regularly criticized as backward and inefficient by whites, paving the way for their further dispossession and economic marginalization. Much of this criticism stemmed from federal Indian agents assigned to the Kiowas, who began to keep records of the Kiowas' efforts at Euro-style agriculture beginning in 1875. The Commissioner of Indian Affairs used these agency reports as the basis of his annual reports on the reservations. Agency records that focused on Euro-style crop production seem contradictory on certain points, reflecting the agents' desire to appear effective to their superiors while also demonstrating their need for more support. Some discrepancy in the agency reports was not intentional but stemmed from inadequate funding for additional personnel, which did not allow the agent to observe what the Kiowas were actually doing on the reservation. Another part of the problem was the distance, in a preautomobile age, from the agency at Anadarko to the areas where bands were located. Another factor was the endless stream of paperwork required of the agent in charge, making him a virtual prisoner in his Anadarko office.[33] Moreover, the KCA agency was unsuccessful in maintaining an agent for longer than one or two years. In the nine years between 1892 and 1901, seven agents were appointed and left the agency. All of these factors make the agency reports and the distilled annual reports created by the Office of Indian Affairs in Washington, DC, somewhat unreliable for historians of Kiowa resource use.

Yet as flawed and incomplete as their reports were, it remains clear that all the agents considered the loss of Indian stock to thieves the biggest obstacle to the tribes' self-sufficiency. Without even the threat of potentially hostile Indians to stop them, white horse and cattle thieves wreaked havoc on the KCA reservation from 1875 until long past allotment in 1901. If we accept the base numbers of stock (horses and cattle) being raised by the Kiowas in the reservation era as reported by the agents, the Indians invested a great deal of energy into this new enterprise. Indeed, even though they received little official encouragement from the Office of Indian Affairs, virtually every agent of the KCA concluded that stock raising was a more efficient and reasonable use of the reservation resources than row crop farming.

Unfortunately, so did unscrupulous cattlemen in Texas. In addition to having their stock stolen outright, the Kiowas had to endure the constant presence of Texas cattle purposely turned out on reservation lands to graze. The unauthorized use of the reservation by cattlemen was a purposeful strategy to force the tribe to give up their herds. At first, federal Indian agents encouraged the leasing of the grass to Texas cattlemen in exchange for animals with which to supplement the Indians' own stock and to bring in some much-needed cash. For some native leaders like Quanah Parker, leases with Texas cattlemen became the basis of personal prosperity. Parker's self-interested behavior was generally not condoned by the Kiowas, and most, like Lone Wolf II, refused their grass money because if they accepted it, it implied their consent to the leasing system.

Against the general wishes of the tribe, Agent Haworth decided that getting something for the grass was better than having it stolen, and he arranged for a number of leases on behalf of the Kiowas. Unfortunately, when the leases expired and the bands wanted to take over the grasslands for their own animals, they found they could not eject the lease cattle from the reservation. Even when the cattle were rounded up, taken back to their owners, and the owners fined, the fine per head was so low that it paid for the cattlemen to simply turn their herds out again at the first opportunity. If this was not enough, J. B. Hunt, KCA agent from 1878 to 1884, also reported that the hay and timber on Kiowa lands were being systematically removed from the reservation by whites who had set up camp on the west side of the reservation expressly for that purpose.

In the meantime, the Office of Indian Affairs continued to cut the amount of rations they would issue to the tribes, right up through allotment. It made no difference to federal officials if drought, pests, lack of equipment, lack of fence, or poor instruction had impeded the Kiowas' ability to farm. The Office of Indian Affairs also refused to supply seed, claiming that the Indians should have saved enough seed from the previous crop—even in years following a complete crop failure.[34] The Office of Indian Affairs' extreme fiscal policies were particularly odious to the Kiowas who regularly traded at Fort Sill and could see firsthand the military and economic power of the U.S. government. A few young men, like I-See-O, took advantage of an army experiment in recruiting Indians into the regular army. This was a very attractive option, given that in the year 1882 the U.S. government was spending nearly $1,000 annually to feed and clothe each regular army recruit, but only $7 a year per Indian.[35]

Overall, the most salient feature of Kiowa farming policy in the reservation period was the government's utter lack of commitment to providing even the most basic needs and rights of the Kiowas, especially in prosecuting white rustlers and thieves. Within this context, the picture that emerges of Kiowa subsistence in this era is somewhat different from that of the agents who stressed either the Kiowas' inability to farm or the government's unwillingness to provide the Kiowas with what they needed to farm. In the larger context of resource use, the fact that the Kiowas survived at all must be largely attributed to their own efforts—and to their knowledge of the environment as a source of food, shelter, and fuel.

Although their agents encouraged the practice, it is clear that most Kiowas did not take up individual family farms after 1875. Instead, they continued to live and work in groups analogous to their former band arrangements. As the Kiowas well understood, common camps helped to solve problems of equipment shortages for farming, protected their herds from white thieves, and helped to concentrate their efforts on lands better suited for agriculture. For all these reasons, the different bands located along creeks and riverbeds, where they could procure water for their stock and their gardens even during periods of drought while attempting to grow things like corn, cotton, and wheat. Every family and settlement had a vegetable garden that, although small, was crucially important for supplementing the meager rations they received every two weeks at the agency. Like the white farmers of Blaine County, who supplemented their incomes by raising cattle after the droughts of the 1890s, the Kiowas were already well aware of the risks involved in depending on either cattle or crops alone and willingly diversified their efforts.

In some years, the delayed shipment of rations, combined with drought, forced the tribe to eat their own cattle herds, thereby adding to their subsistence problems the following year. Under these same conditions, it is doubtful that even the most industrious Euro-American farmer could have survived, and in fact, a great many of the white farmers who took up lands on the KCA reservation after 1904 left after only a few years. The difference between Kiowa farmers and these later farmers was that Kiowa farmers had a greater repertoire of subsistence activities to draw on, and they had nowhere else to go. Allotment of the reservation into individual 160-acre farms would deeply challenge the tribe's ability to survive both materially and culturally after 1901.

Similar to other Plains tribes facing permanent enclosure on reservations, the Kiowas entertained their own version of the fabled Ghost Dance, which promised a return to an earlier existence, by the way of their own prophet Pa-ingya. Pa-ingya claimed in 1888 that all the whites would be taken up by a tornado, everything they had brought with them would be consumed in a great prairie fire, and the bison would be restored to the Kiowa people. After failing to raise his son from the dead (a proposed demonstration of his power), his teachings were abandoned. The Ghost Dance was reintroduced to the Kiowas again in 1889 by the Lakota, but the tribe was understandably skeptical and sent an emissary to investigate the origins of the dance and return to them with some verification of its power. Ahpeahtone, a son of Red Otter and nephew of Lone Wolf the elder, traveled by rail to Rosebud Reservation in South Dakota to discover the origin of the dance. There he learned of the prophet Wovoka of the Paiutes, and he reboarded a train to Nevada to investigate. He returned to the KCA reserve in February 1890 unconvinced of the prophet's authenticity or power. With the exception of a single dance in 1894, the movement was not practiced by a majority of the Kiowas again. Indian office agents rewarded Ahpeahtone for discouraging the dance with medals and other presents and declared him the chief of the Kiowas over Lone Wolf II.[36] In 1906, a town platted in the grasslands known as "big pasture" was named after him by the Department of the Interior.[37]

By the 1890s, then, the Kiowas were faced with a crisis of leadership, subsistence, and belief that lasted well into the twentieth century—crises for which they devised a number of solutions. Even as their choices constricted on the reservation, tribal members continued to interpret and arrange things according to the Kiowa way. As Alice Marriott observed, "No one but a Kiowa would have behaved in that way, at that time, under those conditions."[38] Individual Kiowas reacted to changes in various ways, but it was a limited repertoire of choices firmly rooted in Kiowa values. Although very few Kiowas gave up keeping horses altogether, the most disappointing aspect of reservation life was the Kiowas' realization that stock raising was not going to be tolerated, by either the federal government's agents or by Texas stock thieves. Eagle Plume's acceptance of new things, "to push new things along," was about to come true as the Kiowas looked again to the red earth to sustain them.

7

OWNERS AND TENANTS:
KIOWA FARMING AFTER ALLOTMENT

The plan in a few words is this: That every Indian on the reservation, every man, woman and child, shall have ample land set off for a home that can never be taken away from him, that they can live on and cultivate forever. In selecting these homes and setting them apart to you, your children and yourselves will always have as much land as they can use, even if they get ten times as many as you have now and I do not think that time will ever come.

David H. Jerome to the assembled Kiowas, Comanches, and
Apaches at Fort Sill, Oklahoma, 1898

From a general knowledge of the climatic and topographic features, of the failure of the whites in adjacent portions of Oklahoma, of the success attained only by stock raising, it seems wholly improbable that any considerable community of white men or of Indians can be made self-supporting upon an allotment of the size and character proposed.

Frederick Newell, United States Geological Survey

On his first visit to Mount Scott with Agent Richards from the Wichita agency in 1872, Quaker missionary Thomas Battey was positively impressed with the landscape the Kiowas called home.

We passed through some beautiful valleys, arable, and clear of stone, bounded by mountain ridges, so that, but a few rods from good arable prairie in all appearances clear of rock and suitable for agriculture, those immense piles of boulders arise with only enough soil to supply a foothold for the most scanty vegetation, among which are several varieties of cactus.[1]

Most striking in Battey's description of the Mount Scott region is his optimism about the area's potential for agriculture in spite of the rough and rocky terrain. Battey's enthusiasm at the "good arable prairie" would become part of the federal government's rationalization for the Kiowas' allotment and idealization of western-style farming for the next twenty-five years. Unfortunately, the Kiowas' mixed success with farming their own allotments reflected the broken and uneven landscape of reality.

The Kiowas' adoption of western-style agriculture, beginning with their confinement on a reservation in 1875, was highly pragmatic and self-directed. As a group, the Kiowas had long been noted by army officers, agents, and missionaries for their energy and aggressiveness in pursuing whatever road served their own best interests.[2] The Kiowas' diminished direct control over their own lands by 1907 was not the result of their passivity in the face of incomprehensible change, but of three interrelated factors not within their control. The first circumstance was the ecology of the reservation lands and its division into individual allotments. The Kiowas' selection of allotments frequently reflected their interest and past experience in stock raising, not row crop agriculture. The second factor was the dominant Euro-American economic and legal culture, which did not recognize Indian peoples as equal to whites under the law. From the stingy and paternalistic view of the Indian Office to the abject failure of local white communities to police their own members, Kiowas and other Indians in Oklahoma found it nearly impossible to use the law to their advantage. The third factor in the "decline" of Kiowa farming was the tribe's own inexperience in supporting individual farming enterprises. The generation between 1875 and 1904, when allotment was completed, had little time to adapt "traditional" social obligations, economic relationships, and ecological realities to the changing needs of its members as they tried to enter the wider agricultural community.

The final chapter in the Kiowas' attempt to maintain their prereservation lifeways came in 1898. This was the year negotiations between the Kiowa, Comanche, and Apache (KCA) and the Jerome Commission over allotment were held at Fort Sill and at the Anadarko agency. The minutes taken during the negotiations, which lasted several weeks, are one of a handful of records containing the Kiowas' own words. The commission negotiations speak to the Kiowas' understanding of the resource potential of their reservation during this tumultuous time.[3] Throughout the negotiations, the Kiowa leadership firmly articulated a desire for tribal self-determination and cultural continuity, even as they recognized the need to sustain themselves within unfamiliar economic and social circumstances. This gathering marked a turning point for the Kiowas as it became clear that allotment of their reservation was not something that could be avoided.

Unfortunately for the Jerome Commission, the Cheyennes' and Arapahoes' clear unhappiness following allotment of their reservation in 1892 was a powerful lesson to many Kiowas in what not to do, causing even innocent moves on the part of government to be viewed with suspicion.[4] I-See-O, a Kiowa Indian enlisted with the U.S. Army at Fort Sill, made the Kiowas' skepticism at allotment abundantly clear:

> You have been at the Cheyenne Agency a few years ago. You probably told them what you have told us for the past few days. And the Cheyenne talked amongst themselves and decided to take their allotments. It is only a few months ago that the Cheyenne came to this military reservation . . . What were they here for? They came down to get some cattle and ponies from the Kiowas. They gave us a big dance, so we gave them some ponies. In a few years those Cheyenne Indians will be the poorest Indians, and they will be coming all the time for ponies. Look at them today surrounded by the white men, they will get the Indians drunk and get his money; and the Cheyennes' life in the next three years will be worse than when he was an Indian.[5]

Rather than answer I-See-O's charges directly, Commissioner Jerome blamed the Cheyennes for their lack of thrift and suggested that they had been subsisting on government rations for more than seventeen years already. I-See-O countered Jerome's argument by stating, "They ate deer and turkey and dog besides what the Government gave them." Jerome's final response was that the Cheyennes had swindled and lied to the Kiowas, that they would have told them anything in order to get ponies, and that the Cheyennes were doing very well on their annuities and the production of their farms. But the reformers' obvious disappointment with earlier attempts at assimilation expressed to the Kiowas during the negotiations made even the pretense of good-faith bargaining with the KCA hard to maintain—a pretense made even more difficult by the fact that many of the Kiowas had traveled to Washington and understood perfectly the primary impetus behind the passage of the Dawes Act: the opening of the reservation to whites.

One of the major sticking points of the KCA–Jerome Commission negotiations was, in fact, whether they were replacing the terms of the Medicine Lodge Treaty of 1867 with a new treaty, or whether the Jerome Commission was simply there to work out the terms of allotment as ordered by Congress. For most, if not all, the Kiowas, the choice to sell their lands (as it was presented by the commission) was exactly that: a choice. As Poor Buffalo explained, "You are here to buy our land just like a man would be going to another man's house to ask to buy a horse. The horse belongs to the man; the man coming has the money to pay for the horse but it is the privilege of the man to say whether he is willing to sell the horse or not." Jerome declined to respond to Poor Buffalo's analogy. What began to become clear to everyone assembled was the fact that the negotiations were not contractual, as under a treaty, but de facto. As Quanah Parker (Comanche) put it, "On the right hand is what you are trying to do, and on the left hand is the Dawes Bill."[6]

This realization led the leaders of the KCA to question the commission about what would happen to their "surplus" lands after allotment. Tabanaca, a Comanche chief, was the first to ask what would happen to the mountains, mocking the commissioner's earlier comments about the tribes' surplus of "worthless" lands. When told that they would belong to the government, Tabanaca coyly asked, "If these Kiowas take lands without timber and the Government takes the mountains where the timber is, what will they do?" The commission glibly responded that they could choose timber land if they wanted. But Tabanaca's concern was well founded, as most Kiowas in the Wichita Mountain district were still living in lodges and depended on wood for cooking and heating. Years later, Jenny Haumpty recalled that her parents lived "in them woods, edge of the mountains. The reason they do that, they go because they had no stove. But they go into timber, where there's big timber and a lot of wood."[7] Tabanaca and others at the negotiations were clearly aware of the value of the lands they possessed and the basic resources they contained.

Komalty, a Kiowa, pushed the point even farther. Commissioner Jerome attempted to make allotment sound promising by describing the extensive holdings of Quanah Parker. The difficulty was that everyone knew that Parker made his money through leases with Texas cattlemen on thousands of acres belonging to the Comanche collectively. Komalty made it clear that the proposed 160-acre allotments could not possibly sustain Quanah's lifestyle:

> We have listened to all the talk that the Commission has made and it will make a man rich to listen to it. It is deceiving . . . Remember that we have horses and cattle. These will in a few years die of starvation. We have no machines to put up hay. Your talk is good but that will be the case . . . Eight years from today every one will be afraid to own ten horses and fifty cattle because there will be no grass to eat.[8]

Even Parker was skeptical of the commission's estimation of the future of the KCA reservation, and his concern was far more businesslike than the commission was prepared for. Along with several other KCA representatives, Quanah asked pointed questions about the possible resources to be found on the proposed allotments:

> The Commission speaks of the rocks and hills as being worthless but I have noticed that coal is burned in such localities and that iron, silver and gold and coal are found in such places. If an Indian should take an allotment where any of this should be what would be done with that? Supposing coal is found in the mountains, what will Washington do with that if it is worthless?

In response to the questioning of Quanah and others about the valuation of the potential resources to be found on the KCA reservation, the commission agreed to allow the Indians to ask Congress for a half million dollars more for land that would become "surplus" after the opening of the reservation. The commission declined, however, to answer questions regarding the price per acre the government was willing to pay for the Indians' "worthless" land. Although the arguments presented to the Jerome Commission by the KCA leadership revealed the Indians' full understanding of the nature of the negotiations they were engaged in, they also revealed the extent to which they had familiarized themselves with their reservation environment and the limits it posed for their sustenance in the future.

These two concerns—that the land would not be able to sustain them and that they would not be fully compensated for their "surplus" reservation lands—were at the heart of Lone Wolf II's famous Supreme Court battle with the Department of the Interior.[9] Expressing the concerns of a majority of the Kiowas, Lone Wolf appealed to the commission to uphold the articles of the Treaty of Medicine Lodge until its termination. In this way, Lone Wolf hoped the tribe could avoid allotment through delay and further negotiations in three years' time.

Lone Wolf was not alone in doing everything he could to avoid allotment of the reservation. Upon addressing the commission in Anadarko on October 14, Apeahtone bluntly stated, "These people are my people and not one of them is willing to sign the contract or sell a piece of land . . . I would take the old road. I will ask those that are with me on the Medicine Lodge road to stand up."[10] All the Kiowas stood up in support of Apeahtone. Lone Wolf's own appeal to the Jerome Commission was simple: the Kiowas could not compete with whites, and they were not ready to take up farms of their own. As Lone Wolf pointed out to the commission, very few of the Kiowas had attended school, although the tribe had requested schools, and only a few—himself, Joshua Given, and Quanah Parker—could speak English well enough to be understood. "A white man is taught up from his youth up to work—we are not. And instead of these 160 acres being a blessing, they will be disastrous."[11] As a band leader and a recognized primary chief of the Kiowas, Lone Wolf's concern was not just for himself, but for the majority of the Kiowas for whom he felt responsible.

Although the Kiowas had been confined to their reservation for nearly twenty years, the tribe's traditional band structure had remained intact, much to the chagrin of their numerous agents. Instead of taking up individual farms, most Kiowas had chosen to remain together in a few centralized locations. The only difference was that after 1875, the location of the camps became more or less permanent and they were now identified with natural features—mostly watercourses—instead of with band leaders as before. The permanently placed bands worked collectively to raise stock, put up hay, and plant crops. Albert Horse, who was only a child at the time of the commission meetings, recalled that there were "the Elk Creek Kiowas, the Rainy Mountain Sugar-Creek group, Saddle Mountain and Mount Scott people, Hog Creek, Mud Creek and Stinking Creek Kiowa."[12] Lone Wolf's request that the commission not force the Kiowas to take up allotments was in many ways also a plea for the continuance of tribal social relations. In filing an injunction against the commission, Lone Wolf bought valuable time for the Kiowas in which to begin to prepare for the onslaught of white settlement. But Lone Wolf's and other tribal leaders' requests for being allowed to keep their reservation intact were ultimately ignored.[13]

In 1901, after Lone Wolf had exhausted all his appeals to the Supreme Court, the Office of Indian Affairs began the process of allotment in earnest. By this time, most of the Kiowas had accepted the inevitable and were persuaded to choose their allotments, but others remained adamantly opposed and had to have their lands chosen for them. Even in their choice of allotments, however, the Kiowas strove to maintain their familiar kinship relations as much as possible.

The story of Hunting Horse's experience with allotment is representative of the ways in which the Kiowas negotiated a course between what Eagle Plume called the "old things" and the "new things." After his children were grown and gone, Hunting Horse set up camp with his two wives in the shadow of Saddle Mountain. Here they had good pasture for their horses, a spring that ran all year, a creek, wild cherries, plum patches, and deer that could still be found in the folds of the woods. White missionaries had set up a church nearby, and Hunting Horse and his wives found comfort in their message, "Do good. Help one another. Be kind. Be generous. Live together in peace." It was not long, however, before the missionaries informed Hunting Horse that he was not on the "Jesus road" because he had two wives. This was a serious hardship for the old man, who had been married to the two sisters all his adult life.

Not long afterward, Andres Martinez, whom the Kiowas called Andele, arrived at Hunting Horse's camp.[14] Martinez, a Mexican captive who had worked in the mission school and was now working for the KCA agency, came to ask Hunting Horse about his choice of allotment. He explained again that everyone would get his own allotment; Hunting Horse and his two wives would each get a share, as would all of their children. Martinez suggested that Hunting Horse take up his allotment right there where he was camped. After Andele left, Hunting Horse went into a deep depression. No matter how he tried to reconcile the old and the new, it just didn't feel right.

At last, Hunting Horse's eldest wife came up with a solution—in the Kiowa way. She "threw away" her husband and declared where she would live in the future. As Alice Marriott retells it, Spear Woman declared, "I'll make up your mind for you. That is your allotment up the slope. Next to it is my sister's. Down here at the bottom where the creek is, that's mine. Then we don't have to put up a lot of fences. I can run my horses on your pasture, and you can let yours water at my creek. You and sister can have your house where you want it. I want mine here, where we're sitting."[15] By pretending marital dissatisfaction with Hunting Horse, she ensured the whole family's good standing with the missionaries and kept them physically together, all at the same time.

Guy Quoetone related a similar story about his family's choice of allotments. Quoetone's father was also friendly with Martinez and was advised to choose level land away from the mountains, although most Kiowas did not. According to Quoetone, "Indians didn't have any sense about the value of tillable land. They just wanted to find a place where there was water and timber. They thought they'd just live there about five or ten years . . . Nearly every allotment got a creek on it. They always pick out good water . . . They didn't know anything about digging wells them days."[16] For many Kiowas, their choice of allotments reflected the kinds of resource uses they had always practiced and expected would continue into the future.

Like Hunting Horse's family, most Kiowa families strove to be allotted together. This is clearly shown in the official allotment record, in which family names can be found in series in the first round of allotments.[17] Hicks Boyiddle's family were one of the first to choose allotments. His parents chose allotments for themselves and their children near his cousin's allotments. He remembered that "living was good there" on their combined allotments.[18]

Some families, however, were prevented from choosing land near one another. According to Mary Haumpy, the adult Kiowas were allotted first in 1901. Later on, they were allowed to choose allotments for their minor children. When all the allotments nearby were taken, many Kiowa parents chose a section where there was room to allot all their children together, so they would have each other for company when they were grown up. In some cases, Kiowa families had their first choice of allotment refused because the land had already been taken up by white squatters.[19]

Of course, problems also arose when children married and their spouse's allotment was miles away. In this case, the couple either leased or sold one allotment and lived on the other. Many Kiowa families were unsuccessful in being allotted together in ways that allowed them to share labor and acreage, but their preferences were clear. Choosing allotments together near watercourses that also had a good supply of timber and grass was an effort to replicate in miniature the same socioeconomic band structure that they had been living in for the past century or more.

Although serious study, based on agents' reports, has been done on official Indian policy during this time and the Kiowas' "failure" to become "good" farmers, little attention has been paid to the Kiowa version of this difficult time. Albert Horse, son of Hunting Horse, related that even before allotment, some Kiowas were already convinced of the need to learn to farm. The Horse family was Christian. Albert was a Methodist and his wife Keesa's family had attended a Baptist mission. Schooling had influenced Albert in profound ways. As a youngster, his teacher, Mrs. J. J. Methvin of the Methodist school, took him to her parents' farm in Logan County, where young Albert witnessed firsthand the dynamics of the white agricultural community: "The meals were much different, we had plenty of chicken, pies and cakes . . . While there we went to a country Church and then on to a picnic dinner, where the folks all took baskets of dinner and there were lots of white people and I expect I was the only Indian there."

A sickly child, Albert was eventually sent home, "probably to die." But instead of dying, he spent long hours on horseback with his friends, taking care of his father's horse herd and growing stronger and bigger every day. As a grown man, he took a wife "in the Kiowa way," with the families exchanging gifts to solemnize the affair. Albert and Keesa lived first with her mother for six years, to take care of her. They then moved onto Albert's parents' allotment. Hunting Horse had begun the transition to agriculture when Albert was only twelve or thirteen years old. Hunting Horse adopted a young immigrant boy, the same age as Albert, named Willie Seizek, who said he was from a faraway place, across the ocean, called "Bohemia." Willie was an orphan, and Hunting Horse offered him a home "if he would show them how to farm and raise stock . . . He taught us how to milk cows, raise chickens, hogs, poultry, plow and plant and do all kinds of farm work." Willie taught Albert how to speak English, and the Horse family helped Willie become fluent in Kiowa. Willie eventually married a Kiowa girl, O-pine, and settled down to farm north of Fort Sill.

As a grown man with a large family of his own, Albert farmed and kept stock, hogs, and chickens and took first place one year in a fair for Indian farmers. After several years as a farmer, Albert received a vision while walking in the Wichita Mountains. Albert interpreted his vision as God's calling him to serve the Kiowa people as a Christian minister. Along with his brother Cecil Horse, Albert spent the rest of his life as a minister to numerous Kiowa churches near his birthplace. As a Christian Indian, Albert would not have been regarded as a "blanket" Indian by the whites he worked and lived with. Yet it is also clear that his own description of his calling to the ministry, his traditional marriage, his extended family relations, and his unflagging work as a translator for the Kiowa people were patterned on his own father's role as a medicine man and mediator for the tribe. For Albert Horse, being a farmer or a minister did not diminish his primary identity as a principal member of the Kiowa tribe.[20]

Luther Sahmaunt, a contemporary of Hunting Horse, was a follower of Big Bow, a war leader who led numerous raids on Texan and Mexican settlements and who only narrowly avoided being hanged for murder. Luther, like Hunting Horse, took up farming, but, having only the Anadarko agency farmer to guide him, he gave it up as impracticable. "They felt that they were not suited to farming and much preferred the wild life and traveling around whenever they felt like it, not being tied to one place to tend livestock and crops."[21] Like Albert Horse, however, Luther went to school, first to Carlisle and then to Chilocco on the Kansas-Oklahoma border. While a schoolboy, Luther met and married his wife, Virginia Stumbling Bear. Upon their return to Anadarko, they worked for several years for the KCA agency. Stumbling Bear, Virginia's father, was a peace chief, and eventually Luther and Virginia took up their allotments near Canyon Creek at the base of Mount Scott to farm and raise a family in the Kiowa way.

Between 1875, the year the reservation was founded, and 1901, when the KCA was allotted in severalty, the Kiowa people were forced to radically shift their use of local resources. They moved from an economy based on bison and horses to a mixed economy of stock raising, wild food gathering, domestic agricultural production, cash from leasing and annuities, government rations, and wage labor. Although every aspect of Kiowa society reflected the changes they made to their subsistence regime, these shifts did not cause them to relinquish their traditional forms of resource use or familiar social structure.

It is important to consider that although the Kiowas did not practice row crop agriculture extensively before 1875, neither had they practiced peyotism or Christianity, both of which later became central to their lives. Kiowa families took certain ideas to heart and hand within a very brief period of time (horse keeping and garden farming) while rejecting a widely popular and accepted revival movement (the Ghost Dance) that promised a return to the past. In the same way that the

Kiowas adjusted to new religious ideas, they could, and did, adjust to different subsistence regimes with equal alacrity, whether it was the introduction of the horse, cattle raising, or the production of crops, especially when their survival was at stake. The next challenge to their ability to stay on their land was mechanization, and in this, the Kiowas' ability to adjust to new economic and social structures would not be enough to overcome the dogma of industrialized scientific agriculture.

It is now practically cliché to point out that the educational and provisional efforts of the agents of the federal Indian Office to assimilate Indian peoples before 1934 were obdurately focused on row crop farming, in complete disregard of the environmental obstacles most reservation lands clearly posed. The ideology that prepared the way for the agents' focus on agriculture after 1875 was initially articulated during Thomas Jefferson's administration, which itself was based on earlier experiments with converting the New England tribes into Christian farmers.[22] The perennial solution to the "Indian problem" was always native assimilation into the white population and their eventual "civilization" as they became farmers and God-fearing ideal citizens. In plain language, most solutions to the Indian problem revealed Euro-Americans' inability to tolerate lifeways that differed from their own. In its most virulent forms, assimilation policies were a thin rationalization for whites' acquisition of Native Americans' land and resources.

American Indian policy consistently reflected Jefferson's belief in agrarianism as the foundation of a democratic government of individual landowners within a capitalistic economy. Those peoples that could not assimilate would, regrettably, become extinct, crushed by the inevitable wheels of progress. This same civilizing theory would obtain in Kiowa-federal relations more than a century later. Indian historians of the progressive era generally agree with Russell Lawrence Barsh that "a strong case can be made that Indian policy has been marked by a diversity of forms, but a continuity of effect, at least as far as land and resources are concerned."[23] No one would dispute that Indian peoples lost direct control over millions of acres of land in the period from 1880 to 1930. Indian land loss was particularly acute in Oklahoma after 1889. In this, the Kiowas were not much different from other tribal groups.[24]

But this truism does very little to reveal the story of the process and its consequences from the Kiowas' perspective. Fred Hoxie, an historian of the Crow Indians, has noted that broad generalizations about what happened to Indians at any historical juncture tends to "flatten" the uniquely historical and continuous contributions of distinct peoples in discrete moments in our history.[25] The Kiowas reacted to the loss of their lands in distinctive ways that in turn reordered the landscape they knew so intimately. Contrary to Euro-American predictions of their rapid extinction as a cultural group, the Kiowas of west-central Oklahoma did not become successful commercial farmers, nor did they disappear.

The story of Kiowa Indian farming is distinct from that of other tribal groups in ways that are peculiar to the space and time they occupied. This is especially true in regard to Euro-American Indian policy. Although the ideals expressed by the Indian policies of an Andrew Jackson and a Theodore Roosevelt look remarkably similar on the surface, the provisions of those policies reflected the times in which they were formulated. For example, Indian policy formulated in the 1880s shifted away from a more optimistic ideal based on social uplift to a more negative socially Darwinian view of the Indians' future by 1900.[26] This shift happened at precisely the same moment negotiations were being held for the opening of the KCA reservation in 1898. Similarly, the Kiowas had reached their own negative conclusions regarding the commitment of the federal government to its own policies between 1875 and 1898. The resulting clash between two highly distrustful and skeptical groups working within an antiquated form of discourse was one of the primary reasons for Lone Wolf's suit against the Department of the Interior in 1901, arguably the apex of Indian resistance to federal policy in the twentieth century.

Blacks who came to farm in Oklahoma faced different obstacles to their success than did Kiowa farmers. Most black farmers were primarily interested in becoming economically self-sufficient within the context of a local and national market. They wanted a level of economic security that would allow them to take their place in mainstream American society. The Kiowa Indians who took up farming had a traditional economy that intersected the larger national economy, but was not dependent on it. That traditional economy was stripped from them with the legal allotment of their reservation and the loss of resources they had formerly depended on. For the Kiowas, the adoption of western agricultural methods was an accommodation to a new and unfamiliar economy that they had little experience with. Their efforts to become farmers were directed far more by their desire to maintain their social and cultural traditions in familiar surroundings than any ambition to become part of the mainstream agricultural marketplace.

The continuance of a distinctly Kiowa viewpoint after allotment allows for some generalization of their experience. From an environmental history perspective, the story of the Kiowas after 1901 can also be regarded as a struggle between tribal members and outsiders over the region's primary and secondary resources as they were used according to different cultural values and traditions. The Kiowas' changed relationship with their reservation (and its unwelcome new occupants and elements) is at the center of the story of environmental change in the Washita River valley of Oklahoma Territory. This is especially important because despite the hardships and reversals of the past century, the descendants of the original allottees still make their homes there—and still help shape the ecology of the valley's rural communities and small towns. The story of Kiowa farming, invisible to earlier historians of Oklahoma agricultural history, is in fact integral to understanding the changes to the Oklahoma environment in the twentieth century.

Incredibly, the Kiowas were paid even less heed by the county extension service and the white agricultural community than were black farmers. After allotment, Kiowa farmers were essentially left to themselves to make the best of their situation without any substantial aid from either federal or state government agencies, local farm clubs, or even their own tribe. Visits from county extension agents were rare to nonexistent in Caddo County at the turn of the century, given that the first local county agent was not appointed until 1917. Between 1904 and 1917, counties not assigned their own agent were considered the territory of the state or regional supervisory agent, which meant that their participation in state extension was minimal.

Still, lack of an agent was only part of the story of underserved Kiowa farmers anyway. In Canadian County, which did have an agent, situated just north of Caddo and home to the Cheyennes and Arapahoes, the local extension agent found his best avenue for reaching farmers was working through the local Grange. As he put it, "We believe it is best to have all farm organizations conducted under one head." In other words, the work of the agent was administered and organized exclusively through local Grange chapters. Although this suited most white farmers in the county, Indians and blacks would likely have had some difficulty in gaining membership. As the agent reported, "While the Grange is yet a secret organization, the member-ship fee of one dollar a year will permit any farmer to membership *whose social standing is found to be worthy.*"[27]

Using the Grange exclusively to reach farmers was not a general practice in most Oklahoma counties, but agents were encouraged either to found or to cooperate with local farm clubs wherever possi-ble. In 1918, Caddo agent Nutter reported that the central organization supporting his work was the Caddo County Pure Bred Livestock Association, a private group whose membership was selected.[28] Given the relatively small operations of most Kiowa farmers and the preju-dice against Indian farming in general in Caddo County, it is unlikely that any Kiowa farmers were invited to join the county livestock club.

In any case, white extension agents and farmers believed that the needs of Indian farmers were being supplied by the Office of Indian Affairs. In some ways, this was true, although the level of support for Kiowa farmers by the government, especially in regard to the applica-tion of scientific farming and mechanization of crops, was practically nonexistent. After the last of the allotments were completed in 1904 and the KCA "big pasture" was opened to white settlers in 1906, agency farmers were kept busy most of the time in assessing the value of individual Kiowas' allotments for leasing purposes. This left no time for actual hands-on instruction. Accordingly, Kiowa farming shifted from small homesteading operations to leasing within two years after the opening of the reservation.[29]

Francis Leupp, commissioner of Indian Affairs, best articulated the proposed place of Indians in postallotment society. According to Leupp, although there was much to be admired in the Indian (and his treatment at the hands of whites had not helped him in his path toward civilization), the Indian race still had a long way to go before it could expect to have the same success and privileges whites enjoyed: "In simple terms, the great mass of Indians have yet to go through the era, common to the history of all races, when they must be mere hew-ers of wood and drawers of water."[30] Mechanized commercial farming was not even a remote expectation for Leupp. In essence, the failure of the Kiowas to become successful farmers equal to their white neigh-bors was a foregone conclusion. This was precisely the fate the Kiowas had hoped to avoid in resisting allotment.

Equally disastrous to the level of effective federal help to the Kiowas after allotment was the passage of the Burke Act in 1906, which allowed federal authorities to declare any Indian "competent" to handle his or her financial affairs and to grant them fee simple title to their allotment. This, of course, also made the Indian allottee responsible for taxes. When the Indian owner was unable to pay, his or her land was auctioned off by the local sheriff's office. Similarly, Indian land in fee simple title was open to mortgage liens from creditors or became a quick source of cash for an allottee in dire circumstances. This new law took effect hard on the heels of the opening of the KCA reservation to white settlement in 1904, and it flooded the former reservation with new white homesteaders and business interests. Stock thieves also took advantage of the moment to increase their activities. KCA agent Randlett reported in 1905 that Indian farming

> has been much retarded by the unfavorable influences that were brought among them with the opening of this country, to settlement by the whites. Very many of them who were well supplied with animals with which to work their lands have found themselves stripped of this indispensable advantage by the horse thieves, who took the occasion of the influx of actual settlers to locate themselves in the vicinities where their vocations could most conveniently be practiced.[31]

Predictably, Oklahoma's successful bid for statehood in 1907 further weakened the federal government's ability to protect Indians from unscrupulous whites as local courts took jurisdiction over cases formerly tried by federally appointed territorial judges.[32] Most of these cases involved Indian property. Even when land could not be used as collateral (because it was in trust status), local moneylenders often made loans to Indians at incredibly high rates and then seized their farm implements or stock.[33]

All these changes put allottees at increased risk of legal dispossession of their land if they failed as independent farmers.[34] The vulnerability and foreboding that many Kiowas expressed during the Jerome Commission meetings at the opening of their reservation turned out to be well founded. According to Leonard Carlson, an economic historian, Oklahoma Indian land in trust status (inalienable) fell from 41 million acres in 1881 to a mere 2.9 million acres by 1930.[35] By 1900, the primary purpose of allotment—to place Indian lands under the control of non-Indians who would know best how to utilize it—was not even being questioned by most Americans, including Congress.

One of the most outspoken critics of Indian landownership was a well-known newspaperman named Reynolds, whose pen name was Kicking Bird. Reynolds had deep connections to the railroads: his editorship of the Parson's *Sun* was underwritten by Robert S. Stevens, president of the Missouri, Kansas, and Topeka Railroad.[36] For Reynolds, the primary elements missing in the development of the former KCA reservation were white settlers and the railroads: "The two would serve hand in hand, with the railroads bringing more people and the people providing support for the railroads."[37]

In a brazen bit of chicanery (and in complete disregard of the Kiowas' use of names), Reynolds adopted "Kicking Bird" as a pen name for his articles on Oklahoma development. This left his eastern readers with the impression that he was a civilized and reformed Indian landowner. Reynolds's opinion of Indian land ownership reflected that of most white Americans at the time, which made rare exception for some Indians but generally regarded the rest as backward and a primary obstacle to Oklahoma's rightful place in the economic life of the United States.

As in Blaine County with the Cheyennes and Arapahoes, local whites in Caddo County were critical of Indian farming and complained that the Indians had claimed all the best portions of land, leaving whites with next to nothing. At the same time, however, local whites were pleased to have Indians around to liven up their festivals and parades when appropriate. In 1909, the editor of the *Carnegie Herald* charged his readers for being less than patriotic on the Fourth of July, when the entire town tripped off to watch the Kiowas dance just outside of town, leaving the town parade without any spectators.[38]

The steady progress of the Kiowas—a remarkable achievement given the climatic conditions of the previous quarter century—came undone with the arrival of white farmers, merchants, land speculators, and railroad interests. So long as the reservation was intact and the agency continued to be the primary customer for the sale of the Kiowas' cattle herds and other produce (at fair prices), full-scale commercial production was not central to the Kiowas' maintenance. The reservation was, as Robert Stahl has suggested, an internal economy that was not oriented to the pressure of Euro-American business interests, especially when those interests were supported by an unfamiliar and racially biased legal system that worked in one-way fashion.

The primary change in Kiowa farming practice after 1904, and subsequent use of the lands they owned, was the percentage of Indian lands that were leased by non-Indians. By 1905, nearly half of all the KCA allotments were under lease to white farmers. By 1909, a total of 2,598 leases were granted on 3,716 allotments. Lease money became the Kiowas' main source of income after 1904. This was not a result of the Kiowas' lack of effort at agriculture but was a rational response to an impossible situation. Given that most Kiowas' first priority was maintaining their family and kinship ties within a specific and famil- iar geographical area, leasing provided the best opportunity to live together yet maintain ownership of their land. What they discovered was that farming on a commercial basis opened up Kiowa farmers to a whole host of risks that often ended in their dispossession.

In many instances, Kiowa farmers remained on their allotments and leased the majority of their lands. Unlike African American farmers, who were directed to poorer-quality lands, many Kiowas took up good parcels of land. Their choice of allotments was not generally based on the quality of the soil but on the quality of the water—a reflection of their desire to become stock raisers rather than row crop agricultural- ists. Nevertheless, good water and decent pasture lands tended to con- tain a significant proportion of good cropland as well, and many of the Kiowas' allotments were considered prime farmland after the opening of the reservation.

This was the situation Robert Goombi grew up in near Carnegie, Oklahoma. His father retained between 20 and 40 acres of land and a house for his own use but leased the rest to a cotton and wheat farmer. The Goombi family maintained a large kitchen garden, kept cows, chickens, pigs, and horses for their own use, and supplemented their income with wage labor during the harvest season, picking cotton for their own lessee.[39] Having only horse power and one or two imple- ments, Kiowa farmers could expect to plow and harvest only a very limited acreage—just enough to provide winter feed for their stock. This pattern of partial leasing is revealed in a 1915 survey of Kiowa farmers. According to the survey, of those Kiowas who were farming their allotments, nearly all were living as subsistence farmers on a few acres and leasing the majority of their allotments to non-Indians.

There were some notable exceptions to this general pattern. A few Kiowas attempted to become independent farmers entirely on their own in competition with their white neighbors. One such farmer was Wind Goomda, also known as Medicine Wind. Medicine Wind was only six years old when U.S. soldiers attacked his camp at Palo Duro Canyon. He walked all the way back to Fort Sill and endured the agony of the stone corral winter. As an adult, Goomda raised capital for farming by selling his wife's allotment and moving the family to his allotment on the top of a bluff near Mountain View. Here he built a two-story home, a barn, a garage, and several other structures, including a traditional Kiowa summer arbor. He had corn, cotton, and wheat fields, a large vegetable garden, and a fruit orchard. The family maintained good horses and cows for milk, meat, and power.

At harvest time, Medicine Wind could count on his sixteen children and his own extended family, including brothers and cousins, for help. Occasionally, Wind Goomda hired other Kiowas to help on the farm as well. The Goomdas had converted to Christianity, and their youngest son Howard, born in 1915, was named after one of the local missionaries. But Medicine Wind did not forget his Kiowa upbringing. Respect in Kiowa society came from generosity. Howard Goomda remembered as a child how his father and uncle would set up a tent outside the house and fill it with fresh beef piled high on tables. Local Kiowas would come by to collect the beef and stay to a big supper. Cheyenne travelers often stopped at the Goomda farm on their way south and were treated to a fresh beeve.

But Medicine Wind's prosperity was short-lived. Tuberculosis and pneumonia took all of his children, one by one, after 1899, until only the youngest, Howard, remained. The children would contract tuberculosis at school and would come home to die, thereby infecting their other siblings. The farm itself suffered a similar fate. One night, the hired hands sleeping in the barn accidentally started a fire, and the barn was destroyed. Inside the barn was a brand-new Overland touring car. The pigs were so badly burned that they had to be shot. The chickens roasted in the henhouse and their Kiowa neighbors came the next day with pans to collect the cooked chickens. After the fire and the deaths of most of his children, Medicine Wind sold his farm and moved to town, where he immersed himself in the work of the church.[40]

James Silverhorn was also a full-time farmer, although he started later than Wind Goomda. Silverhorn was able to make a start at commercial farming by securing a loan at an Apache-owned bank and by inheriting several allotments from family members. Silverhorn never bought a tractor. At different times, he and his wife had nine to ten children living at home, as well as eight or nine cousins and nephews. Everyone helped with the work, and they hired help only during the cotton harvest. Like Medicine Wind, Silverhorn was extremely generous, and when friends and relatives came by in search of money or food, he did not refuse them.[41]

Although most Kiowa farmers continued to plant small acreages of wheat and to use horse-drawn machinery, when the price for wheat skyrocketed, a few attempted to enter the wheat market on the same basis as their white neighbors. In 1967, field-worker Julia Jordan interviewed Guy Quoetone, Kiowa, about Indian farming after 1900. Quoetone related that he and other Kiowas raised wheat but had trouble getting it threshed. During the war, Quoetone "had to hire a colored man to help me stack my wheat." Showing Jordan a picture of a custom combining unit, Quoetone explained that "the machinery don't belong to me, I just hired the thresher . . . In those days the white people that owned the threshers, they kind of boycott the Indians. They won't thresh our wheat . . . They wait till all the white people get all theirs threshed and then they thresh ours. It was discouraging for us to raise wheat because we can't get it cut and we couldn't get it threshed."[42] The Office of Indian Affairs responded to the Kiowas' requests for modern agricultural machinery, combines in particular, but their purchase of two combines during World War I was hardly enough to service all of the Kiowa farmers who needed them.[43]

The Kiowas began their transition to agriculture with the demise of the buffalo herds and their confinement to the reservation. Their next big transition was to individual allotments. In this process, their choice of land parcels reflected both the past and their ideas for the future. This resulted in different land use patterns after allotment: stock raising of cattle, horses, or both, leasing of land for grass money, farming for family need and individual commercial crop production.

All these choices reflected a common desire to maintain their connection to the tribe and its internal social, political, and religious structure. The continuing presence today of the Kiowas in the same area that originally comprised their reservation in 1872 is indicative of their success at maintaining their social and geographical relationships. But the effect of the Kiowas' circumstances after allotment on their immediate environment was profound. Before allotment, the Kiowas desired to be stock raisers, living in centralized communities and depending on small acreages of subsistence crops. It is possible that overgrazing might eventually have occurred as the Kiowas' herds grew and much of the old-growth timber was harvested for fuel and other needs. But the Kiowas did not get the opportunity to play out that eventuality. Instead, white thieves and allotment forced the

Kiowas to try to adapt their social structure, which was based on bands, to an unwieldy patchwork of individual allotments dispersed over a wide area. This caused the tribe to lease much of their land to white farmers who managed it in the same way as they managed their acreages of wheat and cotton and corn in counties like Blaine and Logan. For the Kiowas, much like the African American farmers who lived near Langston, the limits of what they could and could not do with the land and its resources was dictated by surrounding white farmers, who profited from their greater access to capital and markets; by the unequal distribution of government help in the form of scientific agricultural methods; by immunity from prosecution for crimes against either blacks or Indians; and by their own initiative in cooperative (and exclusive) capitalization to take advantage of new technologies of scale. In spite of the efforts of black and Indian farmers to organize the resources of the new territory for themselves, it was the needs of white settlers that shaped the agroecology of the red earth.

CONCLUSION:
ORDERING THE ELEMENTS

It does not stand to reason that the hundreds and thousands of houseless and homeless land-hungry immigrants will forever allow these great Indian parks to remain untilled and untouched, while the people are taxed to support the Indian in his idleness. The Indian reservations must go! The tribal relations of the Indians must go! The farce of a blanketed and breech-clouted nation within a nation must go! The home seekers must have homes. The land-hungry must fill the broad prairies and rich valleys of the Indian Territory.

Milton W. Reynolds, aka Kicking Bird

In 1889, Oklahoma Territory was a colorful reflection of the nation's cultural and ecological diversity. Virtually every sort of person could be found there: white, black, American Indian, native-born "mechanics,"[1] and new immigrants. Different classes were there too, from the comfortably wealthy to the desperately poor, although the majority counted themselves somewhere in between. The nonhuman landscape was even more diverse. Dense cross timbers running north and south along the territory's eastern edge gave way to open mixed-grass prairies transected by wide rivers and punctuated by canyons, gypsum hills, and salt beds. The bison and longhorns were gone, but the countryside still contained prairie dogs, snakes, mule deer, elk, pronghorn, coyotes, ducks, geese, turkey, quail, pigeons, and prairie chickens. Indigenous plant varieties numbered in the hundreds, if not thousands.

Less than twenty years later, most of the original elements of the mixed-grass prairie had been neatly rearranged to reflect the well-ordered vision of its white inhabitants: fenced-off farmsteads, straight roads, whitewashed bungalows, white-faced cattle, and row upon row of commercially important crops such as cotton and winter wheat.

Like the countryside, the Indian and African American peoples who lived and worked in the territory were systematically displaced by a largely homogeneous population of white farmers of different backgrounds. By the 1920s, Oklahoma Territory resembled Kansas and Nebraska far more than anything that had existed there in 1889.

That blacks and Indians were sometimes viciously discriminated against, as the Kiowas were in the courts or African Americans were during the land runs, in a society that considered itself a "final island of frontier freedom . . . a kind of America within America"[2] is hardly surprising. The fact remains, however, that most people, even today, are not aware of the ways in which that discrimination played itself out socially and environmentally. The tenacity of the Oklahoma story as the quintessential American dream is a testament to the durability of old notions of racial inferiority and material progress. Of all the ways in which history can be written and remembered, human based environmental change is often a "winner's" history told by the people who remain. Even now, few historians have deeply considered the ways in which historical tensions between social groups, not just culture itself, are reflected in the physical environment.

Oklahoma Territory was not just another space transformed by capitalism. Participation in the national and international agricultural economy long predated the opening of the territory for agricultural settlement. From the time of Indian people's historic appearance through full-scale European-style agricultural settlement, transportation routes in Oklahoma testified to at least three different ways of seeing or evaluating the landscape. Between 1800 and 1865, intertribal trade and Euro-American trade with Indians dominated. That economy centered on two resources, horses and bison, which were in turn dependent on the mixed grasses and watercourses of the southern plains. After the Civil War, the cattle trade intruded on and further exploited this same resource base as cattle retraced the same north-south routes Indian peoples had followed for centuries. At this same time, surveyors from the federal Land Office were busily dividing up the landscape according to the provisions of the ordinance of 1785, whose purpose was the development of uniformly sized, individually held farmsteads.

Finally, the railroads took advantage of all of these visions of the territory. The roads moved cattle north and south parallel with the trails, and then moved settlers and goods into the region and took out their products along east-west routes. The rail system in central Oklahoma was aggressively opportunistic, following rivers and trails and the path of least resistance in one section, then abruptly taking off along the surveyor's lines to intersect with important crossroads that promised higher volumes. These different orientations to the landscape, whether as trade routes, trails, or railways, had a direct and dynamic effect on the agroecology of Oklahoma Territory.

Human migration invariably introduced exotic plant and animal life to the prairie community, consumed or plowed up the grasslands, cut down trees, and created "built" environments in the form of lodges, forts, tracks, fences, and cities. And as each new group of people arrived, they appraised the region for resources to support their particular lifeways or economies. As early as 1821, stories and reports were being circulated in the East by army officers, explorers, cattlemen, and Sooners that Oklahoma Territory was an untapped source of wealth. By the time of the first run in 1889, those places destined to become urban centers had already been decided, instantaneously linking the nascent activities of new settlers with eastern markets.

Similarly, the ecology of Oklahoma Territory can be just as deceptive for contemporary historians. Just as prairie ecologists are fond of saying that we cannot just look at the prairie, we must look inside it, the territory's ecological story cannot be found in studying the wheat and cattle being raised today. It took white Americans, African Americans, and Indian peoples relating to one another in a definable space at a critical moment in the nation's history to shape the territory. Oklahoma Territory, opened in the name of increased opportunity, encompassed everything the nation believed it could be and everything it hoped to avoid. The tragedy of Oklahoma Territory was that the majority of white Americans truly believed in the promise of opportunity but at the same time denied it to those Americans who were arguably the most deserving.

After the enclosure of Indian peoples on reservations in the 1880s, various self-identified groups of people attempted to exploit the territory's vast agricultural resources. An elite group of native-born white farmers were eventually triumphant over all others in ordering those resources into pathways of production and personal prosperity, although the bold traces of black and Indian efforts can still be seen throughout the former territory. Indian and black farmers had little time or room in which to develop their own relationship to the territory. Leasing land or growing cotton was neither the Kiowas' or African Americans' preferred method of land management. For the most part, their decisions to lease their farms or grow an ecologically greedy crop like cotton were negotiated responses to the obstacles placed in their path by white society. In spite of some tantalizing hints at the territory's opening, we will never know how a Kiowa landscape or an unmolested black farm community might have developed over time. Instead, in less than one generation, the collective farming practices of the Kiowas and the mixed-use practices of African American settlers were swept aside in the transition of Oklahoma from a highly diverse ecology of native plants, animals, and people to a more simplified ecology centered on a scientifically approved list of domesticated crops and animals.

That list was largely defined by the newly formed Agricultural Experiment Station scientists at Stillwater and by the Farm Demonstration program. The relationship between Oklahoma's settlers, federal agricultural policy, and the physical environment helps to make sense of the dramatic changes in Oklahoma society and ecology from 1889 to 1907. As this study reveals, federal policy, as administered by the local experiment station and its agents, was a salient feature of many farmers' thinking about nonhuman nature. It was also a force in the eventual dispossession of thousands of would-be farmers.

Local U.S. Department of Agriculture (USDA) histories have been predominantly bureaucratic and political in their focus, documenting the often bitter struggles of local stations with both the national Office of Experiment Stations and pecuniary state officials over inadequate funding.[3] But early USDA policy also contributed to rapid changes in the ecology of central Oklahoma with the introduction of "scientific" agriculture. The agents of the USDA helped to popularize specific technologies and practices that excluded many poor white, African American, and Indian farmers, causing them to lose control over their land or to leave farming altogether.

One reason scholars have not addressed these issues stems from the fact that whatever influence USDA activities may have had on Oklahoma's preagricultural environment or on its subsequent management as an agroecosystem, it was diffuse.[4] As a result of the individualistic and entrepreneurial system of agricultural production that most white farmers in Oklahoma subscribed to, it is easier to assume that farmers were the primary agents in the displacement of Oklahoma's complex ecology of grasses, legumes, and forbs for commercial monocultures of wheat, corn, alfalfa, and cotton. As it turned out, the very presence or absence of the information and support provided by Stillwater to new farmers in the territory turned out to be crucial, not only to their success but also to their confidence in the future.

It was white farmers' acceptance and enthusiasm for mechanized agriculture in particular that initiated and sustained the simplification of the territory. The mechanization of agriculture based on the highly structured, and highly exclusionary, custom cutting system was not solely the result of a belief in scientific farming, but was also pushed along by short-term changes in the ecology of the territory and the ups and downs of the broader agricultural market. The overcapitalization of transportation systems, especially railroads, was a further impetus in territorial farmers' move toward monoculture.

Finally, the ecology of Oklahoma Territory itself created obstacles and opportunities that temporarily aided in the simplification of the landscape. Blaine County farmers' entrance into the commercial agricultural market was slow as a result of a severe drought, their distance from the railroads, and lack of capital, as well as a widespread economic depression. Hard times fell even harder on white tenant farmers and made it almost impossible for African American farmers to stay on their lands. But drought, depression, and hardship also challenged white farmers' preconceived notions about farming the mixed-grass prairie. That uncertainty gave the scientists at Stillwater an entry that might not have existed otherwise and changed the way in which the majority of white farmers would use their land for the next two decades.

Today, the territory looks more like it did in the preagricultural era than ever before. As farms consolidate, railroads pull up their tracks, and frame houses are reclaimed by the red earth, we see through a glass darkly what Washington Irving saw in 1832. Oklahoma today is 95 percent privately owned. There are no red wolves or bison herds, nor are there passenger pigeons flying overhead. Although some fauna have returned, others, like the armadillo, have taken over habitats created by prairie dogs. Fractionalized ownership of much of the territory has left formerly productive fields unmanaged, ungrazed, and unburned, causing an invasion of nonnative eastern red cedar and juniper that is threatening to change the face of the region in only a few decades.

The spread of these two invader species has been dramatic as millions of acres are abandoned by landowners for agricultural use. In 1950 a survey found that 1.5 million acres of red cedar and juniper dominated acres. Today that total stands at nearly 6 million acres, or 30 percent of the total 21 million acres of native plant acres left in the state. This situation has caused problems for the native prairie chickens, white-tailed deer, quail, and bobwhite as well as native plant species. It also poses a grave fire danger to suburban home owners. Juniper encroachment also has a negative effect on water quality through erosion and sedimentation. Finally, juniper and red cedar are heavy pollinators, which has caused a dramatic increase in human suffering from allergies. Moreover, these effects don't even begin to evaluate the damage to biological diversity or forage quality.[5] Perhaps Aldo Leopold's notion that a thing is right when it preserves the integrity, stability, and beauty of the biotic (and I would include human) community is as relevant in Oklahoma today as it was in the territory in 1889. While much has been lost, Oklahoma's unique combination of prairies, shrublands, and forests, as well as peoples of different races, is still intact. It is not yet too late to fulfill the promise of the red earth.

NOTES

INTRODUCTION

1. For histories of the Treaty of Medicine Lodge, see DeMallie and Kickingbird, *Treaty of Medicine Lodge*; and Calloway, *Our Hearts Fell to the Ground.*

2. Oklahoma historian Edwin McReynolds has written that "The entire Indian country . . . was an unused area much in the public mind." McReynolds, *Oklahoma*, 279.

3. Dan Flores contends that human beings often react similarly to particular environments as a condition of their shared genetic code. See Flores, *Natural West*, 13.

4. Stein and Hill, *Culture of Oklahoma*, 198–234.

5. Kolodny, *Land Before Her*, xii.

6. Liebhardt, "Interpretation and Causal Analysis," 33.

7. Geertz, *Interpretation of Cultures*, 5.

8. Sahlins, *Islands of History*, vii–viii, cited in Lewis, *Neither Wolf nor Dog*, 5.

9. McEvoy, *Fisherman's Problem*; Merchant, *Ecological Revolutions*; Kulick, *Socialization, Self and Syncretism*; Diamond, *Fertile Ground.*

10. Gibson, "Oklahoma: Land of the Drifter," 10.

CHAPTER 1
THE PRAIRIE

1. Merriweather Lewis, quoted in Outwater, *Water*, 72.

2. Irving, *Tour on the Prairies*, 105.

3. Webb, *Great Plains*, 1931.

4. A former lack of interest in the complexity of the grassland biome has caused it to lag significantly behind forests, wetlands, mountains, deserts, and watercourses in terms of federal preservation efforts. The first National Prairie Park, a 10,000-acre remnant of tallgrass prairie in Chase County, Kansas, was not authorized by Congress until 1997.

5. Since 1972, over four hundred species of native vascular plants have been identified on Konza Prairie Research Natural Area, located in the transition zone between the tallgrass and mixed-grass prairie areas of Kansas. For an

explanation and description of the density of animals and diversity of plant life in mixed-grass prairie, see Licht, *Ecology and Economy,* 4.

6. For a thorough and opinionated discussion of "climax" theory and its critics, see Worster, *Nature's Economy,* chaps. 11–12.

7. Agnes Chase writes, "Humans are wholly dependent for their living on plants, and of all plants, the grasses are the most important. All our breadstuffs, . . . as well as sugarcane are grasses, and grasses form the principal food of the animals that furnish meat and milk . . . grasses have many other uses, and are also key plants in maintaining the integrity of our landscapes." Chase, *First Book of Grasses.* See also Williams and Diebel, "Economic Value of Prairie," 19–35.

8. Briggs and Knapp, "Interannual Variability in Primary Production in Tallgrass Prairie."

9. Dale E. Lott writes, "We can't understand the ecosystem of primitive North America, or the magnitude of the human rearrangement of that ecosystem without a good estimate of primitive North America's bison population." Lott, *American Bison,* 69.

10. The lowest figure (5.5 million) was proposed by William Hornaday in 1887. His estimate was a simple calculation based on the number of hides (3.7 million) shipped to market between 1872 and 1874. Even though the southern herd was nearly extinct by 1875, Hornaday concluded that no more than 4 million bison could have ever subsisted in the southern Plains. The highest estimate, proposed by Garretson in 1938, was based on the observations of a Robert Wright, who claimed to have ridden with General Sheridan in the late 1860s through a herd 100 miles across and of unknown length. Because Sheridan did not even mention this vast herd, most historians have discounted Wright's claim.

11. Seaton, *Lives of Game Animals.*

12. Flores, "Bison Ecology."

13. Shaw and Lee, "Ecological Interpretation."

14. Omer C. Stewart was one of the first ecologists to make the connection between Indian burning and the evolution of the prairie biome more than fifty years ago. His work on prairie fires has been recently edited by Henry Lewis and M. Kat Anderson as *Forgotten Fires: Native Americans and the Transient Wilderness.*

15. Shaw and Lee, "Ecological Interpretation," 2.

16. Shaw speculates that the north-south movement of the herds, as noted by observers, may have been short-distance moves between watercourses, which generally flow west to east throughout the Great Plains. Observers did not follow herds and so could not have known how far the animals traveled. Shaw and Lee, "Ecological Interpretation," 33–38.

17. Lawson, *Climate of the Great American Desert,* 28; Stahle and Hehr, "Dendroclimatic Relationships."

18. Vehik, "Cultural Continuity and Discontinuity."

19. Flores, "Bison Ecology," 468. Flores accepts the interpretation given by Kavanaugh, *Comanche Political History.*

20. Flores, "Bison Ecology," 471.

21. An oft-neglected feature of the mixed-grass prairie before 1850 was the presence of 20 to 30 thousand shallow wetlands that filled temporarily after a downpour, providing water and habitat for dozens of animals, especially migratory birds like sandhill cranes. Licht, *Ecology and Economy*, 9.

22. Anthropologists have generally defined this as Plains cultures based on mounted bison hunting. Oliver, "Ecology and Cultural Continuity," 2.

23. Kindscher, *Edible Wild Plants of the Prairie*, 184–89.

24. Ibid., 34, 191, 221.

25. Sherow, "Workings of the Geodialectic," 65.

26. Shepard Krech III writes, "This is the rhetoric of buffalo hunting on the Plains: White people wasted and caused the extermination of the buffalo, whereas Indians were skillful, ecologically aware conservationists." Shepard, *Ecological Indian*, 123.

27. The effect of the robe trade on the Omahas' agricultural practices has been well documented: Fletcher and LaFlesche, *Omaha Tribe*; White, *Roots of Dependency*; Holder, *Hoe and the Horse*. Some horticultural tribes' participation in the bison robe trade was based on supplying the trading posts with a dependable food source, either in terms of fresh meat supplies or agricultural produce, especially corn. Wishart, *Fur Trade*, 100, 102.

28. Hoig, *Tribal Wars*; Nye, *Carbine and Lance*.

29. Norall, *Bourgmont*, 71–73. Bourgmont had indeed miraculously transported a great number of items from France to the Plains, including fusils, sabers, axes, gunpowder, Limbourg cloth, Flemish knives, needles, awls, combs, scissors, and dyes.

30. Wishart, *Fur Trade*, 81.

31. Anderson, *Indian Southwest*, 13, 32, 65.

32. Isenberg, *Destruction of the Bison*.

33. Kansas Pacific Railway, "Guide Map."

34. Francaviglia, *Cast Iron Forest*, 107.

35. Ellison, "Traveling the Trail," 539.

36. Knapp et al., eds., *Grassland Dynamics*.

37. Rossel, "Chisholm Trail," 13.

38. Ridings, *Chisholm Trail*, 20.

39. Ibid., 558–59.

40. Skaggs, ed., *Ranch and Range in Oklahoma*, 54.

41. Saunders, ed., *Trail Drivers of Texas*, 71.

42. Durwood Ball, *Army Regulars*, 15–18. Ball notes that "like most federal policymakers, professional soldiers advocated Indian assimilation. However, army officers wanted that end to come through peaceful diplomacy and education, not through war" (18).

43. Leckie, *Buffalo Soldiers*, 46.

44. Price, "Prairie Policemen," 53–55.

45. Opie, *Law of the Land*, 59.

46. Gates, *History of Public Land Law Development*, 472.

47. Anthropologists have studied the ways in which Plains tribes related to one another on different levels. The cooperative use of the bison range was classic interdependence or symbiosis. See Albers, "Intertribal Relationships," 94–132.

48. Saunders, ed., *Trail Drivers of Texas*, 401–2.

49. Hoxie, *Final Promise*, 44.

50. Charles N. Gould, "Oklahoma," 426–30.

51. Gary Thompson, "Changing Transportation Systems," 112.

52. Ecologists have long recognized the importance of the border area between vegetative zones, or ecotones, to certain species of plants and animals, especially browsers and grazers like deer and elk, and their predators. J. E. Weaver, a prolific writer and ecologist of prairie flora and fauna, was one of the first to note this ecological niche. Weaver et al., "Ecological Studies." For a bibliography of early Great Plains ecology publications, see Wali, ed., *Prairie*.

CHAPTER 2
THE PROMISE

1. Danbom, *Resisted Revolution*, 10.

2. Hays, *Conservation*, 263.

3. Worster, *Unsettled Country*, 6.

4. Stubbs, "Relations of the Railroads."

5. Degler, *Out of Our Past*, 262.

6. Kulikoff, *Agrarian Origins*, 55.

7. Rome, "American Farmers as Entrepreneurs," 37.

8. John Ridge to Albert Gelatin, February 27, 1826, in Perdue and Green, eds., *Cherokee Removal*, 34.

9. Bittle and Geis, *Longest Way Home*, 23.

10. Chapman, "Freedmen and the Oklahoma Lands."

11. Fowler, *Black Infantry*; Leckie, *Buffalo Soldiers*; Wickett, "Contested Territory."

12. Stewart, *What Nature Suffers to Groe*, 245. See also Bethel, *Promiseland*.

13. Freedmen and freedwomen took up the promise of landownership even in the most inhospitable reaches of the continental United States. See Jones, "They Call It Timbuctu."

14. Thelen, *Paths of Resistance*, 139.

15. For a survey of black migration themes, see Rodgers, *Canaan Bound*.

16. Hoig, *Oklahoma Land Rush*, 184–85.

17. Oklahoma Historical Society, Living Legends Oral History Project, Oklahoma Historical Society Library, Oklahoma City, hereafter cited as LLP.

18. Transcript of an interview with Sidney Willin Monroe, 1937. In Indian and Pioneer Papers, Grant Forman Collection, Oklahoma Historical Society Archives, Oklahoma City, hereafter cited as IPP.

19. These farms were either rented or purchased, not claimed as free homes under the Homestead Act.

20. Holmes, ed., *Logan County History*, 165.

21. Teall, *Black History in Oklahoma*, 166.

22. *Black* (Oklahoma City) *Dispatch*, April 24, 1954.

23. Edna Randolph Slaughter, LLP.

24. J. H. Crowell, LLP.

25. A portion of the 1890 census covering veterans of the Civil War still exists for Logan County. No black veterans were listed in that schedule. U.S. Department of Commerce, Bureau of Census, "Schedules Enumerating Union Veterans."

26. Hoig, *Oklahoma Land Rush*, 260.

27. *Langston City* (Oklahoma) *Herald*, November 17, 1892.

28. *New York Times*, September 21, 23, 1891.

29. The violence and confusion associated with the runs was the primary argument for the lottery system. Dick, *Lure of the Land*, 294.

30. A. M. Capers, interviewed by Ida A. Merwin, November 13, 1937, IPP 88:62–67.

31. Interview with William Stewart, October 20, 1937, IPP.

32. Tolson, *Black Oklahomans*; Hamilton, *Black Towns and Profit*. Tolson reported that there were actually twenty-nine black towns and a colony by 1907, not twenty-five, as reported in Hill, "All Negro Society."

33. Hamilton, *Black Towns and Profit*, 99. Hamilton claims that Charles Robbins worked hand in hand with McCabe and Eagleson to found Langston City. Although Robbins purchased and platted the town's site, Hamilton offers no evidence that Robbins was ever involved with the promotion of the town or had any further dealings with either of the town's two black founders.

34. Tolson, *Black Oklahomans*, 89. Tolson estimated that between 1889 and 1906, 7,000 to 8,000 blacks entered Oklahoma, in comparison with 250,000 to 500,000 whites.

35. Petterson, *Langston University*. Langston's population averaged 250 residents from 1900 to 1920. Tolson (*Black Oklahomans*, 95) estimated Langston's population in 1907 to be 274.

36. *Oklahoma* (Guthrie) *Guide*, April 11, 1901.

37. Hilliard, *Hog Meat and Hoe Cake*, 21, 36.

38. Teall, *Black History in Oklahoma*, 164.

39. Ibid., 165.

40. Ibid., 162.

41. For an evaluation of black-white-Indian relations in Oklahoma Territory, see Wickett, "Contested Territory."

42. Tolson, *Black Oklahomans*, 69–89.

43. *New York Times*, April 9, 1891.

44. *Langston City* (Oklahoma) *Herald*, November 17, 1892.

45. *New York Times*, April 9, 1891.

CHAPTER 3
THE BLACK FRONTIER

1. *Boley* (Oklahoma) *Progress*, June 8, 1905.

2. Williamson, *Crucible of Race*; Painter, *Exodusters*; Athearn, *In Search of Canaan*. For black migration north, see Grossman, *Land of Hope*.

3. *Langston City* (Oklahoma) *Herald*, August 11, 1894.

4. *Topeka* (Kansas) *Daily Capital*, March 19, 1890.

5. Bethel, *Promiseland*, 18.

6. Tolson, *Black Oklahomans*, 52.

7. Holmes, ed., *Logan County History*, 110. Thomas and Mary's son, Thomas Black Jr., would go on to be the first four-year graduate in agriculture from Oklahoma's Colored Agricultural and Mechanical College in Langston in 1922. He served as the "colored" extension agent for Logan and Lincoln counties from 1930 to 1965.

8. Otto Flasch, interview with author, Langston, Oklahoma, October 9, 1996.

9. Fortunately, the 1904 census for Antelope township in Logan County has survived. It was one of the best years for agriculture in the first decade of the twentieth century, well after the establishment of the town of Langston and three years before statehood and the legal codification of Jim Crow in Oklahoma. Antelope Township Records, Oklahoma Territorial Museum Archives, Guthrie, Oklahoma.

10. Interview with J. H. Crowell, Orlando, Oklahoma, IPP.

11. Interview with Mack McClelland, IPP.

12. Hilliard relates that according to the notes of southern overseers, "there was always time for sowing turnips." Hilliard, *Hog Meat and Hoe Cake*, 39–40.

13. Interview with J. H. Crowell, Orlando, Oklahoma, IPP.

14. Chufas are a relatively unknown crop in the United States even today. In their native Spain, they are called a groundnut or ground almond and are used for various foods and in a distilled drink. They are similar to peanuts in size and habit.

15. *Langston City* (Oklahoma) *Herald*, August 11, 1894.

16. De'Leslaine Davis, LLP.

17. Hilliard, *Hog Meat and Hoecake*, 180–81.

18. Guthrie and Logan County Directory, 1898, Oklahoma Territorial Museum Archives; and Blacks in Guthrie Photograph Collection, Oklahoma Territorial Museum Archives, Guthrie, Oklahoma.

19. Oklahoma Territorial Board of Agriculture, "Oklahoma Peaches for Export Trade," 88.

20. Interview with Nellie Cutler, March 9, 1938, IPP.

21. Hamilton, *Black Towns and Profit*, 114.

22. This is a small fortune in egg money, given that the price of eggs in Logan County at the turn of the century was between 2 and 5 cents per dozen.

23. Hardwick, "Homesteads and Bungalows," 59–60.

24. Ibid.

25. A symposium dedicated to the centennial of the USDA's elevation to cabinet status was held in Ames, Iowa, in 1989. Papers from this meeting were reprinted in the April 1990 issue of *Agricultural History*. Alan Marcus and Richard Lowitt's introduction to this special issue is a good synopsis of the sweeping influence of the USDA in this century, growing from an annual appropriation of just over $1 million in 1889 to a yearly budget topping $50 billion and employing a workforce of 120,000 men and women nationally.

26. Thompson, *Closing the Frontier*.

27. Trachtenberg, *Incorporation of America*, 3–4.

28. One recent study of a single county's readership in New York revealed some surprising trends. Although the subscriptions were initiated by well-to-do farmers, their circulation in the local community followed kinship and

neighborhood connections. This same network moved information from family farm to family farm, mixing new book farming concepts with traditional ideas in Oklahoma at the turn of the twentieth century.

29. U.S. Department of the Interior, Bureau of Census, Tenth Census of the United States, 1891, xxxiii.

30. Bogue actually collected more than a thousand specimens but reported only on those of agricultural importance.

31. Morrow, "Report of the Director," 16–17. A survey of extant weeklies in the collection of the Oklahoma Historical Society confirmed Morrow's claims.

32. Hatch Act, *U.S. Statutes at Large*, 24, 400 (1887).

33. Green, *History*.

34. By 1916, Waugh was a prominent professor of landscape agriculture at Massachusetts' agricultural college. He was also an outspoken supporter of progressive reform. As a member of the American Civic Association, he complained to C. J. Blanchard of the Reclamation Service in 1912 that the service's plans for model irrigation towns "were merely repeating the thoroughly bad types of planning which heretofore prevailed in the prairie states." In this at least, Waugh's time in Oklahoma continued to exert some influence in his thinking. Pisani, "Reclamation and Social Engineering," 54.

35. Donald Green relates attempts by the Board of Regents to usurp the authority of the station. Director Neal's demotion was the most blatant example of the political expediency by the territorial legislature. Green, *History*, 30–32.

36. Franklin, *Journey toward Hope*, 68.

37. Ibid., 75.

38. Ibid.

39. Stoltz, *Terrell Texas*, 90–93; Scott, *Reluctant Farmer*, 211–36.

40. Scott, *Reluctant Farmer*, 216–17; Marks, "Early Days."

41. Ibid.

42. Knapp, "Let Us Enlarge the Domain of Industrial Knowledge."

43. Crosby, "Limited Success against Long Odds," 277–88; Crosby, "Struggle for Existence."

44. Crosby, "Limited Success," 281.

45. Dagley, "Negro of Oklahoma," 104.

46. McLendon and Jones, "Soil Survey," 564.

47. Ibid., 556–57.

48. Tolson, "History of Langston."

49. Brown, "Cultural Ecology."

50. Bruner, "Vegetation of Oklahoma," 109, 142.

51. Therrell and Stahle, "Predictive Model."

52. Brown, "Cultural Ecology," 137.

CHAPTER 4
BLAINE COUNTY BEGINNINGS

1. Stout, ed., *Frontier Adventurers*, 56.

2. Goodman and Lawson, *Retracing Major Stephen H. Long's 1820 Expedition*, 104.

3. Marcy, *Adventure on the Red River*.

4. Berthrong, *Southern Cheyennes*, 372–405.

5. Pennington, "Government Policy."

6. Morris et al., *Historical Atlas of Oklahoma,* 51. For more on the Cheyenne and Arapahoe Indians' use of land and their dissatisfaction with cattle leases, see Berthrong, *Cheyenne Arapaho Ordeal,* 91–117; and Berthrong, "Cattlemen."

7. Berthrong, *Southern Cheyennes,* 132.

8. Ibid.

9. Dan Flores, "Bison Ecology," 479.

10. Sherow, "Workings of the Geodialectic."

11. The problem of maintaining large horse herds was even greater for horticulturist/bison hunters like the Pawnee. As early as the 1830s, travelers noted the poor condition of the grasses surrounding their villages for miles as a result of overgrazing. Maintaining horses too far away from their village sites exposed the tribes' horse keepers, women generally, to attack from marauding tribes, inevitably leading to a decline in population for those seminomadic tribes that attempted to combine their former agricultural economy with seasonal harvesting of bison on horseback.

12. Isenberg, "Indians, Whites and Buffalo."

13. Berthrong, "Legacies of the Dawes Act," 337.

14. Lamar, "Creation of Oklahoma."

15. Wenner, *Homeseeker's Guide.* See also Emmons, *Garden in the Grasslands.*

16. Atack, "Farm and Farm-Making Costs Revisited."

17. Davis, "Present Situation of American Agriculture," 66, 68, 73.

18. Irving, *Tour on the Prairies,* 105.

19. Tom Mosely, interviewed by Frank Beneda, n.d., LLP.

20. Dick Rice, interviewed by Frank Beneda, June 21, 1973, LLP.

21. J. R. Cook, interviewed by Frank Beneda, May 29, 1973, LLP.

22. Dick Rice, interviewed by Frank Beneda, June 21, 1973, LLP. In 1911, Rice's entire corn crop burned in the field and his wife begged him to take the family back to Kansas.

23. Mr. Kimball, interviewed by Frank Beneda, April 20, 1973, LLP.

24. Fred Turner, interviewed by Frank Beneda, May 11, 1973, LLP.

25. Solomon Bill, interviewed by Frank Beneda, May 8 197(?), LLP.

26. Ross Nigh, interviewed by Frank Beneda, April 20, 1973, LLP. For a good overview of this practice, see Underhill and Littlefield, "Quail Hunting."

27. Rice, LLP.

28. *Blaine County* (Oklahoma) *Herald,* June 25, 1896.

29. Merle Rinehard et al., *Their Story,* 47.

30. *Watonga* (Oklahoma) *Republican,* December 21, 1899.

31. Emil Schneider, interviewed by Frank Beneda, n.d., LLP. One historian of Oklahoma contends that any town that did not get a railroad line simply ceased to exist after the territorial period. The classic example of this was the three-town competition for a rail line between Frisco, Reno City, and El Reno. "In the three-cornered battle for local and county honors waged by Reno City, Frisco and El Reno, nature favored Reno City, the politicians favored Frisco but the railroads favored El Reno. And the railroads won by a wide margin." McReynolds, *Oklahoma,* 295.

32. U.S. Department of Commerce, Bureau of Census, Twelfth Census of the United States, 1900; Roark, "Oklahoma Territory."

33. U.S. Department of Commerce, Bureau of Census, Twelfth Census of the United States, 1900. Although this seems exaggerated, a microclimatic study

of Watonga in the early 1970s found that the winds around the city were calm less than 2 percent of the time over the course of several years. Hart, ed., "Planning Document for Microclimatic Modification."

34. Thompson, "Green on Red," 14.

35. Nespor, "From Warlance to Plowshares"; Pennington, "Government Policy."

36. Everhart, "History of Blaine County," 58.

37. David D. Smits, "Squaw Men."

38. Nespor, "From Warlance to Plowshares," 43–75.

39. Earl McBride, interviewed by Pen Woods, 1973, LLP.

40. Everhart, "History of Blaine County," 51.

41. Rice, LLP.

42. McBride, LLP.

43. Everhart, "History of Blaine County," 59.

44. Elmer Epler, interviewed by Frank Beneda, June 1, 1973, LLP.

45. Reggio, "Troubled Times," 205.

46. Berthrong, "Legacies of the Dawes Act," 336.

47. Lavinia Jones, interviewed by Frank Beneda, n.d., LLP.

48. Ibid.

49. Lavinia Jones, LLP.

50. Schneider, LLP.

51. Robertson, *Growing Up in the OK State*, 6.

52. Bill, LLP.

53. Nigh, LLP.

54. Ibid.

55. Jones, LLP; Frank Beneda, interview with author, March 11, 1996.

56. Heritage Book Committee, *Their Story*, 110.

57. Malin, *History and Ecology*, 160.

58. Ibid., 157.

59. Some agricultural philosophers were, of course, more than superficially committed to farming as a lifestyle. This was the assumption behind President Theodore Roosevelt's 1906 Commission on Country Life, chaired by Liberty Hyde Bailey of Cornell. Ellsworth, "Theodore Roosevelt's Country Life Commission."

CHAPTER 5

LAND RUSH

1. Weaver, *Prairie Plants*, 146.

2. Gill, "Thompson Benton Ferguson."

3. *Watonga* (Oklahoma) *Republican*, August 29, 1895.

4. *Watonga* (Oklahoma) *Republican*, May 1, 1895.

5. J. R. Cook, interviewed by Frank Beneda, May 29, 1973, LLP.

6. Blaine County Assessment rolls, 1894–99. Governor T. B. Ferguson House and Museum, Watonga, Oklahoma.

7. Emil Schneider, interviewed by Frank Beneda, n.d., LLP.

8. Saarinen, *Perceptions of the Drought Hazard*.

9. Emmons, *Garden in the Grasslands*, 135, 130.

10. Lynn-Sherow, "Beyond Winter Wheat."

11. *Watonga* (Oklahoma) *Republican*, May 1, 1899.

12. Oklahoma State Preservation Office, Oklahoma Century Farms and Ranches Project, 1989–94, Oklahoma Historical Society, Oklahoma City, Oklahoma.

13. The Oklahoma Experiment Station was somewhat late in taking up wheat pasturing; they did not begin any tests of the practice until 1903. By 1906, it could report that "under favorable seasonal conditions the wheat crop frequently makes a very heavy growth and in such cases it has been found advantageous to pasture." Oklahoma Agricultural and Mechanical College, Oklahoma Experiment Station, Seventeenth Annual Report, 1908, 44.

14. Blaine County Assessment rolls, 1894–99. Governor T. B. Ferguson House and Museum, Watonga, Oklahoma. The manuscript census for Blaine indicates a higher percentage of mortgaged farms by 1900 as well.

15. *Watonga* (Oklahoma) *Republican,* January 4, 1900.

16. John Fields to A. C. True, September 19, 1902. Washington, DC, "General Correspondence with the State Experiment Stations and Agricultural Colleges."

17. Ibid.

18. Ellesworth and Baird, "Combine Harvester."

19. Everhart, "History of Blaine County," 31–36. The agricultural statistics compiled by Everhart were taken from the county assessor's rolls. These rolls are no longer extant, except for a few volumes stored at the T. B. Ferguson Home and Museum in Watonga, Oklahoma.

20. *Watonga* (Oklahoma) *Rustler,* June 8, 1893.

21. Fischer, "Custom Wheat Harvesting," 9.

22. Fisher, "Custom Wheat Harvesting"; Ellesworth and Baird, "Combine Harvester"; Isern, *Custom Combining.*

23. Sellars, *Oil, Wheat and Wobblies,* 33.

24. Dick Rice, LLP.

25. Fernandez, "Critical Study."

26. Danbom, *Resisted Revolution,* 47.

27. Marcus, *Agricultural Science,* 13.

28. Ibid.

29. Pisani, "Reclamation and Social Engineering," 46.

30. Fields was a graduate of the Pennsylvania Agricultural College, which instituted some of the first (1869) short courses designed to bring the scientific results of the college to the average farmer in an intensive four-day course of instruction on a particular topic. Short courses, regarded as an early form of agricultural extension, were a hallmark of Fields's tenure as station director in Oklahoma; Scott, *Reluctant Farmer,* 153.

31. Nelson, *Farm and Factory,* 68.

32. This was true nationally as well. See Danbom, *Resisted Revolution,* 39–40.

33. John Fields to A. C. True, September 19, 1902. Washington, DC, "General Correspondence with the State Experiment Stations and Agricultural Colleges."

34. Ibid. In this regard, Fields's focus was more idealistic than other early station directors. See Rosenberg, "Science, Technology."

35. Fields, "Work of the Experiment Station."

36. U.S. Department of Commerce, Twelfth Census of the United States, "Farms June 1, 1900," 22–26.

37. Oklahoma fits in with the general pattern of station work in regard to correspondence. In 1881, another station scientist wrote his wife, "This is the

very busiest time of the year for us. Farmers are making their plans for the coming year and they write to me on all sorts of subjects. . . . I am a public man, and belong to the people, and the people are exacting and relentless in their demands." Rosenberg, "Science, Technology," 5.

38. John Fields to A. C. True, February 27, 1901. Washington, DC, "General Correspondence with the State Experiment Stations and Agricultural Colleges."

39. Oklahoma Agricultural and Mechanical College, Agricultural Experiment Station, *Report for 1913*, Stillwater, Oklahoma, 4.

40. John Fields to A. C. True, November 10, 1902. Washington, DC, "General Correspondence with the State Experiment Stations and Agricultural Colleges."

41. Danbom, *Resisted Revolution*, 33.

42. John Fields to W. E. Robertson, January 14, 1905; Fields to Guy Sproul, January 16, 1905. Agricultural Experiment Station, Director's Office—Correspondence 1892–1920. Special Collections, Edmon Low Library, Stillwater, Oklahoma.

43. Fields, "Work of the Experiment Station," 22.

44. Hayes, *Iron Road to Empire*, 123–24.

45. U.S. Department of Agriculture, *Annual Narrative and Statistical Reports*, 351–96.

46. Board of Directors, Chicago, Rock Island and Pacific Railroad Company, Report of the Railroad Companies, Stockholders' Report, 1910. Newberry Library, Chicago, Illinois.

47. State of Oklahoma, *Oklahoma Annual Almanac*, 2.

48. McNulty, "Tenderfoot Woman."

CHAPTER 6

RAINY MOUNTAIN: KIOWAS AND THE LAND BEFORE ALLOTMENT

1. Marriott, *Ten Grandmothers*, 129. Marriott's study of the Kiowas is a stylized account based on Mooney's *Calendar History* and oral recollections of Kiowas living in 1935–36, including George Hunt, the son of Hunting Horse. Eagle Plume's actual name was Down on the Breast Plume of an Eagle. According to Mooney, he was given the name Joshua at school as a child. His younger sister was named Julia Given by her schoolmasters.

2. White, *Roots of Dependency*, xiv. White makes the argument that it is too easy to ascribe the collapse of a social system or an environment to simple luck or skill. The real tensions come from the relations of people with their environments.

3. In 1839, the Detroit *Daily Advertiser* carried a story about George Catlin and Henry Schoolcraft's work to record Indian life in the West: "The scene is changing with each year, and the past, with respect to the Savages does not recur . . . those who have seen them most during the last few years, have seen them best." Dippie, *Vanishing American*, 47.

4. Hoxie, "Ethnohistory," 612.

5. Albers, "Symbiosis, Merger and War," 99, 101.

6. Lowie, "Societies of the Kiowas."

7. Levy, "After Custer," 13.

8. For the Kiowas today, the distinction between Christian Kiowas or missionary Indians and peyotists is more important than between classes or military societies. Robert Goombi, interview with the author, April 23, 1996.

9. Olsen, "Furnishing a Frontier Outpost," 52–53.

10. Greene, *Silver Horn.*

11. Mooney, *Calendar History.*

12. Marriott, *Saynday's People.*

13. Kracht, "Kiowa Religion," 86.

14. The evolution of the Saynday tales is beautifully illustrated in one of Marriott's last collections, in which the Indian Saynday outsmarts a "white" Saynday and tricks him into giving him his good clothes and fine palomino horse.

15. Cochrane, "Between a Green Tree and a Dry Tree," 20.

16. "The differences among the True Plains tribes can indeed be related to what kind of tribes they were before moving onto the Plains." Oliver, "Ecology and Cultural Continuity," 67.

17. Vestal, *Economic Botany.*

18. Ware, "First Lieutenant Amiel Weeks Whipple," 145.

19. Ibid.

20. Price, "Prairie Policemen," 47.

21. This was an established practice among Indian tribes by the 1870s. In his description of the Sante Fe Trail crossing in 1864, George Vanderwalker remarked that there were only two stops between Council Grove, Kansas, and Fort Lyons, Colorado. All the stage stops and ranches that were there formerly had "been destroyed by our festive red brother." "Reminiscences of George E. Vanderwalker," in Simmons, ed., *On the Sante Fe Trail,* 91.

22. Hawkins, "When George Saunders Made a Bluff Stick."

23. Ibid.

24. Nye, *Carbine and Lance,* 86.

25. Kracht, "Kiowa Religion," 726–34.

26. Robert Stahl, "Farming among the Kiowa," 92.

27. Ibid., 92–93.

28. Ibid., 114–15.

29. Tatum, *Our Red Brothers,* 199–200.

30. Hagan, *Quanah Parker,* 38.

31. Kracht, "Kiowa Religion," 424.

32. Whitewolf, *Jim Whitewolf.*

33. U.S. Secretary of the Interior, "Report on the Investigation of the Kiowa Indian Agency."

34. Pennington, "Government Farming," 115–17.

35. Swett, "Sergeant I-See-O"; Britten, *American Indians in World War I,* 20. Britten writes, "Among the incentives to enlist in the 1890s was thirteen dollars a month for the first year of military service, a clothing allowance, comfortable quarters, three meals a day, medical care and permission to recreate at the post canteen" (20).

36. Doyah, "Chief Ahpeahtone Chronology." Doyah is a great-grandson of Ahpeahtone's and the chronicler of the family history. The spelling of Ahpeahtone's name in this study is the one used by his descendants.

37. U.S. Department of the Interior, Report of the Commissioner of Indian Affairs to the Department of the Interior, 1907 (Washington, DC: Government Printing Office, 1918), 114.

38. Marriott, *Ten Grandmothers,* xi.

CHAPTER 7
OWNERS AND TENANTS: KIOWA FARMING AFTER ALLOTMENT

1. Battey, *Quaker among the Indians*, 134.
2. Missionaries, reformers, and even the anthropologist James Mooney interpreted the Kiowas' independence of thought as indicative of their less civilized status compared with other tribal groups. They were frequently labeled as warlike, stubborn, and ungovernable. See Tatum, *Our Red Brothers*.
3. "Minutes of the Jerome Commission Meeting," National Archives Southwest Region, Fort Worth, Texas.
4. The government survey of the Kiowa, Comanche, and Apache reservation for the purpose of locating a right of way for the railroad caused a major incident in 1871. The Kiowas led a deadly raid into Texas because, as Satanta put it, "You do not listen to my talk. The white people are preparing to build a railroad through our country, which will not be permitted." Satank, Satanta, and Big Tree were sentenced to prison in Texas for the raid. Satank, a member of the Quoitsenko, preferred death to confinement and was shot by the soldiers a mile or so out from Fort Sill on their way to Jacksboro after he produced a knife and sank it into the leg of the wagon driver. Mooney, *Calendar History*, 329.
5. "Minutes of the Jerome Commission Meeting," September 29, 1892, National Archives Southwest Region, Fort Worth, Texas.
6. Ibid.
7. Jenny Saumpty, interviewed by Julia Jordan, June 13, 1967. Doris Duke Oral History Collection, Western History Collection, University of Oklahoma, Norman, Oklahoma, hereafter cited as DDC.
8. "Minutes of the Jerome Commission Meeting," October 5, 1892, National Archives Southwest Region, Fort Worth, Texas.
9. For more detail on the Lone Wolf case, see Clark, *Lone Wolf vs. Hitchcock*.
10. "Minutes of the Jerome Commission Meeting," October 5, 1892, National Archives Southwest Region, Fort Worth, Texas.
11. Ibid.
12. Corwin, *Kiowa Indians*, 150.
13. Clark, *Lone Wolf vs. Hitchcock*.
14. Guy Quoetone, interviewed by Julia Jordan, March 23, 1971, DDC.
15. Marriott, *Ten Grandmothers*, 216–21.
16. Quoetone interview, March 23, 1971, DDC.
17. U.S. Department of Interior, Office of Indian Affairs, "Kiowa Allotment Books," Washington, DC, National Archives.
18. Stahl, "Farming among the Kiowa," 264–65.
19. Haumpy, interview by Letha Barksdale, July 11, 1967, DDC.
20. Corwin, *Kiowa Indians*, 153–54.
21. Ibid., 107.
22. A good summary of the evolution of this ideology into policy can be found in Lewis, *Neither Wolf nor Dog*, 7–21; and Hoxie, *Final Promise*.
23. Barsh, "Progressive Era Bureaucrats."
24. Carlson, *Indians, Bureaucrats and Land*, 170.
25. Hoxie, "Ethnohistory," 606.
26. Hoxie writes of Walter Camp's report in 1920, "The optimistic expectations of the 1880s by now were long forgotten. Assimilation no longer meant full citizenship and equality. Instead, the term now implied that Indians

would remain on the periphery of American society, ruled by outsiders who promised to guide them toward 'civilization.'" Hoxie, *Final Promise,* 241.

27. U.S. Department of Agriculture, *Annual Narrative and Statistical Reports for Canadian County;* italics added.

28. U.S. Department of Agriculture, *Annual Narrative and Statistical Report,* "Report of the Work of the County Agent for Caddo County."

29. Stahl, "Farming among the Kiowa," 202.

30. Leupp, *The Indian and His Problem,* 46.

31. Randlett, "Report on the Kiowa Reservation, 1905," 300.

32. Berthrong, *Cheyenne and Arapaho Ordeal,* 305–6. Berthrong relates how even the territorial courts were often clearly biased against Indians in enforcing the terms of land leases and other financial contracts.

33. Stahl, "Farming among the Kiowa," 207.

34. Angie Debo's groundbreaking work on land fraud in Oklahoma remains the standard for scholars a half century later. See Debo, *Road to Disappearance.*

35. Carlson, *Indians, Bureaucrats and the Land,* 170, 204.

36. Newsom, *Kicking Bird,* 71.

37. Ibid., 73.

38. *Carnegie* (Oklahoma) *Herald,* July 5, 1909.

39. Robert Goombi, interview with the author, April 23, 1996.

40. Krepps, "Strong Medicine Wind."

41. Stahl, "Farming among the Kiowa," 270.

42. Guy Quoetone, "Indian Farming in the Early 1900s," Kiowa File, DDC.

43. Ibid.

CONCLUSION: ORDERING THE ELEMENTS

1. Common term meaning wage worker, a skilled or semi-skilled person who had not previously farmed.

2. Stein and Hill, eds., *Culture of Oklahoma.*

3. Carstenson, "Genesis"; Marcus, *Agricultural Science;* Louise Boyd James, "Jujubes, Grapes and Grass."

4. Worster, "Transformations of the Earth," 1090.

5. Engles, Bidwell, and Mosley, "Invasion."

BIBLIOGRAPHY

MANUSCRIPT COLLECTIONS

Illinois, Chicago. Bolt, Helen Deister, compiler. "Kiowa Agency Mission Schools." Edward Ayer Collection, Newberry Library.
———. Board of Directors, Chicago, Rock Island and Pacific Railroad Company. Report of the Railroad Companies, Stockholders' Report, 1909. Newberry Library.
Kansas, Topeka. "Oklahoma Files." Library, Kansas State Historical Society.
———. Kansas Pacific Railway. "Guide Map of the Great Texas Cattle Trail from Red River Crossing to the Old Reliable Kansas Pacific Railway." 1874. Library, Kansas State Historical Society.
———. James Stell. *Oklahoma Opportunities.* n.p.: n.p., 1901. Library, Kansas State Historical Society.
Oklahoma, Guthrie. "Antelope Township Records." Oklahoma Territorial Museum Archives.
———. Blacks in Guthrie Photograph Collection. Oklahoma Territorial Museum Archives.
———. Guthrie and Logan County Directory. Oklahoma Territorial Museum Archives.
Oklahoma, Langston. "History of Langston." Special Collections, Langston University Library.
Oklahoma, Norman. Doris Duke Oral History Collection. Western History Collection, University of Oklahoma.
Oklahoma, Oklahoma City. Oklahoma State Historic Preservation Office. Oklahoma Centennial Ranches and Farms Project, 1989–94. Oklahoma Historical Society.
———. Indian and Pioneer Papers. Grant Forman Collection. Oklahoma Historical Society Archives.
———. Living Legends Oral History Collection. Tape recordings. Oklahoma Historical Society Library.
Oklahoma, Stillwater. Walter F. Bentley Collection. Special Collections, Edmon Low Library, Oklahoma State University.
———. Oklahoma Agricultural and Mechanical College. Agricultural Experiment Station, Director's Office—Correspondence 1892–1920. Special Collections, Edmon Low Library, Oklahoma State University.
Oklahoma, Watonga. Assessment rolls, 1894–99, and maps. Governor T. B. Ferguson Home and Museum.

Texas, Fort Worth. "Minutes of the Jerome Commission Meeting with the Kiowa, Comanche and Kiowa Apache." September 28–October 17, 1892. RG 75, Kiowa Agency Files. National Archives Southwest Region.

Texas, Terrell. Vertical file. Porter Demonstration Farm. Carnegie Public Library.

Washington, DC. "General Correspondence with the State Experiment Stations and Agricultural Colleges." U.S. Department of Agriculture Records of the Office of Experiment Stations. RG 164. National Archives.

———. "Station Literature 1890–1921." U.S. Department of Agriculture Records of the Office of Experiment Stations. RG 164. National Archives.

———. "Kiowa Allotment Books." U.S. Department of Interior. Office of Indian Affairs. RG 75. National Archives.

———. Manuscript collections, 1911, 4666, 1910-J, 4525, 2531, and Raoul, Weston, and LaBarre Collection, National Anthropological Archives, Museum Support Center, Suitland, MD.

PUBLIC DOCUMENTS

Oklahoma, State. The Oklahoman Annual Almanac and Industrial Record. 1909. Oklahoma City: Oklahoma State Library.

———. *The Oklahoma Annual Almanac and Industrial Record for 1909.* Oklahoma City: Oklahoma Board of Agriculture, 1910.

Oklahoma, Territory. First Biennial Report of the Oklahoma Territorial Board of Agriculture. 1903–4. Guthrie, OK: State Capital Company, 1905.

Oklahoma Territorial Board of Agriculture. "Oklahoma Peaches for Export Trade." First Biennial Report. Guthrie: State Capital Company, 1905.

Oklahoma Agricultural and Mechanical College. *Agricultural Experiment Station Bulletins*, nos. 1–184. Stillwater, OK, 1892–1928.

Oklahoma Agricultural and Mechanical College. Office of Experiment Stations. *Annual Reports.* Stillwater, OK: Oklahoma Experiment Station, 1892–1924.

U.S. Department of Agriculture. *Annual Narrative and Statistical Reports of the Cooperative Agricultural Extension Work Demonstration Program.* Washington, DC: National Archives and Records Service Microfilm Division, 1909–20.

———. *Annual Narrative and Statistical Report.* "Report of the Work of the County Agent for Caddo County." Washington, DC: NARC Microfilm, 1918.

———. *Annual Narrative and Statistical Reports for Canadian County.* Washington, DC: National Archives and Records Service Microfilm Publication, 1916.

———. Secretary of Agriculture. *Annual Reports.* Washington, DC: Government Printing Office, 1889–1920.

U.S. Department of Commerce. Department of Commerce. Bureau of Census. Eleventh Census of the United States. "Schedules Enumerating Union Veterans and Widows of Union Veterans of the Civil War." Oklahoma and Indian Territories, 1890.

———. Bureau of Census. Twelfth Census of the United States, 1900. Schedule of Population. Oklahoma Territory, T623, rolls 1335, 1339, and 1344.

———. Bureau of Census. Twelfth Census of the United States, 1900. "Farms June 1, 1900 of White and Colored Farmers and of Specified Areas Classified by Principal Source of Income" Statistics for Agriculture, Oklahoma.

———. Bureau of Census. Thirteenth Census of the United States, 1910. Statistics for Agriculture, Oklahoma.

———. Bureau of Census. Fourteenth Census of the United States, 1920. Statistics for Agriculture, Oklahoma.

U.S. Department of the Interior. Office of Indian Affairs. Reports of the Commissioner of Indian Affairs to the Department of Interior. Washington, DC: Government Printing Office, 1900–1915.

———. Bureau of the Census. Tenth Census of the United States. Washington, DC, 1891.

U.S. Secretary of the Interior. "Report on the Investigation of the Kiowa Indian Agency," by Francis E. Leupp, Office of Indian Affairs. Annual Report. Washington, DC: Government Printing Office, 1903.

INTERVIEWS

Beneda, Frank. Lifetime resident and farmer in Blaine County, grandson of Frank Strack. Watonga, OK, March 11, 1996.

Bread, Marilyn. Enrolled member of Kiowa tribe, dean's office, Haskell Indian Nations University, Lawrence, KS, February 16, 1996.

Doyah, Ray. Enrolled member of Kiowa tribe. Anadarko, OK, October 10, 1996.

Flasch, Otto. Lifetime resident and farmer in Antelope Township, Logan County, Oklahoma. Langston, OK, October 9, 1996.

Goombi, Robert. Enrolled member of Kiowa tribe and controller at Haskell Indian Nations University. Lawrence, KS, April 23, 1996.

Rice, Darrell. Assistant editor of the *Watonga Republican.* Watonga, OK, March 12, 1995.

NEWSPAPERS

Black (Oklahoma City) *Dispatch,* 1954.
Blaine (Watonga, Oklahoma Territory) *County Herald,* 1894.
Boley (Oklahoma) *Progress,* 1905.
Carnegie (Oklahoma) *Herald,* 1907–14.
Hitchcock (Oklahoma) *Clarion,* 1911–20.
Langston City (Oklahoma) *Herald,* 1892, 1894.
New York Times, 1891–92.
Oklahoma (Guthrie) *Guide,* 1901.
Oklahoma (Guthrie) *Leader,* 1901–16.
Oklahoma (Oklahoma City) *Farm Journal,* 1908.
Topeka (Kansas) *Daily Capital,* 1890.
Watonga (Oklahoma) *Republican,* 1892–1914.

WORKS CITED

Albers, Patricia C. "Intertribal Relationships among Plains Indians." In *The Political Economy of North American Indians*, edited by John H. Moore, 94–132. Norman: University of Oklahoma Press, 1993.

———. "Symbiosis, Merger and War: Contrasting Forms of Intertribal Relationship among Historic Plains Indians." In *The Political Economy of North American Indians*, edited by John H. Moore, 94–132. Norman: University of Oklahoma Press, 1993.

Anderson, Gary Clayton. *The Indian Southwest: Ethnogenesis and Reinvention 1580–1830*. Norman: University of Oklahoma Press, 1999.

Atack, Jeremy. "Farm and Farm-Making Costs Re-Visited." *Agricultural History* 56 (October 1982): 663–76.

Athearn, Robert G. *In Search of Caanan*. Lawrence: University Press of Kansas, 1978.

Babcock, John Gilbert. "The Role of Public Discourse in the Soil Conservation Movement, 1865–1935." PhD diss., University of Michigan, 1985.

Bailey, Joseph Cannon. *Seaman A. Knapp: Schoolmaster of American Agriculture*. New York: Columbia University Press, 1945.

Ball, Durwood. *Army Regulars on the Western Frontier, 1848–1861*. Norman: University of Oklahoma Press, 2001.

Barsh, Lawrence Russell. "Progressive Era Bureaucrats and the Unity of Twentieth Century Indian Policy." *American Indian Quarterly* 15 (Winter 1991): 1–17.

Bartlett, Richard A. *Great Surveys of the American West*. Norman: University of Oklahoma Press, 1962.

Battey, Thomas. *A Quaker among the Indians*. Williamstown, MA: Corner House, 1972.

Benedict, Murray R. *Farm Policies of the United States, 1790–1950*. New York: Octagon Books, 1966.

Bennett, Hugh Hammond. "Adjustment of Agriculture to Its Environment." *Annals of the Association of American Geographers* 33 (December 1943): 163–98.

Bennett, John W. *Of Time and the Enterprise: North American Family Farm Management in a Context of Resource Marginality*. Minneapolis: University of Minnesota Press, 1982.

Berry, Wendell. *The Unsettling of America: Culture and Agriculture*. San Francisco: Sierra Club Books, 1977.

Berthrong, Donald. "Cattlemen on the Cheyenne-Arapaho Reservation, 1883–1885." *Arizona and the West* 13 (Spring 1971): 5–32.

———. *The Cheyenne and Arapaho Ordeal: Reservation and Agency Life in the Indian Territory, 1875–1907*. Norman: University of Oklahoma Press, 1976.

———. "Legacies of the Dawes Act: Bureaucrats and Land Thieves at the Cheyenne-Arapaho Agencies of Oklahoma." *Arizona and the West* 21 (Winter 1979): 335–54.

———. *The Southern Cheyennes*. Norman: University of Oklahoma Press, 1963.

Bethel, Elizabeth Rauh. *Promiseland: A Century of Life in a Negro Community*. Philadelphia: Temple University Press, 1981.

Bittle, William E., and Gilbert Geis. *The Longest Way Home: Chief Alfred C. Sam's Back-to-Africa Movement.* Detroit: Wayne State University Press, 1964.

Blouet, Brian, and Frederick C. Leubke. *The Great Plains: Environment and Culture.* Lincoln: University of Nebraska Press, 1979.

Bonnifield, Paul. *The Dust Bowl.* Albuquerque: University of New Mexico Press, 1979.

Boone, Robert, and Leo McGee. *The Black Rural Landowner: Endangered Species.* Westport, CT: Greenwood Press, 1979.

Boston, Thomas, ed. *A Different Vision: African American Economic Thought.* Vol. 1. London: Routledge, 1997.

Botkin, Daniel B. *Discordant Harmonies: A New Ecology for the Twenty-first Century.* New York: Oxford University Press, 1990.

Briggs, John M., and Alan K. Knapp. "Interannual Variability in Primary Production in Tallgrass Prairie: Climate, Soil Moisture, Topographic Position and Fire as Determinants of Above Ground Biomass." *American Journal of Botany* 82, no. 8 (1995): 1024–30.

Britten, Thomas. *American Indians in World War I: At Home and at War.* Albuquerque: University of New Mexico Press, 1997.

Brown, Brock J. "Cultural Ecology in the Garber-Wellington Cross Timbers in Eastern Cleveland County, Oklahoma." PhD diss., University of Oklahoma, 1992.

Brown, William Elijah. "Economic and Social Changes Taking Place in a Representative Area in the Wheat Belt of Oklahoma as Disclosed by Surveys Made in the Area in 1924 and in 1930." MS thesis, Oklahoma Agricultural and Mechanical College, 1939.

Bruner, W. E. "The Vegetation of Oklahoma." *Ecological Monographs* 1 (April 1931): 99–188.

Calloway, Colin. *Our Hearts Fell to the Ground: Plains Indian Views of How the West Was Lost.* Boston: Bedford Books of St. Martin's Press, 1996.

Carlson, Leonard. *Indians, Bureaucrats and the Land: The Dawes Act and the Decline of Indian Farming.* Westport, CT: Greenwood Press, 1981.

Carney, George. "Historic Resources of Oklahoma's All Black Towns." *Chronicles of Oklahoma* 69 (Summer 1991): 116–33.

Carstenson, Vernon. "The Genesis of an Agricultural Experiment Station." *Agricultural History* 34 (1960): 19–25.

Cayton, Andrew, and Peter Onuf. *The Midwest and the Nation.* Bloomington: University of Indiana Press, 1990.

Chapman, Berlin. "Freedmen and the Oklahoma Lands." *Southwestern Social Science Quarterly* 29 (September 1948).

Chase, Agnes. *First Book of Grasses.* 4th ed. Edited by Nancy P. Dutro. 1922. Reprint, Washington, DC: Smithsonian Institution, 1996.

Clark, Carter Blue. *Lone Wolf vs. Hitchcock: Treaty Rights and Indian Law at the End of the Nineteenth Century.* Lincoln: University of Nebraska Press, 1994.

Cochrane, Candace Porter. "Between a Green Tree and a Dry Tree: Using Photographs to Explore Kiowa and Comanche Perspectives of their History in the Post-Allotment Period." PhD diss., Harvard School of Education, 1995.

Colbert, Thomas Burnell. "A Most Original Thinker: James C. Malin on History and Technology." *Kansas History* 19 (Autumn 1996): 178–87.

Conrad, David E. *The Forgotten Farmers.* Urbana: University of Illinois Press, 1965.

Cornell, Lloyd, Jr. "Cheyenne-Arapaho Land Leases, 1891–1907." MA thesis, University of Oklahoma, 1954.

Corwin, Hugh. *The Kiowa Indians: Their History and Life Stories.* Lawton, OK: Published by the author, 1958.

Cronon, William. "A Place for Stories." *Journal of American History* 78 (March 1992): 1347–76.

Crosby, Alfred. *Ecological Imperialism: The Biological Expansion of Europe 900–1900.* Cambridge: Cambridge University Press, 1986.

Crosby, Earl W. "Limited Success against Long Odds: The Black County Agent." *Agricultural History* 57 (July 1983): 277–88.

———. "The Struggle for Existence: The Institutionalization of the Black County Agent System." *Agricultural History* 60 (Spring 1986): 123–36.

Dagley, Asa Wallace. "The Negro of Oklahoma." MA thesis, University of Oklahoma, 1926.

Danbom, David. *The Resisted Revolution: Urban America and the Industrialization of Agriculture, 1900–1930.* Ames: Iowa State University Press, 1979.

Davis, C. Wood. "The Present Situation of American Agriculture, Its Relation to the World Food Supply, an Estimate of American Production and Requirements and the Apparently Brilliant Future." *American Agriculturalist* (January 1892): 66, 68, 73.

Davis, Ronald L. F. *Good and Faithful Labor: From Slavery to Sharecropping in the Natchez District, 1860–1890.* Westport, CT: Greenwood Press, 1982.

Debo, Angie. *Prairie City.* Tulsa: Council Oak Books, 1944.

———. *The Road to Disappearance.* Norman: University of Oklahoma Press, 1941.

Degler, Carl. *Out of Our Past: The Forces that Shaped Modern America.* 3rd ed. New York: Harper Torch, 1985.

DeMallie, Raymond, and Lynn Kickingbird. *The Treaty of Medicine Lodge, 1867: Between the United States and the Kiowa, Comanche and Apache.* Washington, DC: Institute for the Development of Indian Law, 1976.

Diamond, Irene. *Fertile Ground: Women, Earth and the Limits of Control.* Boston: Beacon Press, 1997.

Dick, Everett. *The Lure of the Land.* Lincoln: University of Nebraska Press, 1970.

Dippie, Brian. *Catlin and His Contemporaries: The Politics of Patronage.* Lincoln: University of Nebraska Press, 1990.

———. *The Vanishing American.* Middletown, CT: Wesleyan University Press, 1980.

Doyah, Ray C. "Chief Ahpeahtone Chronology." N.d. Anadarko, Oklahoma. Manuscript in possession of author.

Dykstra, Robert R. *The Cattle Towns.* Lincoln: University of Nebraska Press, 1968.

Eighty-Niners, The. *Oklahoma, the Beautiful Land.* Oklahoma City: Times-Journal Publishing, 1943.

Elder, Arlene A. "Swamp vs. Plantation: Symbolic Structure in W. E. B. DuBois's *The Quest of the Silver Fleece.*" *Pylon* (Winter 1973): 358–67.

Ellesworth, J. O., and R. W. Baird. "The Combine Harvester on Oklahoma Farms." *Oklahoma Experiment Station Bulletin* 162 (April 1926): n.p.

Ellis, Clyde. *To Change Them Forever: Indian Education at Rainy Mountain Boarding School, 1893–1920.* Norman: University of Oklahoma Press, 1996.

Ellison, J. F. "Traveling the Trail with Good Men was a Pleasure." In *The Trail Drivers of Texas,* edited by George Saunders, 538–40. Nashville, TN: Cokesbury Press, 1925.

Ellison, Ralph. *Shadow and Act.* New York: Random House, 1953.

Ellsworth, George S. "Theodore Roosevelt's Country Life Commission." *Agricultural History* 34 (October 1960): 155–72.

Emmons, David M. *Garden in the Grasslands: Boomer Literature of the Central Great Plains.* Lincoln: University of Nebraska Press, 1971.

Engles, David M., Terrence Bidwell, and Mark Mosley. "Invasion of Oklahoma Rangelands and Forests by Eastern Redcedar and Ashe Juniper." Circular E-947. Stillwater, OK: Oklahoma County Extension Service, Division of Agricultural Services, Indian Resources, Oklahoma State University, 1996.

Etter, Earl. "A Study of Negro Operated Farms in Oklahoma." MS thesis, Panhandle Agricultural and Mechanical College, Goodwell, OK, 1939.

Everhart, Marjorie Bernett. "A History of Blaine County." MA thesis, University of Oklahoma, 1929.

Ferber, Edna. *Cimarron.* Garden City, NJ: Doubleday, Doran, 1930.

Ferleger, Lou. "Uplifting American Agriculture: Experiment Station Scientists and the Office of Experiment Stations in the Early Years after the Hatch Act." *Agricultural History* 64 (Spring 1990): 5–23.

Fernandez, Grace. "A Critical Study of Periodical Reading in Farm Homes." *Oklahoma Agricultural Experiment Station Bulletin* 176 (May 1928): n.p.

Fields, John. "Work of the Experiment Station." Address before the Oklahoma Agricultural, Horticultural and Irrigation Association, Oklahoma City, Oklahoma, August 19, 1899. Stillwater, OK: Oklahoma Agricultural and Mechanical College, Agricultural Experiment Station Report, 1899–1900.

Fischer, John Louis. "Custom Wheat Harvesting in the Economy of Western Oklahoma." MS thesis, Oklahoma Agricultural and Mechanical College, 1949.

Fletcher, A. C., and F. LaFlesche. *The Omaha Tribe.* Lincoln: University of Nebraska Press, 1972.

Flores, Dan. "Bison Ecology and Bison Economy." *Journal of American History* (September 1991): 465–85.

———. *The Natural West: Environmental History in the Great Plains and Rocky Mountains.* Norman: University of Oklahoma Press, 2001.

Fogelson, Ray. "The History of Events and Non-Events." *Ethnohistory* 36 (Spring 1989): 133–47.

Fowler, Arlen L. *The Black Infantry in the West, 1869–1891.* Westport, CT: Greenwood Press, 1971.

Fox, Richard Wightman, and T. J. Jackson Lears, eds. *The Power of Culture.* Chicago: University of Chicago Press, 1993.

Francaviglia, Richard V. *The Cast Iron Forest.* Austin: University of Texas Press, 1998.

Franklin, Jimmie Lewis. *Journey toward Hope: A History of Blacks in Oklahoma.* Norman: University of Oklahoma Press, 1982.

Franklin, John Hope, and Alfred A. Moss Jr. *From Slavery to Freedom.* 7th ed. New York: Knopf, 1994.

Frederickson, George M. *The Black Image in the White Mind: The Debate on Afro-American Character and Destiny, 1817–1914.* New York: Harper and Row, 1971.

Garretson, M. S. *The American Bison: The Story of Its Extermination as a Wild Species and Its Restoration under Federal Protection.* New York: New York Zoological Society, 1938.

Gates, Paul Wallace. *History of Public Land Law Development.* New York: Arno Press, 1979.

Geertz, Clifford. *The Interpretation of Cultures.* New York: Basic Books, 1973.

Gibson, Darrell. "Oklahoma: Land of the Drifter." *Chronicles of Oklahoma* 69 (Summer 1986): 5–13.

Gill, Jerry L. "Thompson Benton Ferguson, 1901–1906." *Chronicles of Oklahoma* (Spring 1975): 109–27.

Goodman, George, and Cheryl Lawson. *Retracing Major Stephen H. Long's 1820 Expedition: The Itinerary and Botany.* Norman: University of Oklahoma Press, 1995.

Gould, Charles N. "Oklahoma—An Example of Arrested Development." *Economic Geography* 2 (July 1926): 426–30.

Green, Donald E. *A History of Oklahoma State University Division of Agriculture.* Stillwater: Oklahoma State University Press, 1990.

———. *Rural Oklahoma.* Oklahoma City: Oklahoma Historical Society, 1977.

Greene, Candace S. *Silver Horn: Master Illustrator of the Kiowas.* Norman: University of Oklahoma Press, 2002.

Gregg, Josiah. *The Commerce of the Prairies.* Lincoln: University of Nebraska Press, 1967.

Grossman, James. *Land of Hope: Chicago, Black Southerners and the Great Migration.* Chicago: University of Chicago Press, 1989.

Grubbs, Donald H. *Cry from the Cotton: The Southern Tenant Farmers' Union and the New Deal.* Chapel Hill: University of North Carolina Press, 1971.

Gutman, Herbert T. *The Black Family in Slavery and Freedom, 1750–1925.* New York: Pantheon Books, 1976.

Hagan, William T. *Quanah Parker, Comanche Chief.* Norman: University of Oklahoma Press, 1993.

Hahn, Steven, and Jonathan Prude, eds. *The Countryside in the Age of Capitalist Transformation.* Chapel Hill: University of North Carolina Press, 1985.

Ham, George, and Robin Higham. *The Rise of the Wheat State: A History of Kansas Agriculture 1861–1986.* Manhattan: Kansas State University Press, 1987.

Hamilton, Kenneth Marvin. *Black Towns and Profit: Promotion and Development in the Trans-Appalachian West, 1877–1915.* Urbana: University of Illinois Press, 1991.

Hardwick, Jeffery. "Homesteads and Bungalows: African American Architecture in Langston, Oklahoma." MA thesis, University of Delaware, 1994.

Hart, Hoyt E., et al. "Planning Document for Microclimatic Modification." In *The Planning Document for Watonga Oklahoma.* Norman: Oklahoma Center of Regional and City Planning, University of Oklahoma, 1975.

Hawkins, T. T. "When George Saunders Made a Bluff Stick." In *The Trail Drivers of Texas,* edited by George Saunders, 391–96. Nashville, TN: Cokesbury Press, 1925.

Hayes, William Edward. *Iron Road to Empire: The History of 100 Years of the Progress and Achievements of the Rock Island Lines.* Chicago: Simmons-Boardman, 1953.

Hays, Samuel P. *Conservation and the Gospel of Efficiency.* New York: Atheneum Press, 1969.

Heritage Book Committee. *Their Story: A Pioneer Days Album of the Blaine County Area.* Watonga: Heritage Book Committee, 1977.

Hill, Mozell C. "The All-Negro Communities of Oklahoma: The National History of a Social Movement." *Social Science Quarterly* 49 (July 1946): 254–68.

———. "The All Negro Society in Oklahoma." PhD diss., University of Chicago, 1946.

Hilliard, Sam Bowers. *Hog Meat and Hoe Cake.* Carbondale: Southern Illinois Press, 1972.

Hofsommer, Donovan, ed. *Railroads in Oklahoma.* Oklahoma City: Oklahoma Historical Society, 1977.

Hoig, Stan. *The Oklahoma Land Rush of 1889.* Oklahoma City: Oklahoma Historical Society, 1989.

———. *Tribal Wars on the Southern Plains.* Norman: University of Oklahoma Press, 1993.

Holcomb, Gordon Victor. "Some Aspects of Land Utilization among Different Ownership Groups in Osage County." MS thesis, Oklahoma Agricultural and Mechanical College, 1940.

Holder, Preston. *The Hoe and the Horse on the Plains.* Lincoln: University of Nebraska Press, 1970.

Holmes, Helen Freudenberger, ed. *Logan County History.* Topeka: Jostens/American Yearbook, 1979.

Hornaday, William T. *The Extermination of the American Bison, with a Sketch of Its Discovery and Life History.* In United States Natural Museum, Annual Report, 1887. Washington, DC: Government Printing Office, 1889.

Hoxie, Frederick. "Ethnohistory for a Tribal World." *Ethnohistory* 44 (Fall 1997): 595–615.

———. *A Final Promise.* Cambridge: Cambridge University Press, 1984.

Hurt, R. Douglas. *Agricultural Technology in the Twentieth Century.* Manhattan, KS: Sunflower University Press, 1991.

———. *Indian Agriculture in America: Pre-History to the Present.* Lawrence: University Press of Kansas, 1987.

Irving, Washington. *A Tour on the Prairies.* Norman: University of Oklahoma Press, 1985.

Isenberg, Andrew. *The Destruction of the Bison: An Environmental History 1750–1920.* New York: Cambridge University Press, 2000.

———. "Indians, Whites and Buffalo: An Ecological History of the Great Plains, 1750–1900." PhD diss., Northwestern University, 1993.

Isern, Thomas D. *Bull Threshers and Bindlestiffs: Harvesting and Threshing on the North American Plains.* Lawrence: University Press of Kansas, 1990.

———. *Custom Combining on the Great Plains.* Norman: University of Oklahoma Press, 1981.

Iverson, Peter. *When Indians Became Cowboys.* Norman: University of Oklahoma Press, 1994.

James, Louise Boyd. "Jujubes, Grapes and Grass: The USDA Research Station at Woodward, 1913–1987." *Chronicles of Oklahoma* 65 (Winter 1988): 354–79.

Jensen, Joan. *Promise to the Land: Essays on Rural Women.* Albuquerque: University of New Mexico Press, 1991.

Jones, Katherine Butler. "They Call It Timbuctu." *Orion* 17 (Winter 1998): 27–33.

Jones, Thomas Charles. "George Champlin Sibley: The Prairie Puritan." PhD diss., University of Missouri, 1969.

Kavanaugh, Thomas. *Comanche Political History: An Ethnohistorical Perspective.* Lincoln: University of Nebraska Press, 1996.

Kindscher, Kelly. *Edible Wild Plants of the Prairie: An Ethnobotanical Guide.* Lawrence: University Press of Kansas, 1987.

Knapp, A. K., J. M. Briggs, D. C. Hartnett, and S. L. Collins, eds. *Grassland Dynamics: Long-Term Ecological Research in Tallgrass Prairie.* Oxford: Oxford University Press, 1998.

Knapp, Seaman. "Let Us Enlarge the Domain of Industrial Knowledge." 1894. Manuscript, Bentley Collection, Special Collections, Edmon Low Library, Stillwater, Oklahoma.

Knopf, Fritz L., and Fred Samson, eds. *Ecology and Conservation of Great Plains Vertebrates.* New York: Springer-Verlag, 1977.

Kolodny, Annette. *The Land Before Her: Fantasy and Experience of the American Frontiers, 1630–1860.* Chapel Hill: North Carolina Press, 1984.

Kracht, Benjamin. "Kiowa Religion: An Ethnohistorical Analysis of Ritual Symbolism." PhD diss., Southern Methodist University, 1989.

Krech, Shepard, III. *The Ecological Indian.* New York: Norton, 1999.

Krepps, Ethel C. "A Strong Medicine Wind." *True West* 26 (March–April 1979): 7–42.

Kulick, Don. *Socialization, Self and Syncretism in a Papua New Guinea Village.* London: Cambridge, 1997.

Kulikoff, Alan. *The Agrarian Origins of American Capitalism.* Charlottesville: University of Virginia, 1992.

———. "The Transition to Capitalism in Rural America." *William and Mary Quarterly* 46, no. 1 (1989): 120–44.

Lamar, Howard. "The Creation of Oklahoma: New Meanings for the Oklahoma Land Run." In *The Culture of Oklahoma,* edited by Howard F. Stein and Robert F. Hill, 44–46. Norman: University of Oklahoma Press, 1993.

Lawson, Merlin Paul. *The Climate of the Great American Desert.* Lincoln: University of Nebraska Press, 1974.

Leckie, William H. *The Buffalo Soldiers: A Narrative of the Negro Cavalry in the West.* Norman: University of Oklahoma Press, 1981.

Lemaistre, Elise Eugenia. "In Search of a Garden: African-Americans and the Land in Piedmont Georgia." Master of Landscape Architecture thesis, University of Georgia, 1981.

Leubke, Frederick, ed. *Ethnicity on the Great Plains.* Lincoln: University of Nebraska Press, 1978.

Leupp, Francis. *The Indian and His Problem.* New York: Scribner, 1910.

Levy, Jerrold. "After Custer: Kiowa Political and Social Organization from the Reservation Period to the Present." PhD diss., University of Chicago, 1959.

Lewis, David Rich. *Neither Wolf nor Dog: American Indians, Environment and Agrarian Change.* New York: Oxford University Press, 1994.

Licht, Daniel. *Ecology and Economy of the Great Plains.* Lincoln: University of Nebraska Press, 1997.

Liebhardt, Barbara. "Interpretation and Causal Analysis: Theories in Environmental History." *Environmental Review* 12 (Spring 1988): 23–36.

Littlefield, Alice, and Martha C. Knack, eds. *Native Americans and Wage Labor: Ethnohistorical Perspectives.* Norman: University of Oklahoma Press, 1996.

Littlefield, Daniel F., Jr., and Lonnie E. Underhill. "Black Dreams and 'Free' Homes: The Oklahoma Territory, 1891–1894." *Phylon* (Winter 1973): 342–57.

Lott, Dale E. *American Bison: A Natural History.* Berkeley: University of California Press, 2002.

Lowie, Robert. "Societies of the Kiowas." *Anthropological Papers of the American Museum of Natural History* 11 (1916): 839–51.

Lynn-Sherow, Bonnie. "Beyond Winter Wheat: The USDA Extension Service and Kansas Wheat Production in the Twentieth Century." *Kansas History* 23 (Spring–Summer 2000): 100–111.

Mahnken, Norbert R. "Economic Beginnings: Making a Living in the Cherokee Outlet." *Chronicles of Oklahoma* 71 (Summer 1993): 203–23.

Malin, James C. *History and Ecology: Studies of the Grasslands.* Edited by Robert P. Swierenga. Lincoln: University of Nebraska Press, 1984.

———. *Winter Wheat in the Golden Belt of Kansas: A Study in Adaption to Subhumid Geographical Environment.* Lawrence: University of Kansas Press, 1944.

Marcus, Alan I. *Agricultural Science and the Quest for Legitimacy.* Ames: University of Iowa Press, 1985.

Marcy, Randolph B. *Adventure on the Red River.* Edited by Grant Forman. Norman: University of Oklahoma Press, 1968.

Marks, Tom. "Early Days of Extension Work, 1928." Manuscript, Bentley Collection, Special Collections, Edmon Low Library, Oklahoma State University, Stillwater, Oklahoma.

Marriott, Alice. *Saynday's People.* Lincoln: University of Nebraska Press, 1963.

———. *The Ten Grandmothers: Epic of the Kiowas.* Norman: University of Oklahoma Press, 1945.

McConnell, Grant. *The Decline of Agrarian Democracy.* Berkeley: University of California Press, 1953.

McDonnell, Janet A. *The Dispossession of the American Indian 1887–1925.* Bloomington: Indiana University Press, 1991.

McEvoy, Arthur F. *The Fisherman's Problem: Ecology and Law in the California Fisheries.* Cambridge: Cambridge University Press, 1986.

McLendon, W. E., and Grove B. Jones. "Soil Survey of Oklahoma County, Oklahoma, 1906." Washington, DC: U.S. Department of Interior, Department of Agriculture, Bureau of Soils, 1906.

McNulty, Irene Beatty. "Tenderfoot Woman, Pioneer Horse." Archives, Oklahoma Historical Society.

McReynolds, Edwin E. *Oklahoma: A History of the Sooner State.* 5th ed. Norman: University of Oklahoma Press, 1964.

Meagher, M. "Evaluation of Boundary Control for Bison of Yellowstone National Park." *Wildlife Society Bulletin* 17 (1989): 15–19.

Meier, August, and Elliot Rudwick. *From Plantation to Ghetto.* New York: Hill and Wang, 1976.

Merchant, Carolyn. *Ecological Revolutions: Nature, Gender and Science in New England.* Chapel Hill: University of North Carolina Press, 1989.

Miner, Craig. *The Corporation and the Indian: Tribal Sovereignty and Industrial Civilization in Indian Territory, 1865–1907.* Columbia: University of Missouri Press, 1976.

Mooney, James. *Calendar History of the Kiowa Indians.* Seventeenth Annual Report of the Bureau of American Ethnology 1895–96. 1898. Reprint, Washington, DC: Smithsonian Institution Press, 1979.

Moore, John H., ed. *The Political Economy of North American Indians.* Norman: University of Oklahoma Press, 1993.

Morgan, Anne Hodges, and Rennard Strickland, eds. *Oklahoma Memories.* Norman: University of Oklahoma Press, 1981.

Morris, John W., ed. *Geography of Oklahoma.* Oklahoma City: Oklahoma Historical Society, 1977.

Morris, John W., et al. *Historical Atlas of Oklahoma.* Norman: University of Oklahoma Press, 1986.

Morris, Rosamond. *Oklahoma: Yesterday–Today–Tomorrow.* Guthrie, OK: Cooperative Publishing, 1930.

Morrow, G. "Report of the Director." *Agricultural Experiment Station Report 1899–1900.* Stillwater, OK: Oklahoma Agricultural and Mechanical College, 1900.

Nelson, Daniel. *Farm and Factory: Workers in the Midwest 1880–1990.* Bloomington: Indiana University Press, 1995.

Nespor, Robert P. "From Warlance to Plowshares: The Cheyenne Dog Soldiers as Farmers 1879–1930." *Chronicles of Oklahoma* 65 (Spring 1987): 42–75.

Newsom, D. E. *Kicking Bird and the Birth of Oklahoma: A Biography of Milton W. Reynolds.* Perkins, OK: Evans, 1983.

Norall, Frank. *Bourgmont, Explorer of the Missouri, 1698–1725.* Lincoln: University of Nebraska Press, 1988.

Nye, Wilber S. *Carbine and Lance: The Story of Old Fort Sill.* Norman: University of Oklahoma Press, 1937.

Oliver, Symmes. "Ecology and Cultural Continuity as Contributing Factors in the Social Organization of the Plains Indians." *University of California Publications in American Archeology and Ethnology* 48, no. 1 (1962): 1–90.

Olsen, Sarah M. "Furnishing a Frontier Outpost." In *Bents Old Fort*, 139–68. Denver: State Historical Society of Colorado, 1979.

Opie, John. *The Law of the Land: Two Hundred Years of American Farmland Policy.* Lincoln: University of Nebraska Press, 1987.

Oubre, Claude F. *Forty Acres and a Mule: The Freedman's Bureau and Black Land Ownership.* Baton Rouge: Louisiana State University Press, 1978.

Outwater, Alice. *Water: A Natural History.* New York: Basic Books, 1996.

Page, Brian, and Richard Walker. "From Settlement to Fordism: The Agro-Industrial Revolution in the American Midwest." *Economic Geography* 67 (October 1991): 281–315.

Painter, Nell. *Exodusters: Black Migration to Kansas after Reconstruction.* New York: Knopf, 1977.

Pennington, William. "Government Farming on the Kiowa Reservation, 1869–1901." PhD diss., University of Oklahoma, 1972.

———. "Government Policy and Indian Farming on the Cheyenne and Arapaho Reservation: 1869–1880." *Chronicles of Oklahoma* 62, no. 2 (Summer 1979): 170–89.

Perdue, Theda, and Michael Green, eds. *The Cherokee Removal.* New York: St. Martin's Press, 1995.

Petterson, Zella. *Langston University: A History.* Norman: University of Oklahoma Press, 1979.

Phillips, John Bartell. "Sources of Oklahoma Agricultural History." MLS thesis, University of Oklahoma, 1973.

Pisani, Donald. "Reclamation and Social Engineering in the Progressive Era." *Agricultural History* 57 (January 1983): 46–63.

Price, Byron. "Prairie Policemen: The United States Army's Relationship to the Cattle Industry in Indian Territory, 1866–1893." In *Ranch and Range in Oklahoma,* edited by Jimmy M. Skaggs, 53–55. Oklahoma City: Oklahoma Historical Society, 1978.

Prucha, Francis Paul. *The Great Father: The United States Government and the American Indians.* Vol. 2. Lincoln: University of Nebraska Press, 1984.

Rader, Brian F. *The Political Outsiders: Blacks and Indians in a Rural Oklahoma County.* San Francisco: R and E Associates, 1977.

Randlett, William. "Report on the Kiowa Reservation, 1905." In *Annual Reports of the Commissioner of Indian Affairs,* 300. Washington, DC: Government Printing Office, 1906.

Ransom, Roger, and Richard Sutch. "The Ex-Slave in the Post-Bellum South: A Study of the Economic Impact of Racism in a Market Environment." *Journal of Economic History* 33 (March 1973): 131–48.

———. *One Kind of Freedom: The Economic Consequences of Freedom.* Cambridge: Cambridge University Press, 1977.

Reggio, Michael G. "Troubled Times: Homesteading in Shortgrass Country, 1892–1900." *Chronicles of Oklahoma* 55 (Summer 1979): 196–211.

Ridings, Sam P. *The Chisholm Trail: A History of the World's Greatest Cattle Trail.* Guthrie, OK: Cooperative Publishing, 1936.

Rikoon, J. Sanford. *Threshing in the Midwest, 1820–1940.* Bloomington: Indiana University Press, 1988.

Rinehard, Merle, et al. *Their Story: A Pioneer Days Album of the Blaine County Area.* Watonga, OK: Heritage Book Committee, 1977.

Roark, Michael Owen. "Oklahoma Territory: Frontier Development, Migration and Culture Areas." PhD diss., Syracuse University, 1979.

Robertson, Ken. *Growing Up in the OK State.* Published by the author, 1996.

Robinson, Elwyn B. *History of North Dakota.* Lincoln: University of Nebraska Press, 1966.

Rodgers, Lawrence. *Canaan Bound: The African American Great Migration Novel.* Urbana: University of Illinois Press, 1997.

Roe, Frank. *North American Buffalo.* Toronto: University of Toronto Press, 1970.

Rome, Adam Ward. "American Farmers as Entrepreneurs, 1870–1900." *Agricultural History* 56 (January 1982): 37–49.

Rosenberg, Charles E. "Science, Technology, and Economic Growth: The Case of the Agricultural Experiment Station Scientist." *Agricultural History* 45 (January 1971): 1–20.

Rosengarten, Theodore, ed. *All God's Dangers: The Life of Nate Shaw.* New York: Knopf, 1974.

Ross, Earle D. "Retardation in Farm Technology before the Power Age." *Agricultural History* 29 (Winter 1955): 11–27.

Rubright, Lynnell. "Development of Farming Systems in Western Kansas, 1885–1915." PhD diss., University of Wisconsin-Madison, 1977.

Saarinen, Thomas F. *Perceptions of the Drought Hazard on the Great Plains.* Chicago: University of Chicago Press, 1966.

Sahlins, Marshall. *Islands of History.* Chicago: University of Chicago Press, 1985.

Sameth, Sigmund. "Creek Freedmen." MA thesis, University of Oklahoma, 1940.

Saunders, George, ed. *The Trail Drivers of Texas.* Nashville, TN: Cokesbury Press, 1952.

Schlebecker, John T. "Grasshoppers in American Agricultural History." *Agricultural History* 27 (July 1953): 77–84.

Schlesier, Karl H., ed. *Plains Indians A.D. 500–1500.* Norman: University of Oklahoma Press, 1994.

Scott, Roy Vernon. *Railroad Development Programs in the 20th Century.* Ames: University of Iowa Press, 1985.

———. *The Reluctant Farmer: The Rise of Agricultural Extension to 1914.* Urbana: University of Illinois Press, 1970.

Seton, Ernest Thompson. *Lives of Game Animals.* 4 vols. Garden City, NJ: Doubleday, Doran, 1929.

Sellars, Nigel. *Oil, Wheat and Wobblies: The Industrial Workers of the World in Oklahoma, 1905–1930.* Norman: University of Oklahoma Press, 1998.

Shannon, Fred. *The Farmers' Last Frontier.* New York: Farrar and Reinhart, 1945.

Shaw, J. H., and T. S. Carter. "Bison Movement in Relation to Fire and Seasonality." *Wildlife Society Bulletin* 18 (1990): 426–30.

Shaw, James H., and Martin Lee. "Ecological Interpretation of Historical Accounts of Bison and Fire on the Southern Plains with Emphasis on Tallgrass Prairie: Final Report to the Nature Conservancy of Oklahoma." Stillwater, OK, 1997. Photocopy.

Shepard, R. Bruce. *Deemed Unsuitable: Blacks from Oklahoma Move to the Canadian Prairies in Search of Equality in the Early 20th Century Only to Find Racism in Their New Home.* Toronto: Umbrella Press, 1997.

Sherow, James E. "Workings of the Geodialectic: High Plains Indians and Their Horses in the Region of the Arkansas River Valley, 1800–1870." *Environmental History Review* 16 (Summer 1992): 61–84.

Simmons, Charles A. "A Comparative Look at Four Black Newspapers and their Editorial Philosophies during the Eras of the Northern Migration and World War I, World War II and the Civil Rights Movement." PhD diss., Oklahoma State University, 1995.

Simmons, Marc, ed., *On the Sante Fe Trail.* Lawrence: University Press of Kansas, 1986.

Skaggs, Jimmy M. *The Cattle Trailing Industry: Between Supply and Demand, 1866–1890.* Norman: University of Oklahoma Press, 1985.

Skaggs, Jimmy M., ed. *Ranch and Range in Oklahoma.* Oklahoma City: Oklahoma Historical Society, 1978.

Slotkin, Richard. *Regeneration through Violence.* Middletown, CT: Wesleyan University Press, 1973.

Smits, David D. "'Squaw Men,' 'Half Breeds' and Amalgamators: Late Nineteenth-Century Anglo-American Attitudes toward Indian-White Race-Mixing." *American Indian Culture and Research Journal* 15, no. 3 (1991): 29–61.

Southern Society for the Promotion of the Study of Race Conditions and Problems in the South. *Race Problems of the South.* Proceedings of a conference held in Montgomery, AL, May 8–10, 1900. New York: Negro Universities Press, 1969.

Stahl, Robert John. "Farming among the Kiowa, Comanche, Kiowa Apache and Wichita." PhD diss., University of Oklahoma, 1978.

Stahle, D. W., and J. G. Hehr. "Dendroclimatic Relationships of Post Oak across a Precipitation Gradient in the South-Central United States." *Annals of the Association of American Geographers* 74 (1984): 561–73.

Stein, Howard F., and Robert F. Hill, eds. *The Culture of Oklahoma*. Norman: University of Oklahoma Press, 1993.

Stewart, Mart A. *What Nature Suffers to Groe: Life, Labor and Landscape on the Georgia Coast, 1680–1920*. Athens: University of Georgia Press, 1996.

Stewart, Omer C. *Forgotten Fires: Native Americans and the Transient Wilderness*. Edited by Henry Lewis and M. Kat Anderson. Norman: University of Oklahoma Press, 2002.

Stoltz, Jack. *Terrell Texas, 1873–1973*. San Antonio, TX: Naylor, 1974.

Stout, Joseph A., Jr., ed. *Frontier Adventures: American Exploration in Oklahoma*. Oklahoma City: Oklahoma Historical Society, 1976.

Stuart, Paul. *Nations within a Nation*. New York: Greenwood Press, 1987.

Stubbs, J. C. "The Relations of the Railroads to the Trans-Mississippi Territory." Speech given in San Francisco in 1908. Library, Kansas State Historical Society.

Surface, Frank M. *The Grain Trade During the World War*. New York: Macmillan, 1928.

Swett, Morris. "Sergeant I-See-O, Kiowa Indian Scout." *Chronicles of Oklahoma* 13 (Spring 1935): 346–54.

Tatum, Lawrie. *Our Red Brothers*. 1899. Reprint, Lincoln: University of Nebraska Press, 1970.

Teall, Kay M. *Black History in Oklahoma—A Resource Book*. Oklahoma City: Oklahoma Public School, 1971.

Thelen, David. *Paths of Resistance*. New York: Oxford University Press, 1986.

Therrell, M. D., and D. W. Stahle. "A Predictive Model to Locate Ancient Forests in the Cross Timbers of Osage County Oklahoma." *Journal of Biogeography* 25 (1998): 847–54.

Thompson, Gary. "Changing Transportation Systems of Oklahoma." In *Geography of Oklahoma*, edited by John W. Morris, 112–24. Oklahoma City: Oklahoma Historical Society, 1977.

———. "Green on Red: Oklahoma Landscapes." In *The Culture of Oklahoma*, edited by Howard Stein and Robert Hill, 3–28. Norman: University of Oklahoma Press, 1993.

Thompson, John. *Closing the Frontier: Radical Response in Oklahoma 1889–1923*. Norman: University of Oklahoma Press, 1986.

Tobey, Ronald. *Saving the Prairies: The Life Cycle of the Founding of the American School of Plant Ecology 1895–1955*. Berkeley: University of California Press, 1981.

Tolson, Arthur Lincoln. *The Black Oklahomans: A History, 1541–1972*. New Orleans: Edwards Printing, 1966.

———. "A History of Langston, Oklahoma, 1890–1950." MA thesis, Oklahoma Agricultural and Mechanical College, 1952.

———. "The Negro in Oklahoma Territory, 1889–1907." PhD diss., University of Oklahoma, 1966.

Trachtenberg, Alan. *The Incorporation of America*. New York: Hill and Wang, 1982.

Travis, Paul Dee. "Charlatans, Sharpers, and Climatology: The Symbolism and Mythology of Late Nineteenth Expansionism in Kansas." PhD diss., University of Oklahoma, 1975.
True, Alfred Charles. *A History of Agricultural Extension Work in the United States 1785–1923.* New York: Arno Press, 1969.
Underhill, Lonnie F., and Daniel F. Littlefield Jr. "Quail Hunting in Early Oklahoma." *Chronicles of Oklahoma* 49 (Autumn 1971): 315–33.
Vehik, Susan. "Cultural Continuity and Discontinuity in the Southern Prairies and Crosstimbers." In *Plains Indians A.D. 500–1500,* edited by Karl H. Schlesier, 239–63. Norman: University of Oklahoma Press, 1994.
Vestal, Paul Anthony. *The Economic Botany of the Kiowa Indians.* New York: AMS Press, 1981.
Wali, Mohan E., ed. *Prairie: A Multiple View.* Bismarck: University of North Dakota Press, 1974.
Walker, Alice. *In Search of Our Mothers' Gardens.* New York: Harcourt, Brace, Jovanovich, 1983.
Walther, Thomas Robert. "Social and Economic Mobility in Rural Kansas, 1860–1905." PhD diss., University of Oklahoma, 1971.
Ware, James. "First Lieutenant Amiel Weeks Whipple, 1853." In *Frontier Adventures: American Exploration in Oklahoma,* edited by Joseph A. Stout Jr., 138–50. Oklahoma City: Oklahoma Historical Society, 1976.
Waugh, Frank A. *The Agricultural College.* New York: Orange Judd, 1916.
Weaver, J. E. *Prairie Plants and Their Environment.* Lincoln: University of Nebraska Press, 1968.
Weaver, J. E., A. F. Thiel, R. J. Pool, and F. C. Jean. "Ecological Studies in the Tension Zones between Prairie and Woodland." *Botanical Survey of Nebraska* 1 (1917): 1–60; 2 (1918): 1–47.
Webb, Walter Prescott. *The Great Plains.* Boston: Ginn Publishing, 1931.
Wenner, Fred. *The Homeseeker's Guide: Eighteen Million Acres of Indian Land for White Settlers.* Guthrie, OK: n.p., 1890. Library, Kansas State Historical Society.
Wetsell, Dick. *Pasture and Range Plants.* Fort Hays: Fort Hays State University, 1989.
White, Richard. *It's Your Misfortune and None of My Own: A New History of the American West.* Norman: University of Oklahoma Press, 1991.
———. *Roots of Dependency.* Lincoln: University of Nebraska Press, 1983.
Whitewolf, Jim. *Jim Whitewolf: The Life of a Kiowa Apache Indian.* Edited by Charles S. Brant. New York: Dover, 1969.
Wickett, Murray. "Contested Territory: Whites, Native Americans and African Americans in Oklahoma 1865–1907." PhD diss., University of Toronto, 1996.
Wiebe, Robert. *Search for Order.* New York: Hill and Wang, 1967.
Williams, J., and P. Diebel. "The Economic Value of Prairie." In *Prairie Conservation: Preserving North America's Most Endangered Ecosystem.* Edited by F. B. Samson and F. L. Knopf. Covelo, CA: Island Press, 1996.
Williamson, Joel. *The Crucible of Race: Black-White Relations in the American South since Emancipation.* New York: Oxford University Press, 1984.
Wishart, David. *The Fur Trade of the American West, 1807–1840.* Lincoln: University of Nebraska Press, 1979.
Woodward, C. Vann. *The Origins of the New South.* Baton Rouge: Louisiana State University Press, 1971.

Works Projects Administration. *The WPA Guide to 1930s Oklahoma.* Lawrence: University Press of Kansas, 1986.

Worster, Donald. *Dust Bowl.* New York: Oxford University Press, 1979.

———. *The Ends of the Earth.* Cambridge: Cambridge University Press, 1988.

———. *Nature's Economy.* 1977. Reprint, Cambridge: Cambridge University Press, 1985.

———. *An Unsettled Country.* Albuquerque: University of New Mexico Press, 1994.

———. "Transformations of the Earth: Toward an Agroecological Perspective in History." *Journal of American History* 76, no. 4 (March 1990): 1087–1106.

INDEX

Abert, J. W., 71
Agricultural Journals, 101
  American Agriculturalist, 70
  *Oklahoma Annual Almanac and
    Industrial Record*, 104
  Oklahoma Farm Journal, 56
Anadarko, Okla., 7, 113, 118, 120, 125,
  129
Antelope Township, 37, 52–54
Apeahtone, 122, 123, 129
Army. *See* United States Army
Aughey, Samuel, 86, 87

Battey, Thomas, 118, 124
Beneda, Frank, viii, 81
Bentley, William, 58, 103–4
Berthrong, Donald, 66
Bethel, Elizabeth Raun, 42
Bison, 5–6, 11–12, 17, 72, 144
Black Kettle, 3
Black newspapers
  Black Dispatch, 39
  Boley Progress, 41
  Langston City Herald, 35, 37, 40, 42
  Oklahoma Guide, 37
  Western Age, 51
Black settlers, 30–64, 78, 135, 143
  "Colored" Immigration Bureau, 38
  Lincoln Town, 32
  New Dora settlement, 39
  New York Times description of, 35
Blaine County, 3, 65, 70–73, 77, 79, 82,
  83, 85, 87, 90, 95, 102, 104. *See also*
  Hennessey, Okla.; Watonga, Okla.
  banking and credit, 73
  cantonment, 19
  cash crops, 85
  Cedar Springs, 19
  cheese factory in Watonga, 88
  custom threshing, 89–91
  drought, 84–85
  ecology, 72
  stock raising, 87–88, 92
  wheat, 92

Bogue, Earnest, 55
Bourgmont, Etienne de Veniard, 16
Broom corn, 49, 101
Burtis, Frank C., 55

Caddo County, 113, 136
Caddo Indians, 108, 116
Cattle trailing, 72
  Cedar Springs and, 19
  Jesse Chisholm and, 18, 113, 114
  Chisholm Trail, 18, 103, 113
  Edward Everett Dale and, 21
  ecology of, 17–19
  Great Western Trail, 18
  Joseph McCoy and, 113, 114
Centennial Ranches and Farm Project,
  Oklahoma Historical Society, 97
Cheyenne-Arapahoe Indians, 2, 3, 75–78,
  81, 110, 126, 136, 141
  cantonment, 66, 76
  Darlington Agency and, 65, 66, 76
  as original inhabitants of Blaine
    County, 4
  stock raising, 66, 75
Chisholm, Jesse, 18, 113, 114
Clark, William, 9
Comanche Indians, 2, 66, 114, 118
Commissioner of Indian Affairs, 119
Coyle, Okla., 44
Culture of Oklahoma, 4
Custom threshing, 49, 89–91

Dale, Edward Everett, 21
Danbom, David, 26
Danhoff, Clarence, 69
Darlington Agency, 65, 66, 76
Dawes Act, General Allotment Act,
  130–37
  Burke Act and, 137
  Jerome Commission and, 68, 124–27, 138
Degler, Carl, 29
Demonstration program
  agricultural extension and, 57, 136,
    147–48